A HAPPY HAS-BEEN

Exciting Times and Lessons Learned by One of Canada's Foremost Entertainment Journalists

BILL WELYCHKA

FEATURING A FOREWORD BY
THE TRAGICALLY HIP'S PAUL LANGLOIS

One Printers Way
Altona, MB R0G 0B0
Canada

www.friesenpress.com

Copyright © 2023 by Bill Welychka
First Edition — 2023

All rights reserved.

No part of this publication may be reproduced in any form, or by any means, electronic or mechanical, including photocopying, recording, or any information browsing, storage, or retrieval system, without permission in writing from FriesenPress.

Photo Credits:
Thanks so much to the following for permission for photos…Amanda Alves, Catherine Lash, TJ Champagne Photography, SkEye Stream, James C McColl, MuchMusic, MuchMoreMusic, CTV - Bell Media, Corus Entertainment, Global News Kingston

Front Cover Design by Jason Rees, www.facebook.com/jaybird.digital.arts/
Jaybird Digital Arts (Belleville, ON)

ISBN

978-1-03-918346-9 (Hardcover)
978-1-03-918345-2 (Paperback)
978-1-03-918347-6 (eBook)

1. BIOGRAPHY & AUTOBIOGRAPHY, ENTERTAINMENT & PERFORMING ARTS

Distributed to the trade by The Ingram Book Company

QUOTABLE QUOTES ABOUT BILL WELYCHKA A HAPPY HAS-BEEN

"Bill's memoir is both a creative workbook and an authoritative musical reference. 35 years after it all began, he shares his richly textured and enduring up close & personal music memories. It is a *fanfreakintastic* reminisce of yesteryear. This notable book is a must-have piece to add to your collection of highly addictive reads. It will thrill all his fans!"

—The Wire MEGAzine

"Bill has proven to be an exceptional writer. This book will excite any fan of music or Bill's fans or any avid reader of Bios. This book is chock-full of information about the music business."

—*Rick Revelle/ Author Algonquin Quest series*

"I love that he chronicled his story in book form. There were laughs and there were lessons, tales and tears. And Bill is the same guy from all those years ago – charming and genuine. You'll love this book. I sure did!"

—*Kevin Shea / Hockey historian and Author*

"If you grew up in the heyday of the nation's music station, you understand the impact the VJs had on your life. Bill Welychka was one of the greats. In his book, we're blessed with inside access to the life and times of Bill, who it turns out is much more than a beloved VJ. He's a beloved human being."

—*Toronto Mike'd Podcast*

This book is dedicated to *you*. I know that seems like pandering but your interest in my life brings me joy. So, thanks for purchasing a copy and being curious. Everything I have done on-air and everyone I have interviewed has always been for the viewer's pleasure and providing some semblance of entertainment. I hope I have entertained you.

This book is also dedicated to every musician and music artist who has entertained me, and whose music has been a companion in times when I needed it most. These times include long drives alone and in moments of utter despair. Your music has saved my life and has also provided me a soundtrack to glorious times, when I have spent countless hours of air-drumming and air-guitaring. I can't imagine a world without music.

Thank you!

CONTENTS

IX	Foreword
XI	Preface
1	Chapter One — A Flask Full of Whisky
5	Chapter Two — Music as a Badge
12	Chapter Three — I'm an Adult?
19	Chapter Four — On the Air and a Manuel Jacket
25	Chapter Five — Gram Parsons's Corpse
30	Chapter Six — A Message from Garth
38	Chapter Seven — Slash's Porn
47	Chapter Eight — Dead Skin Cells
57	Chapter Nine — A Cowboy's Bullet and Bodyguards
66	Chapter Ten — Elevating Women and A White Ribbon
73	Chapter Eleven — Madonna's Monitor
84	Chapter Twelve — A New York City BDSM Club
89	Chapter Thirteen — Booze Cans and Floor Hockey
106	Chapter Fourteen — A Sad Border Crossing
118	Chapter Fifteen — Pooping Alpacas
147	Chapter Sixteen — A Bow from Prince and a Hug from Liam
175	Chapter Seventeen — Kingston's Saddest Day
185	Chapter Eighteen — Death and Gord Downie
195	Chapter Nineteen — A Singlet and Black Wrestling Boots
206	Chapter Twenty — Egos and Empathy
215	Chapter Twenty-One — Advice and Tips
220	Chapter Twenty-Two — Birthdays and Goodbye
229	Acknowledgements

FOREWORD

Bill Welychka. What to say...

He's a great guy, obviously, anyone can see that, whether you're watching him interviewing someone or you're talking to him on the street. He actually always looked to us like a guy that could've gone to our high school.

He kinda had the same hair as me too.

We in The Hip *never* wanted to do interviews, like ever. We looked at it as a chore and an extreme chance to embarrass ourselves. So, we always did the same thing: short straw had to do it, and then we'd take turns after that.

But Bill was a revelation to us. He was super friendly, had a kind smile and vibe and yet he asked questions that kind of woke you up and made you realize that you'd better up your game and stay on the ball. He was that good, and his questions were always interesting and usually fun.

He made you feel really good, special, safe. You felt like you were talking to a buddy, one who was very interested in you and your band in a very personal way.

His long and curly locks continued to be a signature for him back then and, come to think of it, he was actually close to being as cute as (MuchMusic VJ) Erica Ehm at times. Quite an achievement!

Gord Downie and I lived beside each other in Toronto in those days, and I actually remember the two of us walking home from MuchMusic after an interview with Bill and agreeing that he was a cool cat and a great interviewer—of course, we said he looked a little too much like us, but we'll forgive him for that because he's really good at what he does.

You'd be hard-pressed to find anyone in music that Bill hasn't interviewed. He's rubbed shoulders with Madonna, Cher, Kiss, Michael Jackson, David Bowie(!) and Prince, just to name a few!

But from personal experience, he doesn't bring it up or brag about it—you have to dig it out of him. And when you do ask, "What was Bowie like!?" he always has an interesting and highly respectful answer. A highly unique and interesting life he's had for sure.

After such an illustrious career in TV and radio and all other kinds of media, Bill eventually settled here in Kingston in 2012, and our hometown has been so very lucky for that.

He immersed himself in everything here immediately—he's currently got a great morning time TV show and interviews everybody who's got anything going on. To this very day, he does so much for our community—like, constantly!

You see him everywhere, especially at events designed to raise money for those in need. He looks for places to help and he finds them. He has leveraged his celebrity status to help all kinds of charities and individuals here, and just as importantly, he has lent his emceeing talents to numerous charitable causes countless times. From what I know, Bill's mom Barb instilled in him the importance of charity and community.

Bill uses these inherited gifts daily as he graciously gives so much of his time to great causes, and he also quietly supports events financially behind the scenes in addition to what he has already been asked to lend his talents to.

He's a gem. I know this to be true. He sorta likes me I think, which makes me like him even more. All The Hip guys consider him part of the family, and I'm proud to call him a friend.

You'll enjoy taking this journey with Bill in his book. I promise.

Paul Langlois, The Tragically Hip
Kingston, Ontario
February 2023

PREFACE

Most people reading books flip straight to Chapter One. I know I usually do. So, thanks for reading the always important Preface. If you skipped past the Foreword, I invite you to please, go back and read it. It was a true honour to have The Tragically Hip's Mr. Paul Langlois offer a few kind words. Paul joked that I "sorta like" him. Of course I do! But one time at a benefit concert I emceed in Kingston several years ago, I kidded from the stage that I had a hetero man-crush on Paul. Paul was performing later in the evening. His wife Joanne was in the audience. I think she found my comment quite humorous as we still laugh about it to this day. Thanks again, Paul, for the awesome words. Hearing nice things about oneself can do wonders for one's spirit.

I suppose I could start Chapter One here and not have a Foreword or Preface, but all the biographies I have read have a Preface and/or Foreword. I certainly do not want to deviate too much from the long-held traditions of the literary world. Especially because this is my debut book. And depending on its reception, maybe *only* book? I do hope to have a second edition, but that all depends on *you*. Anyway, I would hate to make book or publishing purists upset that I didn't include a Preface. I live my life with the goal to avoid anyone getting upset with me about anything, ever! So, enjoy this Preface. I do believe the following sets up the rest of this book nicely.

About twenty-five years ago, I remember first being told, "You should write a book! You have some great experiences and a great story!"

I have been told that same sentiment many times since. My inner voice and ego (or lack of ego?) would always warn me, "No one will care about what you write. You didn't save lives. You didn't create a cure for cancer. All you did was be on some people's TV screens interviewing rock stars."

However, I learned a long time ago and have always maintained that *everyone* has a great story worthy of a published book. We all possess experiences that we can learn from and share with others. We all have moments in our lives that are funny, sad, heartbreaking, fantastic, wondrous, glorious, momentous, shocking, enlightening, surprising, educational and unbelievable.

I really didn't believe my story was worthy of a published book until being asked to share some of my past with *The Kingston Whig-Standard* newspaper for what would become a popular monthly column. The writings would be published nationally from 2014 to 2019 by parent company Postmedia Network Canada. It was a fun chance to look back and share some of my background and interesting experiences that would previously only occasionally be randomly shared with close friends. Or sometimes with strangers. For many years and even now, I will meet strangers at bars or grocery stores or bus stops or gas stations, and they will proceed to ask me questions about my career or be curious about specific interviews I had conducted. Sometimes, I would forget that I had interviewed someone that they admired, but *they* remembered the interview fondly. That remains a huge thrill to me.

One gentleman in an Edmonton pub in 2006 kept asking me questions about my 2004 interview with Velvet Revolver. He wanted to know more about my time spent in Los Angeles with ex-Guns N' Roses members Slash, Duff McKagan and Matt Sorum when I had interviewed them about their newly formed band. I realized he had obviously seen the special I had hosted, edited and produced for MuchMoreMusic. He admitted to me that he had videotaped my Guns N' Roses/Velvet Revolver special, and he had sold many duplicated VHS and DVD copies of it online. My only reaction was, "Wow. Very industrious of you. I guess you should buy me a beer!" I recall actually buying *him* a beer for being so honest with me. He also complimented me on my interview abilities and thanked me for the enjoyment the many interviews I had done over the years had brought him. So, I bought him two beers.

In writing the nationally syndicated column, retelling some of my past and sharing stories, I had concluded that I was fortunate to have started writing so much shit down before it was forgotten and lost forever. There were many more stories and experiences that came to mind, and most were never printed in the columns nor previously told.

Maybe, just maybe, I do have some stories to tell and moments to share that will make people smile and perhaps even inspire. That is the goal with this book you are holding (or reading on your computer or e-reader).

By the way, the "lessons learned" part in the book's subtitle won't be overtly listed. The lessons I have learned were never handed to me, so I will let you extrapolate them from reading my words and stories. But, towards the end of the book, I try my best to highlight and explain some of them.

· · · · ·

I was working in Ottawa at the CHUM Limited TV property A-Channel as a 6 p.m. news weather anchor and on-air host in 2006. The station has since been rebranded as CTV 2, a Bell Media Inc. TV station. A co-worker (who wasn't very well-liked or respected among his work peers) asked me, "How does it feel to be a washed up has-been?" He knew of my somewhat esteemed past and was awkward in his curiosity as to why I was in Ottawa on local television and not having a national presence anymore.

It really was no wonder why this co-worker (who held a producer position) was largely disliked. I replied, "I don't know. It must be shitty for you to be working at the same level as a washed up has-been. What does that say about *your* career?" He had no response, and his cocky smirk was quickly replaced by a blank and confused look.

At the time, his comment really hurt. No one wants to be regarded as a has-been or (to quote a Bay City Rollers cover song) a "yesterday's hero." I could somehow relate a tiny bit to Bruce Springsteen's 1985 hit "Glory Days." It was a musical tale of looking back at someone's big accomplishments and how they didn't bring to fruition the possibility of growing their stature and notoriety into something *bigger*. But when does that desperate desire to be "rich and famous" stop? At what point does one get to a level of satisfaction and contentment and be grateful for what they achieved, without having to further climb the ladder of (especially perceived) success and expectations?

For most of the 1990s, I had gained national attention as a VJ (video jockey) at MuchMusic, Canada's groundbreaking and highly influential music TV station. To be honest, I actually never liked having my role or title distilled down to two letters. *VJ*. To me, it always sounded too sophomoric and juvenile. If I could magically change the letters that described my career, I'd have chosen PhD, it certainly pays more and comes with more respect.

I was at MuchMusic from 1988 to 2000. In those twelve years, I was a video dubber, a video editor, sometimes a camera person, an interviewer, a show creator, an on-air presenter, a VJ (ugh!), a voice-over talent, a post-production director and a producer. In 2000, I was granted my request to transfer to the more adult-contemporary version of MuchMusic, the then-newly launched sister station, MuchMoreMusic. The middle *M* in MMM was unofficially a nod and implication to the radio format genre MOR (middle of the road). MuchMoreMusic was skewed towards an older audience and was less poppy and trendy than MuchMusic. The focus was on the *music* and not how it was presented.

After five years at MuchMoreMusic, I began questioning my place and role in life. You will read that my life was grand. Travelling the globe. Bonding with every music idol I ever had. Getting free drinks at bars. Being given an endless supply of concert tickets. Attending all night parties. Having many alcohol-fueled sexual encounters with consenting women who I let pick me up. I am ashamed to say I could not remember all the names of the girls I have spent intimate time with. I recall meeting a girl at the Wheat Sheaf Tavern on King Street in Toronto in 2004 (my neighbourhood then). She was excited to see me and came up to say hello as I was sitting at the bar, conversing with Patrick, the bartender. I was confused and said, "Ummm, hi. How are ya?" She replied, "You don't remember me, do you? We had sex at your place two months ago! You don't remember? You're an asshole!" She then stormed off back to her table at the other end of the pub. I was embarrassed and angry at myself. Patrick shook his head and said to me, "Wow. I've never seen that before!"

Yes, I was a bit trampy in my twenties and thirties, but I was and remain always very respectful of whom I consider the better and smarter sex. I could become enamoured very quickly, but no matter how beautiful and intelligent and successful my partner would be, I would always eventually want to move on. I preferred being alone. Honesty and respect always prevailed, and I always let my intentions and feelings be known that a long-term relationship wasn't easy for me.

Something was missing from this (some might say) "fabulous" life. I began looking for a purpose to exist without solely being known for what I did for a living and what I was nationally recognized for. Being on TV and gaining attention for award-winning interview skills were proud benchmarks in my life, but there was more to me than what most people knew. Or thought they knew.

When I realized I wasn't satisfied with my role, I began to look for reasons why I felt that way. There were actual tangible signs that spoke volumes to me. You will read why I left that coveted post at MuchMoreMusic. I decided to walk away from my role, and I began a search to find something else that didn't define me, something away from so many esteemed projects. I began what would become a long search for something aside from fame. A search for a place away from my spacious, kick-ass, twentieth floor, two-bedroom condo in downtown Toronto with a wood-burning fireplace and floor-to-ceiling windows that faced Lake Ontario. A place away from out-of-control parties that lasted entire weekends.

I have always loved creating television. It is all I have ever known in my adult life. My move away from Toronto took me to co-hosting a morning show for the newly branded Citytv Edmonton. That was followed by a move to Ottawa's A-Channel TV station. Sure, to many, I had dropped in rank in my TV career. I had gone from national exposure, travelling the globe, to a regional/local presence. That's not how a career's trajectory is supposed to go. But it was imperative to me that I reinvent myself. I didn't want to be a one-trick pony, only interviewing rock stars. I found a path that excited me to pursue lifestyle interviews and learn weather forecast broadcasting.

It was in Ottawa working with news director Peter Angione and 6 p.m. news anchor Sandra Blaikie that I came to an earth-shattering realization.

I was actually very happy with my *diminishing* status. I had found myself at a new level in life, and I was satisfied for the first time in a long time.

I didn't need to be national to be happy. I didn't need fame. Besides, I'd always looked at fame as something very minor and not very worthy of adulation. I never really cared for fame or aspired to be what a celebrity is.

Like everyone, all I ever wanted was happiness. Surprisingly, I have achieved it.

It is my pleasure to share with you some interesting and fun career moments I've had, and more importantly, share with you what I believe happiness is and why I have embraced the concept of being a "has-been."

Bill Welychka
Kingston, Ontario
March 2023

CHAPTER ONE
A FLASK FULL OF WHISKY

Cameraperson Dave Hurlbut and I had just wrapped up a week-long assignment in Monte Carlo, Monaco covering the 1999 World Music Awards. It was my fourth year out of six consecutive years travelling to the Principality of Monaco on the Mediterranean Sea, covering the renowned spectacle. Unlike the Grammys or other award shows that recognize the music world's best by way of an insider industry jury, the World Music Awards handed out the hardware simply to the world's biggest selling music artists. No awards for best producer, engineer or liner notes. Only the biggest sellers were celebrated and lauded over.

I was working for the Canadian TV channel MuchMusic as host, editor and producer. MuchMusic had repeatedly purchased the broadcast rights for the World Music Awards in Canada. I was lucky enough again to spend a week covering the rehearsals, the parties and champagne receptions at the Hôtel de Paris Monte-Carlo and the Monaco Yacht Club, the red-carpet arrivals and of course, the actual moments backstage during the taped broadcast. The previous five days were spent interviewing Cher, Janet Jackson, Britney Spears, Celine Dion, Will Smith, Mariah Carey, Barenaked Ladies, Pam Anderson, Tommy Lee and many more. During the week we would have to interview these artists sometimes two or three times at various places.

It was a very busy week. We also caught up with many A-list actors, athletes and supermodels. I also interviewed Prince Albert II of Monaco. I know what you are thinking: "Those people aren't music makers. Why were they part of a music awards show?" You are correct. Many of the attending celebs didn't record albums or sell music, but they would share the stage as presenters. Actually, Prince Albert's younger sister Princess Stéphanie did have a minor vanity music project in the '80s. I interviewed her in Monaco at the 1996 World Music Awards. She offered then that she was done with music professionally. Probably a good thing—I don't think she sold many records at all.

All these recorded moments and interviews would be used to air a thirty-minute "pre-game" show prior to the MuchMusic national broadcast, interspersed with my backstage interviews with artists holding World Music Awards trophies.

During the week when not covering the rehearsals and parties, we would shoot "throws" in our spare time. Throws were introductions to videos to be played on MuchMusic. We taped several afternoons of programming for MuchMusic. For the national TV audience in Canada, they would see snippets of the interviews we acquired with the big stars, and me at various locations around the Mediterranean (from Nice, France to Northern Italy) introducing music videos.

Looking back now, I am embarrassed to say those weeks were exhausting. Yes, the days were long. But c'mon, I wasn't digging ditches for a living! I was holding a microphone, asking questions and conversing and bonding with the interview subject. To the viewer at home, it looks like I am having the best time ever, hanging out with all the famous, cool and beautiful people at the ritziest and swankiest of parties. These scenes were always funny to me because my personality dictates, quite proudly, that I prefer living a more average person existence. These ostentatious parties were the furthest thing from what I personally enjoy. Yes, I can dip a toe into that world if the need arises and I will blend in well. But I never really cared for high-end social celebrity events. Friends would always convey jealousy when I would tell them about these parties. After the interviews were done and the microphone was put away, you'd find me hanging out at the bar conversing with some servers and staff or having a smoke out on the street alone. I became an expert at faking my way through some pretentious celeb events. My goal was to create compelling television, not to feed my ego. I have never based my self-worth on who I have met or who I have hung out with.

At the end of the long week, the actual World Music Awards would be mostly live-to-tape. This meant it was not broadcast live internationally, but taped, edited and aired in dozens of countries weeks later.

Literally moments after the taping had ended and we had collected all the great recorded moments we needed of everyone with their World Music Awards trophies, we started packing up our gear. It was 1 or 2 a.m.

I remember thinking to myself, "Wow! I must have one of the best jobs in the world. I just travelled to Europe and interviewed Britney Spears, Ricky Martin and so many more. We achieved the goal of securing some awesome and amazing moments to entertain Canadian viewers." I expressed to Dave out loud, "Thanks, man. Great job this week. Fun times, huh?"

I was waiting for an answer from Dave. No answer came. I looked over and smiled as I watched him sucking on the spout of his silver flask, which was raised high above his head. He eventually said, "It was an amazing week! Great interviews!" before going back to nursing his flask. I realized this was his personal ritual to wind down and relax after a long week of supporting a heavy video camera on his shoulder. I had seen him do it before on previous international assignments. I asked him what was in the flask this time. He smiled and said, "Wild Turkey." I felt grateful when he handed it to me. I knew Wild Turkey was a type of bourbon from Kentucky. I learned to love Jack Daniel's many years prior while on assignment in Tennessee, its home state. I don't think I had ever had Wild Turkey before then though. Dave continued to educate me about bourbons, whiskies and sour mash as I sipped some down.

As I drank from Dave's flask while helping him pack up his lights and gear, I told him the spout looked filthy. It wasn't silvery, like the rest of the flask. It had a greenish tinge that circled the top. He said, "It's OK. It's alcohol. It cleans itself." Who am I to argue with the logic of a seasoned vet? To me, Dave was a road-weary elder with much wisdom. He was one of my favourite camerapeople to work and travel with. I always believed, and I knew Dave thought the same, that *work* was the priority.

But downtime meant taking a breath and relaxing. And perhaps indulging in some bourbon. Or beer. Or wine. Or a little of each.

I sat down exhausted. And a little tipsy. I felt so much appreciation for where my life had taken me thus far. I was loving life and grateful for every opportunity offered to me. One can't help but look back on their life and roots and be thankful during a rare moment like I was experiencing in that moment.

But in time, something would not sit right. In time, I would walk away from what I considered, and what most people would consider, *the best job in the world.*

CHAPTER TWO
MUSIC AS A BADGE

I have always loved music. Sometimes I amaze myself with my taste in music. I love rock in all its varied forms and eras ('50s, '60s, '70s, '80s, '90s, the 2000s), punk, heavy metal, alternative, new wave, blues, hip hop, world and ethnic, roots, folk, gospel, pop, country, experimental, dance etc.

My earliest memories of falling in love with music go back to kindergarten in Welland, Ontario. My family lived on Centennial Drive. I was the youngest of six kids. There was me, then Ed, Gerard, Dave, Lenny and Maria. My oldest sibling, Maria, had already fled the nest to Toronto years before to get married. It's a cliché to admit that one's parents worked hard to raise their kids, but it was true in the case of my middle-class parents. My dad worked at a steel company and my mom was a schoolteacher. Yes, Barb and Alex worked very hard to support and raise us. Both of my parents are now deceased. It is sad to note that I attended many funerals by the time I turned thirty. It was painful to watch my beloved mom (or as I affectionately called her for many years, Barb) bury two of her kids and my father before she passed away in 2012.

The second youngest sibling is Ed, who is seven years older than me. I was always closest to him. It needs to be said that I am proud of him and his accomplishments. He is a successful geologist, he has a beautiful wife named Jan and I am a proud uncle to his sons Quinn (the owner of a popular sports clothing line called bCLUTCH) and Brett (a pro hockey player).

My next three older brothers have all passed on. Gerard was shot and killed when I was in the seventh grade. I was told he hung out with some bad people. No kidding! The next two older siblings, Dave and Len, have also passed on. Dave had two kids, Vanessa and Mikey. My nephew Mikey passed away several years ago. My oldest sibling is my sister Maria, and she has two successful kids, Karen and Kevin. Me? No kids. Although, a psychic once told me that I have three kids I don't know about. Another psychic also once told me that I'd be a millionaire by age thirty. That didn't happen, so I am pretty sure I don't have any kids.

I do have distinct memories of sneaking into my older brothers' rooms and being interested in their vast album collections. I was fascinated by the artwork and photography and stared at and examined album covers by Led Zeppelin, Rod Stewart, Lynyrd Skynyrd, David Bowie, Bad Company and many others.

On the clock radio in the bedroom I shared with my older brother Ed, I listened to CHOW-AM (pronounced on air as "See-How"). Back then in 1973, it offered an easy listening format. I heard some songs by a band called The DeFranco Family, who were from nearby Port Colborne. A friend in the first grade showed me a record she had brought to school that had one of their songs on it. It was a K-Tel collection of hits, and the song was "Abra-Ca-Dabra". It occurred to me right then that *anyone*, not necessarily older people but anyone, even people *my* age, could actually be in control of the songs they wanted to hear! One doesn't *have* to listen to a radio, waiting in anticipation to hear their favourite song. One could *own* the song on these black phonograph record platters! It was a realization I found hard to fathom. I could play songs I wanted to hear, anytime I wanted to, just like my much older brothers did. I would hold on to that new revelation and prove it to be true sooner rather than later.

My family had a cottage in Port Maitland on Lake Erie. It was the summer of 1975, and a short walk away from our cottage was a convenience store that had a jukebox outside under a canopy. The nearby cottagers and older teenagers would sit on the benches, and I would sometimes join them, listening to songs by Jim Stafford, Grand Funk Railroad, Elvis Presley, Stevie Wonder, Paul McCartney and Wings, Andy Kim, Linda Ronstadt, Glen Campbell, Elton John, The Guess Who, The Eagles, Bo Donaldson and other artists with big hits from that period.

Later that year in 1975, I saw a new group on TV. It was the Bay City Rollers performing their song "Saturday Night." It was a premiere show on NBC entitled *Saturday Night Live with Howard Cosell*. The Scottish band used this show as their North American TV debut, and I was further hooked with music. I became enamoured with how music was presented on TV—the colourful and flashing lights, the frantic screaming audience, the sound mixes of it all and how it was directed. I begged my mom to take me to our local Seaway Mall to the record store. I pleaded with her to buy their record for me. Barb obliged! It was the 1975 self-titled *Bay City Rollers* album. It was the band's first full-length album to be issued in the US and Canada. Years later I would find out it was a compilation of previously released UK hits. The band would release further albums in the next few years and further begging to my mom for them ensued.

In grade three, I would begin conversations with fellow classmates about music and this new Scottish group. I realized my classmates didn't care much about music. No one else in grade three talked about music. I did! They would look to me as a fan of music.

My parents separated in the spring of 1976 and I moved with my mom to a small apartment in Richmond Hill, Ontario. A new adventure with music began in the fourth grade at my new school, Our Lady Help of Christians.

Richmond Hill is located just north of Toronto, so CFTR-AM and CHUM-FM were radio staples for me between grades four and eight. I fell in love with the music I heard. It excited me, with songs by Bruce Cockburn, Robert Palmer, Queen, Chic, Rush, April Wine, T. Rex, The Tubes, Leo Sayer, Pink Floyd, the soundtrack for *Grease*, Hall & Oates, Bee Gees, Fleetwood Mac, Bob Seger, The Guess Who, James Brown, The Spinners, the soundtrack for *The Blues Brothers*, Lionel Richie, Electric Light Orchestra, Genesis, Trooper, The Monks and so many more. I would make regimented trips to Hillcrest Mall where Sam the Record Man became paradise for me. I would always purchase 45 rpm singles and sometimes even full-length albums by the artists mentioned above. Also purchased were: Sweet, "Fox On The Run"; Billy Joel, *52nd Street*; Aerosmith, "Come Together"; The Who, "Squeeze Box"; Billy Thorpe, "In My Room"; Meat Loaf's *Bat Out of Hell*, The Kings, "This Beat Goes On/Switchin' To Glide"; Kiss, "I Was Made for Lovin' You"; Blondie, "Heart of

Glass"; The Clash, *Sandinista!*; and Gary Numan, "Cars." The Boomtown Rats, Elvis Costello and Talking Heads also became favourites. These and so many more singles and albums became part of my collection. I listened to them over and over again. I had a growing assortment of music, and I was freakin' proud of it!

As I type these words, it has become apparent to me that at a very young age, I was curious about all genres of music. Not just the Top 40 hits of the day, but artists with a harder edge or a folk tinge to their style or some funk or punk leanings. Many of these musical acts that were part of my large and growing music collection would eventually become my interview subjects years later. As an adult, I would establish deep connections on a cerebral level with many of them. That's really cool to think about.

My mom and I would move to Thornhill in 1979. In time, I would eventually enroll at Thornlea Secondary School for grade nine. Suddenly, I was attending a new school with absolutely no friends. I had learned and trusted that music was my friend. In 1980, The Police album *Zenyatta Mondatta* became a favourite, and I would bond with some other students who also loved that record and their 1981 follow-up, *Ghost in the Machine*.

Grade nine brings back many memories of a fresh genre of music called "new wave." It was synthesizer based and very pop driven with memorable, dance-worthy hooks. The bands that stood out for me at this time were The Fixx, The Jam, Orchestral Manoeuvres in the Dark, Men Without Hats, Talking Heads, Duran Duran, The Human League, INXS, The English Beat, Tears for Fears and David Bowie with his venture into this new, *experimental* sound. I became a fan of other new wave bands that had a more punk influence to them like The Knack, the Ramones and Canada's Teenage Head.

By grade ten, I had become transfixed by harder sounds. I would become a devout follower of Led Zeppelin, The Who and The Rolling Stones. These classic artists were older, and although some of these giants had disbanded, their influence was undeniable. These were the artists that my older brothers listened to as well, and I understood then that music can be timeless and that great artists transcend trends and decades. These influential musical acts would always be picked up and adored by younger people. My tastes turned even harder in discovering and loving AC/DC,

Ozzy Osbourne, Iron Maiden, Judas Priest, Black Sabbath, Van Halen, Rush, KISS, Def Leppard, the Scorpions and many others. Again, these artists would become some of my interview subjects many years later. If a magical and mysterious person would've told me in the tenth grade, "Hey, you like Zeppelin, Ozzy, AC/DC, Rush and the Scorps? You'll be bonding with them and interviewing them in fifteen years," I would've laughed. And then I would've said to this mystical person that if they could predict the future, then they should give me some winning lottery numbers!

By grade ten, music became integral and so important to me. I embraced all the genres I listened to, but harder and heavier music became a badge. All through high school, music for me was a way to let others know what I was about. It became a way to identify myself. My taste in music was proudly displayed in my locker with pictures I had cut out from *Creem* magazine. That trend carried over with rock band logo doodles on my notebooks and rock band patches and pins on my jean jacket. During these times, I was proud of my ever-increasing collection of records and tapes. I had also become proud of a solid group of friends I had bonded with since grade nine at Thornlea Secondary School. Even to this day, one of my closest friends from that period is Jeff Parissi. We played hockey together in grade four and reconnected in high school. I have remained very close to Jeff and his parents, Janet and Peter. Janet passed away a few years ago and I was very saddened by her loss. "Honey-Bunch" (as Jeff and I called her since high school) would sometimes cut my hair and feed us at lunch in those early years.

Halfway through high school, my mom and I moved to Barrie, Ontario. She was planning her retirement in a few years and bought a small house. These were the delicate, formative years for a teenager. I understood *why* she wanted to move, but I really couldn't agree with the concept of changing schools halfway through grade eleven to a region two hours north of Thornhill. To me, it might as well have been a move to Jupiter. I became depressed. Not just saddened by the upheaval in my life, but looking back, truly depressed. Depression was something I would be diagnosed with much later in life, but I truly believe that the recognizable signs began around this time. Depression and how to deal with it is a big part of my life, even now as I type these words in early 2023.

By grades twelve and thirteen in Barrie at Innisdale Secondary School, I had discovered alternative and goth music. That music scene opened my eyes to the concept of *individuality*. I felt alone in Barrie and to me, the logical extension of being comfortable with being alone was to embrace solitude. To live with solitude is to appreciate one's own thoughts and be open to understanding that you are not part of a group anymore. I believed that if I wasn't going to be part of a group and conform, I would further that concept by dressing *different*. Looking back though, dressing as an *individual* meant emulating the looks of my favourite musicians who I would see in music videos on the newly launched Canadian TV channel MuchMusic. Copying fashions and hair to look like an individual wasn't very individual at all. Oh, the irony.

Alternative and goth music became my life saver. The alt-music genre was in its infancy, led by acts like a young U2, early R.E.M., The Cult, The Cure, Howard Jones, Depeche Mode, Morrissey and The Smiths, Simple Minds, New Order, The Jesus and Mary Chain, Bauhaus (and its off-shoots, Love and Rockets and lead singer Peter Murphy's solo career), Lloyd Cole, Hüsker Dü, Billy Bragg, The Mission, The Sisters of Mercy, Violent Femmes (who weren't violent or feminine), The Lords of the New Church and others. In Canada, Images in Vogue, Breeding Ground, Blue Peter, Spoons and Platinum Blonde contributed some to the alt and new wave scene. Around this time I also discovered early Lou Reed. The former Velvet Underground musician's work was a constant for me in my rented room during my first year of college.

The band that spoke volumes to me at this time was UK act The Cure and its leader Robert Smith. The Cure's early music became a huge focal point for me. I didn't discover The Cure until 1984. They had formed six years previous with very little commercial success and only a cult following. I immediately started buying their back catalogue as imports at Sam the Record Man in downtown Toronto whenever I could take advantage of long bus rides from Barrie. By 1985, their North American breakthrough, *The Head on the Door*, was released. This band, their music and Robert's lyrics became all-encompassing to me. It was comforting. The Cure's music became a friend and a cherished escape into something meaningful, after feeling like an outsider and not truly fitting in at my new school in Barrie. The music offered security and provided confidence.

For a grade thirteen history project, I rented a video camera from the local library. It was a camera with cables connected to a portable VHS deck for recording. The class project's theme and topic was racism. I videotaped myself wearing strange makeup and mismatched clothes having a one-way conversation, and when I presented the project as myself in class, I was able to have a dialogue with my videotaped self in the TV monitor.

The end result was two people who looked nothing alike, having a conversation and realizing that they have more in common than they thought. It was my naive but creative attempt at making a statement about racism. The timing of the live dialogue with the monitor and taped one-way dialogue was perfect! I received a great mark too.

The experience with the video camera piqued my interest in videography and the art of shooting. In my final year of high school, I made the decision to enroll in a radio and television broadcasting program. I applied to a few colleges and accepted the first offer I received. It was from Seneca College in Toronto.

College introduced me to yet another genre of music I really hadn't been exposed to before, and it would alter my life forever.

CHAPTER THREE
I'M AN ADULT?

I began a two-year radio and television broadcasting course in Toronto at Seneca College in the fall of 1986. The beginning of a post-secondary education is an important time in anyone's life, but for me it meant having to overcome an affliction I'd had since childhood: stuttering and stammering.

I remember being called "B-B-B-Billy" in grade school because I stuttered. I was surprised that many classmates found it funny or odd. I had two older brothers that also stuttered, so to me, it wasn't a terribly big issue. I had been aware that most people didn't stutter when talking, but I hadn't really paid too much attention to it or noticed it until trying to communicate in class or with friends at recess.

By high school, I tried to control it and somehow improved my speech from stuttering to stammering. Stuttering means being stuck on a consonant. The most difficult letters are *B*, *D*, *K*, *P*, and *T*. Words like "dish" would come out as "d-d-d-dish." Stammering involves repeating syllables. If I was talking about the rock group Def Leppard, it would come out as "Def Def Def Leppard."

The worst part for me in my teen years was picking up the phone to say hello. It got to the point where I actually feared the phone ringing, and when it did, true panic would set in. If I was home alone and the phone rang, I was unable to say hello. My mouth would be open, but it would be like gagging on air and no sound would come out. The person calling would hear the ringing tone stop and expect a normal, "Hello?" on the other end, but there wouldn't be one available. They would ask, "Ummm, anyone there? Hello?" If they didn't hang up first, I could eventually let out a "hi." A ringing phone caused more distress to me as a teenager than any acne ever could.

During radio and television broadcasting college courses, I somehow found a way to force words to come with some effort. I had to. We had to give live classroom presentations, do voice-over lessons and act in other students' video projects. I am grateful I found a way to speak without stuttering or stammering when I needed to. I credit college with helping me overcome those previously lifelong challenges.

Another change was happening to me during college. My fascination with alternative music had grown to include a fashion expression involving wearing makeup like foundation and eyeliner and a hairstyle that was medium length with bangs that covered my face. It was sort of the opposite of a mullet. Even mullets didn't have a name at this point. In my mind, the makeup, plaid pants, long black overcoat and buckled, pointed-toe, black leather ankle boots I wore were a statement about the importance of expressing one's individuality.

One afternoon in the large college cafeteria, I realized I had run out of cigarettes. Smoking was allowed in public places back then, so when I recognized a guy from some of my classes sitting, reading a newspaper and smoking, I approached him. Paul Boynett was a normal-looking and quiet dude who wore cowboy boots. No one I knew wore cowboy boots. I stood across from him at the table and said, "Hey man, can I bum a smoke?"

He lowered his newspaper to just below his eye level. He looked me up and down, lifted the paper back up to cover his face, then slid his pack of Player's Lights under the newspaper to me. It was his way of saying, "Yeah. Take a smoke. But you look weird. Now bugger off."

It struck me that this was one of the coolest people I had ever met. He was disapproving of how I looked, yet suave and generous with his actions. Within a month, Paul and I would become best friends. I would often sleep at Paul's place (he was closer to Seneca than I was), and we would feature each other in our college video projects.

In that first year of college, my circle of friends grew to contain girls and guys with varying tastes in music, fashion, hobbies, outlooks and backgrounds. Paul and I would eventually acquire back-to-back campus radio shifts. After my show at CRSC Seneca Radio (The Byl's Asylum Show) in which I played mostly alternative music and some classic rock and metal, Paul would come in and play country music for his two hours. I would stick around during his show, and I soaked up the country music tunes he was playing. Paul would play cuts from new artists at the time, like Randy Travis, Steve Earle and Dwight Yoakam.

The new-traditionalism movement of country music saw a pivotal year in 1986. The early '80s' country music scene had become watered down, and the Nashville establishment attempted, in a sloppy and confusing way, to go pop. Randy, Steve and Dwight came along with their debut records and brought something new and fresh and exciting to the genre. These were young cats that proudly borrowed from the legends. They were unabashedly sounding like their influences. But they framed their sound in a no-holds-barred contemporary style with production and musicianship that was groundbreaking for Nashville at the time. These music artists and a few others at the time introduced country music to an entirely new audience. Many young people would get turned on to country music for the first time in 1986, myself included.

Steve Earle and Dwight Yoakam were just some of the artists that got me hooked on country music. From there, I went back and did much research and homework, and I discovered the beauty that is country music. I would eventually fall deeply in love with the legends, like George Jones, Waylon Jennings, Conway Twitty, Johnny Cash, Patsy Cline, Hank Williams Sr. and Jr., Merle Haggard, Willie Nelson, Billy Joe Shaver and many others. I also began to follow newer stars like Emmylou Harris, Joe Ely, The Judds, Ricky Van Shelton and Keith Whitley.

No one I knew (besides Paul) listened to country music at this time, so this entirely exciting new world of music was, to me, alternative! Around 1987, I stopped wearing makeup. I grew sideburns and started to dress a bit like Dwight Yoakam, but without the cowboy hat. And without the $2000 Manuel couture jacket. Although, a Manuel jacket *would* come. More on that later in the book.

My goal in college was to learn the discipline of shooting, videography and mastering a video camera. During my first year of college, I fell in love with editing. The process involved VHS tape-to-tape editing on an edit controller, picking the best audio and video and mixing it all together for whatever project was assigned. Shooting was fun, but I learned that the real magic was in editing. I picked up the intricacies of editing fairly quickly.

Seneca College had a hallway of four or five edit bays alongside each other. If someone had a problem with their edit controller or was confused, they could easily step out and check in on another student who was editing and ask for help. The edit bays were open twenty-four hours a day. It was always a thrill to be in an edit bay at school, working on a project and hearing a knock on the door. I was always ready and willing to assist a fellow student that required assistance. Often, I would sit in their chair and take over, eventually editing their project for them. This happened many times. I never thought of it as doing someone's work for them though, as I would explain every little step as I went, and I would oversee their attempts at what I was teaching.

Heading into my final year of college, I had become close with a classmate named Brian T. James (he always insisted on the T. initial). He organized a student council for all of Seneca College's communication arts students and asked me to join it. I agreed to be part of this fresh collective, only because I had never been part of a concerned group of people before. It was a surprising move for me, as joining any club in high school, let alone a student council, had always been way beyond my interest. Mostly, listening to music and spending time alone had been my existence. But I was, dare I say it, growing up and perhaps maturing? At least, I was now giving people a chance and increasing my desire to be more social.

Towards the end of college, I took on a part-time baking job at the now-defunct chain, Mister Donut. My schedule was: take a subway and bus to school in the morning and back in the afternoon to a room I was renting in Thornhill, shower, change and then take another bus to Mister Donut to bake until 11 p.m. This went on for a couple months.

During this time, I heard from a friend who had dropped out of Seneca during the first year. Roger had taken an editing job at MuchMusic but was now leaving it to work for the newly launched French version of MuchMusic, MusiquePlus. He let me know that an editing position might be coming open. I submitted my short resume. I had no idea if mentioning on my resume that I was a baker at Mister Donut would matter, but jeez, I hadn't had a whole lot of work experience!

Eventually, I heard back from a manager at Much and was told there was no editing position available, but they asked me if I was interested in volunteering for MusiquePlus. The task involved dubbing all of MuchMusic's videos for Plus, as it was nicknamed (pronounced "pl-oose"). MusiquePlus was broadcasting out of the same building as MuchMusic (and Citytv) at 299 Queen Street West in Toronto, but they were getting ready to move to a new facility in Montreal. They needed dubs of all of MuchMusic's videos and archived interviews. The not-very-glamorous and tedious job of dubbing required making copies: press play on one deck and record on another and clearly label the beta tape with artist/song title, length, time to first vocal and record label. The only catch was the hours—it involved volunteering overnight.

I said yes to the volunteering gig. It meant my new schedule for the final month at Seneca College was: get up, go to school, go to my baking job, head downtown to 299 Queen Street West, dub music videos, take the subway north, catch a bus, return home, sleep for a few hours and repeat.

The end of college couldn't come soon enough. After several hours of dubbing videos at MuchMusic downtown, I would catch the subway northbound to the final stop at Finch Station. There were a couple of times where I was so tired, I fell asleep on the subway. I would wake up and realize the subway had already reached Finch Station and continued on its southbound route. I had missed my stop! After shaking away the confusion, I would get off at the next available stop, cross the platform and enter the next subway going north again.

Finally, graduation. No more intense, sleep-deprived schedule. I received my diploma with high honours and was even voted Most Outstanding Student by my peers. I am pretty sure most were recognizing me for helping them at desperate times with editing assignments. I was very grateful for the gesture, and the $100 cash bonus that came with the award was awesome.

The week I graduated I was hired full-time as an editor at MuchMusic. This was in the spring of 1988. The hard work had paid off. It was sad to say goodbye to my Korean bosses at Mister Donut. It was also sad saying goodbye to free donuts! My bosses were very nice and accommodating with my busy schedule and I was going to miss them. I was caught off guard when they gave me a beautiful goodbye present, a new watch. That week was filled with major accomplishments and some cool free stuff. It was a very fine week!

Beginning my career at MuchMusic, "The Nation's Music Station," was surreal. The editing equipment was a far cry from what I was accustomed to in college. Of course, it involved professional broadcast gear in high-end video suites and different video formats. Us professionals in the biz (bahahaha) were using broadcast-quality one-inch reel-to-reel video tape, Beta and three-quarter-inch video tape, not VHS tapes.

The first couple years at MuchMusic involved packaging commercial break blocks, dubbing the new videos that came in from the record companies (I was one of the first in Canada to see the brand-new music videos!) and eventually editing interviews, stories and features for both MuchMusic and Citytv News.

I eventually acquired a small bachelor apartment on Queen Street East at Logan Avenue over Angie's Steakhouse, which is no longer in business today. I recently looked up that old bachelor apartment on Google Street View and saw that good ole Angie had been eventually replaced by a Korean BBQ and bubble tea restaurant. I became a little sad, but my spirit was lifted a bit when I saw that Eddie's Convenience corner shop was still in business! I was in my very early twenties and living life as a responsible adult, having my own apartment with my own furniture, doing my own laundry and buying my own groceries. I was already doing some of these things during college and even in high school, but it seemed somehow more adult while paying bills and having a full-time job.

While I worked behind the scenes at Much, I joined the Toronto Citytv/MuchMusic charity hockey team. I hadn't played ice hockey for years, and I missed it. In one particular game, we went up against an Ontario women's championship team. There was no hitting allowed of course. It was a charity game! Early in the first period, we realized these girls were tough—they came out strong, banging all of us into the boards with clean hits. On the bench, I remember a teammate, Jonathon, panting heavily, saying to me, "Screw this! I'm hitting back!" I warned him not to and reminded him that it was a charity game and that the crowd loved seeing the girls hitting the guys. He replied, "Watch me!" On the next shift, I cringed as Jonathon tried to check his opponent. He missed. The opposing team swarmed him, screaming for his blood! We were outscored 17–1.

I was involved in charity hockey at Maple Leaf Gardens with that City/Much team a few months before the historic rink closed. I am proud to say that I played hockey at that legendary arena. Doug Gilmour, Stan Mikita, Bobby Hull and I all have that in common! Cool.

I couldn't believe it . . . I was a recent college graduate, employed full-time in a career of my chosen field. The biggest thrill for me was knowing that I was working at a national TV station that I used to watch while I was in high school. I was also working with some of the personnel and VJs I used to watch on MuchMusic.

I started to recognize what I called "perfect circles." I've always been fascinated by these moments that reminds one of the past, in relation to where one is currently. Everyone has them. But it was always special for me to recognize a tangible moment that would bring the past up to date. It's the special moment that happens when one is engaging with a touchstone in one's life. I love those perfect circles. They are always "aha" moments for me.

My life would soon become filled with a lot of perfect circles, aha moments and experiences way beyond my imagination.

CHAPTER FOUR
ON THE AIR AND A MANUEL JACKET

I picked up the more advanced skills of video editing for MuchMusic and the Citytv entertainment department very quickly, just like I did in college. But unlike college, the skills needed and the equipment used were vastly different. My tasks never seemed like work, ever. I loved editing video clips for the late news. The evening cameraperson would be assigned to cover one or two live shows and return to the station with the raw footage. Often, by the time the cameraperson had come back to the station, I would have ten minutes to cut the visuals before it was actually on the air. I never missed a deadline.

When I had much more time, I loved the challenge of using live music footage, shot from a single camera, to edit forty-five seconds' or a minute's worth of visuals and sound. I am not a musician, but I know well enough to understand beats and rhythms and that a song structure is based on verses, a chorus and a bridge. It was a skill to edit the singer, guitarist, bass player and drummer all into forty-five seconds, and make it look like there were multiple cameras shooting footage from different angles. I learned that great editing is an art and a craft, and it takes a skilled cameraperson to shoot live music. I perfected and loved working on the craft of music performance editing.

My absolute most satisfying moments in television have been and continue to be spent organizing, producing and editing. That is when I am most satisfied: when I am *creating* television. I have mild OCD, so video editing a story and telling a tale complete with pictures, music and creative editing, satisfies my penchant for proper placement and context. It becomes a perfectly framed, beautiful puzzle.

I also learned that it is a skill to edit music with interviews. I loved the artistry that went into conveying a thought or story using words and music and I became accomplished at utilizing spacing and timing and evoking emotion simply by editing. It was unreal to think that I was getting paid for this.

MuchMusic's broadcast content was live from noon to 8 p.m. EST. That eight-hour block would be repeated twice to make up twenty-four hours. It wasn't just filled with VJ flow (music videos with introductions) but sometimes with live interviews with musicians and artists. If an artist was coming to Toronto, MuchMusic was the priority for the record label. Any other TV show or print or radio coverage was secondary.

While at 299 Queen Street West, after a live appearance, Citytv News would sometimes grab a few minutes of their entertainment reporter with the visiting musician and other shows would also do separate interviews. Artists visiting Toronto had busy days, especially in our building.

Besides the live programming, we had packaged shows that ran for thirty minutes or an hour. This was original programming that would sometimes be genre specific. While dubbing all the new music videos that came into the MuchMusic library, I noticed a rise in high quality country music videos being released. The genre was exploding, and every music label had a large number of established and new country artist signings. I knew we had a vast library of a lot of older country music videos and a large collection of previously taped interviews with many country artists. I thought, "I'm young and I fit MuchMusic's demographic. I love country music! We have all these old country videos and we're being serviced with so many new country videos each week . . . Why not a weekly country music video show?"

I did some research and formatted a proposal for a country music video show and placed it on John Martin's desk one late evening. John Martin was responsible for Citytv's *The New Music*, a music magazine show that was broadcast on Citytv starting in the late '70s. It would be recognized as the precursor to MuchMusic. John would become the director of programming for MuchMusic, the station's highest position. John only answered to Moses Znaimer, Citytv and CHUM Limited's president and executive producer. (In addition to John Martin, Moses was another creative genius I grew to admire, respect and appreciate.) At this point in my very young professional career, I had never met John Martin. He didn't have a clue who I was, but I remained in awe of his stature and was always impressed by his creativity and love for producing music-related television. If MuchMusic was going to launch a country music show, or *any* new show, it had to come from him.

Within weeks of the proposal being placed on his desk, MuchMusic introduced the new weekly country music video show, *Outlaws & Heroes*. I have been credited with creating Canada's first country music video show, but I was told months after the launch that John had wanted to launch a country music show for a while. I tend to believe it was already in the planning stages in John Martin's mind. Some co-workers I shared my plans with early on say it was my idea and the proposal jump-started the process. Either way, I was just happy country artists and videos would have a home in Canada. Everything MuchMusic did was groundbreaking. And so was the sixty-minute weekly national show *Outlaws & Heroes*. Eventually, it expanded to ninety minutes.

Outlaws & Heroes launched in 1988 with host and MuchMusic VJ Christopher Ward. One of the people assigned to program and produce the show was Sherry Greengrass. Sherry had worked on *City Limits*, an all-night music video show with host Christopher Ward on Toronto's Citytv. That show pre-dated the launch of MuchMusic. *City Limits* and *The New Music* were the spark plugs that fired up Canada's first music TV station.

Sherry Greengrass and I had totally different schedules. I was usually working all night shifts and Sherry started in the morning. We sometimes would exchange friendly greetings while I was leaving the building and she was entering. At some point, we actually stopped to talk, and we became very good friends. Our mutual love of country music, especially the legends, was our bond. Eventually, I was asked to help program the music videos for *Outlaws & Heroes* and be the show's only video editor.

Video editing *Outlaws & Heroes* meant taking the taped interviews by Christopher Ward and editing a story, with Sherry producing the pieces. When Sherry and I had similar shifts, we would end our workday by finding an empty edit suite or a screening machine and watch hours of country music videos—old and new—from the Much library. We would plan theme shows and work ahead, programming many shows featuring our favourite country artists.

Christopher Ward was one of my favourite interviewers. He could interview any major music legend and make it seem effortless. He was gracious and polite and never talked down to the viewer. He didn't have an annoying ego and he conveyed a personality of someone you'd love to talk about music with over drinks. Eventually, he became very busy as a songwriter and would leave MuchMusic. He had co-written Alannah Myles's Grammy- and Juno-winning debut album and was riding high on the success of that release, becoming an in-demand songwriter for other artists.

His replacement for *Outlaws & Heroes* was Citytv's Denise Donlon, the host and producer of *The New Music*. She was also an expert interviewer, and someone who also loved the craft of creating compelling television. I had followed Denise's career for many years, and I was grateful that she would be hosting *O&H*. Around this time, I was asked to conduct off-camera interviews for *Outlaws & Heroes*. This simply meant the viewer might occasionally hear my question, but mostly it would feature only the artist's answers. I was never seen, which was fine with me. I had no aspirations to be on TV. I loved my roles of editing and producing.

I conducted many off-camera interviews. The Nitty Gritty Dirt Band, Sawyer Brown, Clint Black, Rodney Crowell, Aaron Tippin and Marty Stuart were just some of my favourite stand-out experiences during this time. Marty Stuart had just released his debut recording with MCA Records, *Hillbilly Rock*. But even prior to the album, he had a long and storied past playing mandolin as a kid with Lester Flatt in the early '70s, being in Johnny Cash's band in the '80s, marrying Johnny's daughter Cindy and working with Carl Perkins, Roy Orbison and Jerry Lee Lewis. He had limited success with his first few releases on US indie labels and CBS, but his 1989 *Hillbilly Rock* album became a commercial hit and resulted in four hit singles. *Outlaws & Heroes* played a lot of Marty Stuart's videos in the show's early days.

A HAPPY HAS-BEEN

Marty Stuart would become a favourite of Sherry and mine. We were offered an interview with Marty when he came to Toronto to play a concert in the summer of 1990.

The interview was prior to showtime on his tour bus, a country music museum on wheels, once owned by country legend Ernest Tubb. It was an amazing experience. My questions and his resulting answers were edited into a lengthy feature for broadcast on *Outlaws & Heroes*. I learned a long time ago that it's a sign of a successful interview when the interview subject still wants to talk and bond even when the camera is put away. Marty and I began a friendship that would last for many years.

After the feature aired on *Outlaws & Heroes*, I eventually sent a VHS copy to Marty's manager in Nashville. A few weeks later, I received a handwritten letter from Marty. I had it framed and it has adorned the wall of every place I have lived in since 1990. Today in Kingston, it hangs with much pride in my basement man cave/sanctuary, among my collection of many treasures.

> Oct 1, 1990
> Nashville
>
> Dear Bill,
> There's been a lot of television cameras on me and interviews done with me throughout my career—but the one that you put together is without a doubt the very best yet!
>
> I am very proud of this piece, and you did an incredible job.
>
> Once again, fantastic! Please stay in touch . . . new album out in Jan . . . called *Tempted*. It's pretty hot!
>
> Keep rockin',
> Marty Stuart

Wow. In the exact moment I finished reading the letter, I must have been the happiest person on earth. I knew it was a great interview that would result in a great segment. The cool thing about the interview was I didn't have lengthy notes. I didn't want to rely on a question/answer interrogation style of interview. I knew enough about Marty that I wanted it to be a *conversation*. I wanted him to talk and be comfortable sharing. I had spent a year and a half watching and editing great interviews with artists conducted by Christopher and Denise, and I put into practice what I learned from them. It was all about research, listening and engaging. A conversation!

Whenever Marty Stuart came to Toronto, we always had a camera available. One of my favourite moments with Marty was before a Garth Brooks show in Toronto. Marty opened for Garth at Maple Leaf Gardens in 1992. We had already done an interview earlier in the day, but he invited me to his bus before showtime. We sat and talked and laughed. He credited MuchMusic and Sherry and I for achieving more album sales in Canada (per capita) than in the USA. Eventually, he stood up, excused himself and went to the back of the bus. He returned moments later to present me with a gift . . . a Manuel jacket. It was a moment I would never forget. I was so appreciative of the gesture because I loved Manuel's work but could never afford his clothing.

Manuel Arturo José Cuevas Martínez is a famous designer to many A-list musicians, actors and even some politicians. He is the man who made Johnny Cash the "Man in Black." His client list is mind-blowing. Manuel designs have been worn by Elvis Presley, Hank Williams, Waylon Jennings, Porter Wagoner, John Wayne, Clayton Moore (the Lone Ranger), Dwight D. Eisenhower, John Lennon, Loretta Lynn, George Jones, Glen Campbell, Ernest Tubb, Gene Autry, Dolly Parton, Linda Ronstadt, Emmylou Harris, Neil Young, Elton John, The Rolling Stones, Bob Dylan, George H. W. Bush, George W. Bush, the Bee Gees, Dwight Yoakam, Janis Joplin, Jimi Hendrix, Salvador Dali and many more.

Marty proudly wore many pricey Manuel jackets on stage, on his album covers and in his music videos. To be given a Manuel jacket from Marty's own closet remains a career highlight. Marty was very generous and bestowed upon me a couple more Manuel creations in time.

CHAPTER FIVE
GRAM PARSONS'S CORPSE

Outlaws & Heroes would find a large and faithful audience on MuchMusic, hosted by Chris Ward and then Denise Donlon. In 1992, Denise stepped away from the cameras to go on maternity leave. I was asked to be the show's host. The concept was me, the show's editor, filling in for Denise while she was away.

At this time in the country music industry, the gawd-awful "new country" tag rose to prominence. Sherry and I hated the term. While there was a large proliferation of newer acts being signed to record labels and being played on the radio, the movement shut out older, established acts. *Outlaws & Heroes* took enormous pride in featuring newer acts, but it was important to us to remind viewers and newer fans to the genre that there was a large number of legends who shouldn't be ignored.

I would sometimes host the show from the edit bay, rewinding tapes and video clips to illustrate whatever I was talking about. To this day, it's a concept that has never been repeated. Sometimes it worked, sometimes it didn't, but it was always fun experimenting with the concept. On a trip to Nashville, we shot a great segment at a local honky-tonk bar. I interviewed one of the bouncers, I think his name was Tex. Tex was telling me that he was in the Marty Stuart and Travis Tritt music video for "The Whiskey Ain't Workin'." When the segment aired, at this point in the interview, we cut to me in the edit bay forwarding through the video, then stopping it where Tex was featured in a crowd shot. The viewer even saw me blow up the shot to a larger frame to show Tex up close, with me pointing at the monitor. On air, the segment looked seamless, smooth and fun, but the amount of shooting and editing required to *show* me editing a segment was a little exhausting and at times pretentious.

Another fun instance of using editing for the presentation of a music video for *Outlaws & Heroes* happened in 1993. I introduced Emmylou Harris's video for "High Powered Love" from the edit bay. I cited that this was a catchy tune with a great beat to dance to and said, "Heck! I might even dance myself right here while watching the video!" As the video played, I edited in a ten-second split-screen of me dancing with co-producer Sherry Greengrass in the edit bay. We actually received a lot of mail about that moment with viewers mentioning that they loved the dance sequence.

I was officially hosting *Outlaws & Heroes* in 1992 while also doing a regular editing shift for MuchMusic. I was loving my behind-the-scenes duties just as much as I loved doing all the interviews for *O&H* and being seen conversing with the likes of Marty Stuart, Diamond Rio, Tanya Tucker, Randy Travis, Dwight Yoakam, Billy Ray Cyrus, Michelle Wright, Waylon Jennings, Mark Chesnutt, Conway Twitty, Johnny Cash, George Strait, The Mavericks, Alan Jackson, Martina McBride, Travis Tritt, Garth Brooks, Shania Twain, Stompin' Tom Connors and every other major American and Canadian country star at the time. The job also involved many assignments to Nashville or across Canada to do interviews.

One of the things I noticed immediately was the connection to viewers. I started getting a lot of letters from followers of the show from across Canada, citing that they enjoyed the show and loved my interviews. Viewers of all ages would send me gifts and pictures and scrapbooks. One year, a viewer sent me a handmade wooden Christmas tree ornament of *me*. It was painted, and the details were incredible, right down to the tiny features of my sideburns and colourful cowboy boots.

I easily recognized the importance of the relationship between on-air personalities and viewers. That vital connection has stayed with me to this very day, especially with the advent of social media, which has made communication and interaction easier and quicker. I have never taken the role lightly, nor have I ever taken it for granted. It was always surprising to me, and it still is, to hear from a viewer that they enjoy my work. I have always said that the viewer is doing us a huge favour by watching, but I have worked with too many on-air people whose egos dictate that they are the ones doing the viewer a favour, simply by being on their TV screen. I am repulsed by that thought.

Over the years, viewers have told me that their mothers or grandparents asked about me on their death beds. Viewers have requested me to send them letters or videos of greetings and encouraging messages. Please note, I will never use the word "fan." To me, anyone that watches and appreciates my work is a faithful viewer or social media follower of mine. I believe that "fan" implies one-way respect and affection, but I return the same respect and affection to *anyone* who enjoys my work.

Parents have told me that they told their kids that they were only allowed to watch me if their homework was done, and that their kids obeyed and received great marks. Parents have requested me to visit their terminally ill children in the hospital. Those are moments I will never forget, and it makes me grateful that I can be the source of a smile for someone that needs one.

I learned to realize that my simply meeting someone might be a perfect circle for them—where they watched and enjoyed me on TV, and then eventually met me. I will never understand why me specifically, but I know now to just accept it and be very appreciative that I have a job that can inspire someone to smile.

It really is a blessing to look back and understand that my new role was more than a mere job. My recently bestowed on-air position at MuchMusic came without warnings that there would be responsibilities to nurture and foster connections with sponsors, record labels, music artists and (most important) the viewing audience. I embraced it. Being on the air at MuchMusic with *Outlaws & Heroes* even provided some signs that I may have even made it!

"Making it" or feeling one has *made it* is very subjective. To some, feeling that you are successful and that you've arrived or made it, might mean owning property. Or making your first million dollars? Hell yeah, you made it! To me, there were several instances in my life when I felt *I made it*. These moments didn't involve money or cars or real estate. They were small celebrations of tangible fun significances. MuchMusic gave stacks of personalized postcards to the VJs, to sign for viewers or to sign at appearances. My first batch of postcards had a colour picture of me in an edit bay wearing a Manuel jacket. I had my own postcard!? Wow, I made it! That postcard would be the first of five MuchMusic postcards in eight years, each with a different haircut and look.

When I first started hosting *O&H*, I once clipped out the page of the weekly nationally published 'TV Guide'. Each Sunday at 8 PM, it read *MM Outlaws & Heroes - Bill Welychka*. My name in TV Guide's national listings surely means I made it! Right?

I couldn't believe it when I read my name in Stompin' Tom Connors' massive autobiography, 1995's 'The Legend Continues'. Tom wrote about our MuchMusic interviews during his comeback period. It was an honour to think Canadian icon Tom Connors wrote about *me?* Man, I sure did make it!

During the 90s and well into the 2000s, I was the subject of dozens of articles and interviews in newspapers and magazines across Canada. What? People want to interview *me?* I am worthy of press attention and features? Wow! I must have made it!

Years later, I stopped thinking about if "I made it". It didn't matter. But I was reminded of the idea again in 2014, when I was an answer in a cross-Canada syndicated crossword puzzle published in Metro News by Torstar. The clue was 41 Down, *Canadian broadcaster Bill of MuchMusic and MuchMoreMusic*. What the hell!? WELYCHKA was the correct response in a national crossword puzzle!? Surely THIS means I made it!

To me, looking back at a large number of perfect circles, allows me to think I am somewhat sort of *maybe* successful. I have always returned to the concept of perfect circles, as a means to explain my personal version of *making it*.

A perfect circle moment for me was when I was interviewing Emmylou Harris in 1993. I have always loved her approach to songwriting, her wide range of eclectic influences and her ability to colour outside the lines given Nashville's strict establishment rules. She was an inspiration of mine from many years prior. She came to Toronto to promote her album, *Cowgirl's Prayer*. In a downtown hotel room, we talked about her new album, songwriting, her storied past, learning from the greats and her first start in 1971 working with the legendary Gram Parsons. Gram helped pioneer the late '60s' and early '70s' California country-rock sound. Emmylou Harris toured as a member of Gram's band, The Fallen Angels, and worked with him on his album, *Grievous Angel*.

After a great and thoughtful interview, our cameraperson stopped recording and proceeded to collapse the lights and pack up the gear. Also in the room was another gentleman who became busy talking on the phone and looking at notebooks. I assumed he was her tour manager. Emmylou and I continued to talk at length about Gram Parsons, even after the interview. She recounted to me Gram's final days. Before his death, Gram stated that he someday wanted his body cremated at Joshua Tree National Park and his ashes spread over nearby Cap Rock. In 1973, Gram died in his California motel room near Joshua Tree from an accidental overdose of drugs and alcohol.

As the legend goes, Gram Parsons's manager, Phil Kaufman, and a friend of Kaufman's, stole Gram's body from the Los Angeles International Airport before it could be flown to Louisiana, which is where Gram's family wanted to have the funeral. Kaufman and the friend somehow acquired a hearse and drove Gram's body to Joshua Tree, as per Gram's prior wishes. They attempted to cremate Parsons's corpse by pouring gasoline into the coffin and throwing a lit match inside. This resulted in a huge fireball, drawing police attention. Kaufman and his friend were only fined a small amount for stealing the coffin, since there was no law at the time against stealing a dead body. Oddly, they were not even prosecuted for leaving Gram's charred remains in the desert. Most of Gram Parsons's remains were eventually buried in Metairie, Louisiana.

Emmylou could easily see I was fascinated by this tale, and she was surprised by my knowledge of the legendary story. Manuel, the country designer, even made a custom suit for Gram, way before his death. As Emmylou and I stood up and said our goodbyes, I started to follow the cameraperson out the door. She called me back into the room. "Bill, meet my bus driver. He is Phil Kaufman's friend. He was there to grant Gram's final wishes."

CHAPTER SIX
A MESSAGE FROM GARTH

In 1992, country music artists had exploded with unprecedented album sales and sold-out tours around the world. The Billboard album charts would routinely have country music alongside rock, pop and hip-hop in the Top 10. On television, MuchMusic's *Outlaws & Heroes* was Canada's go-to source for all things country.

Garth Brooks became the biggest selling artist on the planet at this time. *O&H* was a big supporter of Garth. Sherry Greengrass and I played a lot of Garth in *O&H*'s early days. His talent, charisma and artistry were undeniable. His music videos were groundbreaking. But more than anything, his message of universal love, inclusivity and equality were relatively new for the country music genre. In 1992, "We Shall Be Free" was released, the new single and video from Garth to support his album, *The Chase*.

I was asked to go to Nashville and interview Garth. It would be my biggest interview to date in my burgeoning music journalist career. It was a whirlwind same-day trip, and all things went perfectly. The interview remains one of my favourite experiences, only because Garth is the dream interview subject. He is thoughtful, intense, funny and a proud humanitarian. The interview happened about three weeks after a Barbara Walters international TV special with Garth. In my opinion, my single-camera interview was way better than her massive, multiple-camera, fifteen-person, big-bucks American network production.

My interview was turned into a thirty-minute prime-time special for Canada on MuchMusic. It would have been a huge source of pride to have merely conducted the interview, but I also hosted, edited and produced the final product. Our publicity department at MuchMusic sent out screening copies to various major media outlets before the broadcast. This was my first experience seeing my name in a newspaper clipping (I am not counting my name being printed in the Richmond Hill Liberal for being the Third-Best Cub Scout of the Year). My Garth clippings file was two inches thick and included a very positive review by Canadian News Wire Services. My Garth interview was promoted in virtually every newspaper in Canada.

I heard from Garth's record label in Canada, Capitol/EMI, that Garth loved the special. I had hoped he would. More importantly, I had hoped Canadian viewers would love it! And they did, with huge, record numbers reported in the national ratings.

I would have several interviews with Garth Brooks in the next two years or so. He has a rare, God-given talent to make *everyone* feel special. A handshake from Garth came with direct, eye-to-eye contact from him where you might believe he was looking into your soul. It was the first time I realized that meeting *anyone* meant that they were being present in the moment and appreciating and welcoming you into their space, even if only for a split second. I began to find it fascinating that no matter how important a figure was or how big their personality shone, that there could be a fraction of time, frozen, where their energy and presence and space is centered and focused on *you*. This interaction is special and happens to every one of us multiple times daily. Isn't this a wonderful realization?

On one of Garth's trips to Toronto, he invited me back to his hotel room following an interview. He had a business idea he wanted to talk about. Later in the evening, Garth buzzed me up to his suite at the downtown Four Seasons hotel. After some drinks and catching up, he wanted my opinion on a business venture he wanted to pursue. He loved watching MuchMusic whenever he came to Canada. He thought it was way more entertaining and credible than MTV or even CMT (Country Music Television) in the US. He explained to me his new concept for a music television station. He wanted to bring MuchMusic's energy and vibe to the US with a new station that would offer a twist: viewers would be able to order CDs via a 1-800 number while a music video was being played or while the artist was being interviewed. His idea was for a music channel that combined elements of a home-shopping channel. This was around the mid '90s when everyone was buying CDs. All music labels were making record profits, and Garth believed in the concept of TV and music working together in a way that furthered CD sales for markets and in rural areas that didn't have access to record stores. He had partners that wanted to invest and partners that could handle marketing, promotion and distribution of music, but he wanted to know what it took to run a national TV station with equipment, resources, personnel and other factors.

I listened intently while he spoke. On the outside, I am sure I looked like the pro he thought I was, never looking or reacting like a "fan." I remember I offered my suggestions on what a TV studio would need to offer the best sound and how many production people it would require to pull off this new venture. On the inside, I was thinking, *FACK! The biggest selling artist in the world values my opinion!* This was the dude that had made me dance and cry with his music. I thought to myself, *There are millions of people that would kill to be in my position right now.* Thankfully, I was really good at centering myself and summoning calm and concentration when I needed it.

We exchanged numbers and I wished him a safe trip home. I never did call him, and I figured if he needed to talk to me, he now had my number. About three months later, I received a voice message from Garth. The message was on my answering machine. This was before cellphones and texting and voice mails. I still have the answering machine microcassette that contains Garth's message: "Hey Bill! It's G.B.! Remember that thing we were talking about when I was there in To-Ronno? I haven't forgotten ya. It looks like things are happening! Talk to ya soon, pal!"

I didn't hear from Garth after that. His business venture, which was groundbreaking and ahead of its time, didn't materialize. Music tastes shifted, my roles at MuchMusic were changing and Garth eventually went into hiding for a short period of time after his *Garth Brooks in . . . The Life of Chris Gaines* concept album was deemed a flop. It was painful for me to learn that Garth's brilliant idea for marketing music didn't come to fruition. In my opinion, I thought it was brilliant for the mid-90s.

It wasn't until what seems a lifetime later in 2016 when I was in Kingston at CKWS-TV, that Garth and I would see each other again. I was sent to

A HAPPY HAS-BEEN

Ottawa for a Garth Brooks press conference prior to his sold-out show and launching point for his Canadian tour at the Canadian Tire Centre. It was a packed room full of national and local media, and Garth made everyone present feel important and welcomed. After the press conference, both Garth and his wife Trisha Yearwood focused on me and called me over to them. Garth immediately offered a hug and asked, "Bill, buddy! How ya been?" We proceeded to talk while our cameraperson rolled on what was a great interview and catch-up, and even Trisha was excited to be part of our reunion. It was great television. But it was especially fun for me and my crew knowing that no one else was allowed a one-on-one interview.

Garth was born to make people feel good and he has a God-given gift to inspire. He has a magic and positive energy swirling around him. There are few people in this world that can offer what Garth brings to the table.

· · · · ·

Denise Donlon would return from her mat leave in 1993, and we became co-hosts for *Outlaws & Heroes*. She was impressed with the viewer feedback regarding my presence on *O&H*, but our pairing wouldn't last long as Denise would step up to become MuchMusic's director of music programming. To this day, Denise Donlon remains one of my favourite bosses of all time. She introduced a drive for relevance in MuchMusic's programming. She would prove that music wasn't necessarily mere entertainment, but that it could change lives, bring awareness, create discussion around many social issues and be used as a platform for charity. As my boss, Denise once told me, "I wish I could clone you." It's a memory I have held on to dearly for decades. From then on, in every work situation, I would conduct myself in a professional manner that I hoped would have every boss feeling the same way.

I would helm hundreds of interviews as the sole host for *Outlaws & Heroes*. Most interviews were in Toronto, but there were more than a few trips to Nashville to conduct interviews. On one of my trips to Music City, USA, I interviewed Polygram/Mercury star Ronna Reeves at a location of her choosing, the Country Music Hall of Fame. I had interviewed Ronna a few months prior in Toronto when she opened for Billy Ray Cyrus at Maple Leaf Gardens. Our interview in Nashville went extremely well. So well that I asked her to dinner. I had never asked any interview subject out on a date before. I was already a big fan of her powerful voice and was very smitten with her intelligence, wit, charm and beauty. She kindly rejected my offer, citing that she was already in a relationship.

A couple of months went by before her publicist reached out to me. Ronna would be in Toronto for a nationally syndicated country radio show and wanted to know if I was available for dinner later in the evening. I was very excited and happy to realize she hadn't forgotten about me! We made plans for dinner in Toronto. Weeks later, I attended the radio taping as part of the studio audience. As instructed, I waited for the show to be over and hung around until her manager came and got me and invited me into the dressing room.

Ronna and I got caught up with some small talk and I sensed a strong connection. Later in the evening, we met for dinner. One couldn't have scripted a more romantic and beautiful experience. I learned more about her than was included in the standard press releases that accompany each artist's release and more than I had learned through our previous TV interviews. She openly shared with me details about her life growing up in west Texas, about opening many shows for country legend George Strait in her teen years and about getting a major label deal and moving to Nashville. The evening turned to late night, and we eventually saw the morning together. I was sitting on the floor against the side of the bed in her downtown hotel, watching the sun break through the clouds straight into our window. I felt grateful to be alive and appreciative of this perfect moment, yet felt unbelievably sad that we would have to say goodbye soon. I recognized that I had transitioned from being smitten, to having a crush, to falling in love. I was happy to hear her words when she said, "I don't want this to end. This *can* happen! We can do this. It will be long distance, but I want this! Do you?"

I replied, "Yes! I sure do."

We would take turns visiting each other. I would take some days off and visit Ronna in Nashville when she wasn't touring, or she would visit me in Toronto for a few days. The lapses in between visits became a repeated cycle of emotions. Ultimate joy, elation and bliss when we were with each other, and then pain and depression when saying goodbye. The depression would slowly diminish only when we started making plans for the next visit. Anticipation and excitement would build as the days grew closer to finally seeing each other again. Being in her presence meant feelings of ecstasy. This exhausting pattern would repeat every one to two months. It was the first time in my life that I experienced a love and commitment I had never felt or dreamed of having before. Ronna was extremely close to her family, and it didn't take long for me to be welcomed into it by her mom, dad and older brother. I spent Christmas holidays in Nashville and her parents gave me my first-ever Christmas stocking. Stockings were never a thing at Christmas in my family, so I was deeply touched by the gracious gesture of finding candy, small toys and fruit in my personalized Christmas stocking.

Our lives were spent talking on the phone, writing letters and planning the next trip to see each other. There were times when I would even join her on the road, flying in to one city, meeting her at the concert, travelling for a few days on the tour bus, then flying back to Toronto from another city. On one trip, I flew into Shreveport, Louisiana. After the show, her band and I got acquainted at the bar. They wanted to bond with me, and I wanted to do the same with them. They tested my mettle by doing shots with me. Many shots. While Ronna was off signing autographs at her merchandise table, I was getting hammered, thanks to her equally hammered band. On a tour bus, there is a front lounge; in the middle, there are sleeping bunks on both sides; and in the back is the stateroom, complete with a large, pull-out bed. Ronna got angry at her band for getting me in such an altered state. She put me to bed in the stateroom, kissed me goodnight and then retired to a bunk. I tried my best to not vomit. Mission successful. To her band, I was this awesome dude from Canada that could out-drink any of them. To myself, I was ashamed that Ronna and I began our week with me having a hangover. Her band and I behaved much better at the shows that followed in Kansas, Oklahoma and Texas.

Somewhere in south Texas, Ronna headlined a county fair concert. While she was at the hotel getting ready, I was on the bus with the band. Some of us ventured out to walk around the fair grounds. It was the first time I sampled gator meat. Back at the bus, two Texas State Troopers were assigned as security. When we returned to the tour bus, one of her band members said to the troopers, "This here is Bill, visiting from Canada. He ain't seen a gun before! They have no guns in Canada."

One of the friendly troopers looked at me, unholstered his weapon and said, "Serious? We here in Texas are pretty much born with a gun in our hands. It's not a weapon, but a tool we grow up with. Hell, you ain't never seen one up close? Take a look! Hold it if you wanna!" He handed me his gun and it felt heavy. I looked at it and turned it over in my hand, holding tight on to the handle. I carefully examined it and felt its weight. I noticed its shine, and I studied its grooves and details. I turned it towards my eyes to look down the long barrel. "WHOA, SON! Gimme that! Whatcha doin'? You never look at a gun like that!" the trooper yelled, as he grabbed it from my hand. I was embarrassed, knowing immediately that how I handled the gun was very wrong. I apologized, wished them a good day and climbed back onto the bus, thinking, *I hope these Texans don't think all Canadians are dumb-asses.*

In a few days, I would fly back to Toronto from Houston, the day after Ronna's gig there. That familiar depression hit hard as we said our goodbyes. As the plane gained altitude, my spirit and emotions plummeted. I was actually getting used to the depression that would accompany our goodbyes.

I was assigned to travel to Jamaica with MuchMusic in 1994 for our spring break broadcast. Ronna flew down to meet me and stayed with me for the week. We taped an episode of *Outlaws & Heroes* with us co-hosting. We didn't necessarily try to keep our relationship a secret, but I certainly didn't want viewers to think Ronna's videos were being played because we were dating. Yes, I was partial to seeing Ronna being featured on *O&H*, but viewers didn't mind. We even saw a large increase in viewer mail requesting even more Ronna! Perhaps they enjoyed the co-host episode where they got to see her in a bikini on the beach?

The music press in Canada would publish pictures of Ronna and I at various Toronto country shows, and although not fully trying to keep our relationship hidden, the audience and industry would know.

By the fall of 1994, *Outlaws & Heroes* would come to an end. The show was cancelled after the introduction of a new Canadian TV country music channel, The New Country Network. NCN would be renamed Country

Music Television (CMT), after partnering with the US-based station. The MuchMusic bosses felt that our ninety-minute weekly country show could not compete with an entire new rival network devoted to country music. The final *O&H* broadcast showcased many moments from the show's six-year history and featured many artists like Ian Tyson, Marty Stuart and Aaron Tippin calling in to say thanks for the support.

That period also meant the end for Ronna and me. After a few weeks of trying to figure out every possible angle where our relationship could work, I made the decision to break things off as I wouldn't get to Nashville as much anymore. I certainly wasn't going to move there, and she definitely couldn't move to Toronto. Everything she did was based around Nashville. It was her home, and it included her manager, touring band, record company, publicist, friends and family. I was devasted and heartbroken. The only love I had ever really known came to a grinding halt *not* because of falling out of love, but because of long distance. It was excruciating for me to not only be the one to bring what was a beautiful relationship to an end, but to also explain this to Ronna and to my close friends.

At this point in my life, 1994 would feature the highest of highs and lowest of lows that I had ever experienced. Despite the success of *Outlaws & Heroes* and how hard Sherry and I had worked to create a recognizable and respected national and international brand and a ratings winner, it was now gone. I still maintained an editing and producing shift for MuchMusic, but I didn't care either way if I continued an on-air presence or not.

My boss Denise Donlon became my saviour. She would go on to ask me something that would turn my life completely upside down.

CHAPTER SEVEN
SLASH'S PORN

When my world was seemingly coming apart in late 1994, my boss at MuchMusic, Denise Donlon, asked me to put aside my experiences with *Outlaws & Heroes*. She said be proud of what it was and of what Sherry and I had created, but that it was time to look forward. She asked me to become a regular flow VJ. She saw enough in me to think that I could become part of an esteemed few. Being a regular flow MuchMusic VJ meant being the face and focus of live, four-hour shifts a few times a week. It required a love and knowledge of all kinds of music. It meant having a sense of style and knowing and predicting trends. It was compulsory to be creative, to take control of programming and to offer fun and spontaneous deliveries of the music. It was imperative to work well and play well with others, especially the live crew of camera operators, directors, graphics people, audio operators, tape operators, producers and others.

I was extremely flattered to be offered this amazing opportunity, but my biggest concern was the audience. How would I be accepted, going from being known as "the country guy" to regular daily programming? Would our national audience accept me introducing rock and hip hop videos and interviewing artists in these other genres? I had my concerns, but my fears would be unfounded. It worked just fine.

Around the time I started being a MuchMusic regular flow VJ, a band from York, Pennsylvania called Live came out with a song entitled, "Lightning Crashes." The song's atmosphere, lyrics and mood grabbed me and soothed me. I sunk into the video and the band. Their 1994 album

Throwing Copper became a favourite. It was an album I would fall asleep to on many nights. I eagerly shared my love of the song's video with viewers each time I introduced it. I became MuchMusic's biggest supporter of the band, and it was a treat to eventually interview them many times in the following years. I credit the band Live as being a powerful muse for me in crossing over to being a MuchMusic VJ.

In my first month or two of being a MuchMusic VJ, I would go live interviewing Chris Isaak, Sophie B. Hawkins, Bob Seger, Spacehog, Weezer, Tom Cochrane, Simple Minds, Blur, the Goo Goo Dolls, Foreigner, The Stone Roses and many others. They were great live interviews that were televised across Canada. My goals were simple: make sure the artist enjoyed the encounter and make sure the artist appreciated my original questions and the ensuing dialogue. I wanted to ensure that viewers who were fans of the artist would be rewarded with an engaging experience and would love watching the interview. I also wanted the live segment and interview to be compelling enough for viewers who didn't know the artist or their songs to watch and perhaps be led to learn more about the artist.

While VJing for MuchMusic, I knew damn well how fortunate I was. I could live in both worlds, involved behind the scenes with editing and producing *and* active on air. Creating television was all I cared about. I noticed that some other VJs had higher aspirations than to simply work in TV. Some wanted to use their on-air experience to move into acting or to pursue a career in music. I was totally content to work on both sides of the camera. I had also noticed that some VJs would develop personas that made them easily identifiable to the audience. I was never the wacky one. I also wasn't the cute one. Or the political one. If I did have *any* persona to offer, it was that I was the one that loved music, loved interviewing and loved creating television.

Sometimes, I would use my editing skills to incorporate a fun presentation of the music videos. When I wasn't on air during a VJ shift, I would be in one of the edit bays, pulling soundbites (short interview clips) to be played before an artist's video. In the first month of being a MuchMusic VJ, we had Van Halen's "Don't Tell Me (What Love Can Do)" on high rotation. It was a gritty, conceptual video that featured a Van Halen performance interspersed with a storyline having to do with gangs and prison life. It was a big departure from Van Halen's previous reputation as being a fun party band. The band's musical statement with their video was to show that being in a gang is not glorious. The video featured numerous gang members at various times showing scars on their bodies with full-frame graphics proclaiming, "drive-by victim," "knifing victim" or "gunshot victim." I re-edited the video for a one-time play, adding scattered dramatic zoom-in shots of a scar over my left eyebrow and another on my elbow with graphics reading, "recess playground accident with a wayward swing" and "fell off his bike in third grade." My shots and the accompanying graphics matched the texturized shots in the Van Halen video.

After the video aired, the normally jaded live MuchMusic crew was laughing and clapping. I think they and the viewers appreciated the humour I set out to create. I certainly was not poking fun at the serious plight of gang life, but was making fun of myself as being the opposite of tough and threatening. I wished I had saved the clip to show Eddie Van Halen, Alex Van Halen, Sammy Hagar and Michael Anthony. I would interview Van Halen a couple times in later years, with one interview conducted in Eddie Van Halen's house in LA.

Around this time, I thought it best to cut my hair. It reached halfway down my back, and the long curly locks became an inconvenience. I started getting it cut in stages. I am only referencing my hair now because for thirty years, people have asked me about having long hair. My reaction to questions about my hair is, "What about those interviews? What about those international assignments?" Nope. It's weird to me that many people might only remember me for having long hair.

Transferring to a live, main flow MuchMusic VJ shift was challenging in terms of confidence. I was given a lot of support at this time by MCA Records rep Andrea Orlick. We had become close during the *Outlaws & Heroes* period. Her music tastes were very aligned with mine: she loved country and The Cure, and we had a ton of other bands in common in our record/CD collections. We dated for a short period, but like with many women I went out with, we broke up and developed a friendship afterward. We have remained very good friends over the years.

One day in early 1995, she came to visit, and she looked exhausted. She told me that she'd just dropped Slash off at the airport. Andrea had set up

Slash's three-day media blitz for Toronto and was responsible for the Guns N' Roses' guitar player's schedule to promote his new solo release, *It's Five O'Clock Somewhere*. Andrea took Slash around town while he did media appearances and interviews. She also spent free time with him, going to dinners, bookstores (he's an avid reader), pinball arcades *and* a stop-in at an adult video store.

Andrea told me that Slash had bought about fifteen porn videotapes and brought them back to his hotel room to watch, but the next morning had asked her to return them because he didn't like them. They weren't the type of porn he liked. Apparently, they were "too tame." At that time, Andrea still had the videos that needed to be returned. I said, "What? You still have Slash's porn in your car? Ummm, can you leave them with me?"

Hesitantly she replied, "Really? Okay, but I need to get them back to the store soon." I grabbed the bag of VHS tapes from her trunk and brought them inside. Admittedly, I watched the tapes over a period of about a week. Slash watched most of them in one night. Slash is not only one of the world's greatest guitar players, but he's also one of the fastest viewers of porn! Then again, as Andrea had said, he wasn't digging them, so he was likely fast-forwarding through them. It was funny though, seeing a Visa receipt still in the bag, showing that the tapes were purchased by Saul Hudson (Slash's real name).

I did eventually return the bag to Andrea, and it still amuses me to admit that I had Slash's porn for about a week.

I would interview Slash many times following that experience. I was always tempted to say something about temporarily having his porn, but I never did.

· · · · ·

In early 1996, I was asked to interview Dave Grohl live on MuchMusic. It would be a live, thirty-minute interview spread out with Foo Fighters videos. I was sure that every rock fan in Canada would be tuning in to view the spectacle because it would be the first time he was talking about his life post-Nirvana. He had formed a band to tour, supporting his self-titled Foo Fighters debut. That Foos debut was in the truest sense, a solo album. Dave played all the instruments on the recordings that were done in secret in late 1994, the same year as Kurt Cobain's untimely passing. Dave would prove that there was life beyond being Nirvana's drummer. The album is, quite simply, brilliant. It solidified my love, respect and admiration for Dave Grohl, someone who I adore to this day.

There is a delicate balancing act in interviewing someone like Dave, who's life was turned upside down after his friend and bandmate's much-publicized apparent suicide. Kurt Cobain and Nirvana's music was a global phenomenon that ushered in new music trends and would influence a whole new generation to rethink how music was produced, written and marketed. *Anything* Nirvana following the band's demise was of major interest worldwide. That huge interest included Dave Grohl's debut solo outing. At this stage in Dave's career, he was trying really hard to downplay his role in Nirvana while wanting everyone to know about his new Foo Fighters project.

MuchMusic had allowed a live audience of about fifty young people into the building to watch the live interview. Many more were watching through MuchMusic's famous Queen Street windows. I was a big Nirvana fan, but I also thought Dave's solo debut outshone much of Nirvana's work. It was brave and bold. It was bombastic and yet poppy at times. It was the work of someone who obviously loved songwriting and creating music with huge passion. One got a sense that in Nirvana, Dave was merely a drummer. The Foo Fighter's debut proved that Dave was a gifted musician with a knack for writing original yet highly accessible tunes.

The live interview began with a visibly nervous Dave Grohl, soon relaxing and enjoying the moment, thoroughly delighted in our talk and seemingly grateful to be surrounded by so many excited fans.

We talked about how he wrote all the songs in his own studio and how he wanted to assemble a band to play live shows. He explained how silly it would be to say yes to any of the hundreds of interview requests he was getting when no one had heard a single note from his album. He said he knew people just wanted him to dish the dirt.

I knew everyone watching at home and those gathered in the MuchMusic environment were wanting and waiting for him to just say the word "Nirvana" or utter the name "Kurt Cobain." I also sensed that Dave knew that people wanted him to say those words. I knew it was my job to appease the audience and satisfy my own curiosity, but also to make Dave feel like this live interview was a great experience. I didn't want Dave to punch me in the mouth!

I brought up the fact that Nirvana's "Smells Like Teen Spirit" was already being called the anthem of the '90s. Things got real quiet. Dave responded with, "Hey, if people got off on it, great. To me, it was just this . . ." and he mimicked, in a boring fashion, playing drums. Things got quiet again.

In my mind, I thought, *Really? That song meant nothing to you?* It was as if he was implying that all his contributions to a globally massive-selling and highly influential band was at best an exercise in merely moving his arms in a robotic fashion. I know he didn't mean that, but for anyone watching, I was hoping they would get a more thoughtful answer. See? It was a delicate balancing act to lead a conversation into a territory where everyone could be satisfied.

After a second or two of him downplaying his involvement in Nirvana's legacy, I asked point blank, "Does it hurt to talk about it?"

Uh-oh. More silence. But only for a moment, as he came back with, "Wouldn't you think it would? Why would you even ask?"

I replied "Time? Maybe enough time has passed." After saying it, I felt ashamed for trying to get an answer or anything resembling a response, but it was the best I could do in that split second moment. Watching the tape back later that day and even years later, it wasn't the disaster I thought it was at the time. It was actually great television.

Dave deflected the question perfectly. He explained how some things should remain private and how not having a bleeding heart when being in a band is fun and games, but mostly it's just about the music. In my opinion, he answered the question by explaining why he didn't want to answer the question. It was brilliant and honest and endearing and sweet and heart-felt. I felt good with his response, and I am sure everyone watching felt the same way.

The rest of the interview went very well. At the end of the live segment, before we said goodbye, I gave him a box of Girl Guide cookies (it was Girl Guide cookie week) and I presented him with a signed copy of Stompin' Tom Connors's autobiography. I knew he was a fan of the Canadian country legend. He truly loved my gifts, embracing them both in his arms as if he was holding newborn twins. He was grateful and I could tell he enjoyed his time with us, and he said goodbye to a loud and appreciative cheering studio audience.

The next day, Denise Donlon called me into her office. She asked me why I brought up Nirvana. I explained that there is no Foo Fighters without Nirvana and I felt that it was important to reference it somehow. I also reminded her that I never actually mentioned the word "Nirvana." She explained that Dave Grohl's record company and management was livid with me because they told me before the interview to not go anywhere near the subject of Nirvana.

I said, "Ummm, no. Not true. No one issued that request to me. And if they did, I would have come to you telling you and I would have asked for your guidance."

She said, "I thought so. You did well. We can't be dictated to. We can't be told what subjects are deemed off-limits. I am proud of you." There really is no wonder at all why I cite Denise Donlon as one of my favourite bosses of all time.

I would interview Dave Grohl many more times following that first interview in 1996. He was always gracious and kind. We would easily establish a great rapport and years later in 2005, he hosted me at his newly built recording studio north of Los Angeles for what would become one of the television special projects I am most proud of.

· · · · ·

In 1996, I became borderline-obsessed with TV's *The X-Files*. The sci-fi drama had already been on the air since 1993, but I became an ardent viewer a few years later. I loved the show's concept and mythological, convoluted story arc about government conspiracies, aliens and paranormal occurrences. I also quickly became enamoured by its lead co-star, Gillian Anderson (portraying FBI Agent Dana Scully). I would sometimes talk about *The X-Files* and my crush on Gillian live on air during my MuchMusic VJ shifts. Viewers even started sending me homemade scrapbooks of magazine pictures of Gillian.

It turned out that a friend of mine knew someone that worked on the show behind the scenes. Scott Steyns had worked on the show as a

A HAPPY HAS-BEEN

playback coordinator since the series' pilot episode. Scott called me one spring day in 1997 and invited me to come out to tour the show's set in Vancouver and attend the season four wrap party. My presence there was not for a TV assignment, but just to attend as an invited guest on vacation. I said, "Absolutely! And thanks so much!" In a few days, after booking a hotel and return airfare at the last minute, I was off to Vancouver. It was an expensive vacation but well worth every penny.

Meeting Scott was awesome. He was very cool and we got along great. He took me to the large studio where *The X-Files* was filmed. The sets for *The X-Files* were in the process of being torn down as the season was about to wrap. But, I did recognize FBI Assistant Director Walter Skinner's desk. It was easy to spot because the nameplate on the desk read FBI Assistant Director Walter Skinner. (Agent Skinner was played by actor Mitch Pileggi.) I also spotted FBI Agent Dana Scully's bed. I took the opportunity to stretch out on it and get a picture. I have a huge smile on my face in the pic.

The next night, it was time for *The X-Files* season four wrap party. At the private function, I met *The X-Files* creator and executive producer Chris Carter. He thanked me for talking about his show so much on TV. I also met actors Mitch Pileggi and William B. Davis (Cancer Man). Later in the evening, Scott introduced me to Gillian Anderson. I swore I heard angels from heaven singing. Her silhouette was surrounded by a beautiful blinding glow. Standing in front of me, she was even more beautiful than I could imagine. (Did I mention I had a big crush on Gillian Anderson?)

We began to talk, I had to lower my head down to hear her over the loud music. As I looked down to listen to her words, I noticed her perfect, pretty feet in her open-toed dress sandals. She told me she watched a lot of MuchMusic and she admitted that she had seen me talking about the show and specifically about her. She said thanks for all the kind things I had said. After a few minutes of talking, she asked me if I wanted to dance.

First, I didn't even expect to meet Gillian. I was surprised and grateful to even get more than a kind hello from her. Now, we were conversing. What the hell!? And then she was asking me to dance? I just about dropped my bottle of Heineken. I didn't expect this at all. Second, I don't dance. I'm a terrible dancer. But I couldn't say, "No thanks." Instead, I nodded to her invite to dance and bravely led her to the dance floor. This was not going to be pretty.

It felt as if my soul had left my body. It got too surreal for me. After about two minutes of dancing, I excused myself and went to the bar. And stayed there.

After about five minutes, Scott came up to me and said, "Bill! What happened? She just broke up with her husband and you left her on the dance floor? Not cool!" I was ashamed of myself. I replied, "I don't know. I didn't expect to dance with her or begin a relationship! I got nervous."

I was such an idiot. Gillian, if by chance you are reading this, I am so sorry I left you on the dance floor. It was a huge thrill meeting you. I was blown away by your amazing presence. You were so sweet and kind and generous with your time. I apologize for being a huge moron.

CHAPTER EIGHT
DEAD SKIN CELLS

Many of my favourite experiences at MuchMusic involved the opportunity to travel. In the '90s, the record labels had huge budgets for promoting their artists' releases. They would pitch a project to Denise Donlon and if she believed in the artist and project, we would discuss how the resulting interview would be showcased. Usually, it meant sending me and a cameraperson out on assignment to interview the artist outside of Toronto, and often outside of Canada.

I have had the pleasure of visiting every province and territory in Canada. I have visited about twenty-five US states. For a time, I was in New York City or Los Angeles every other week. (I have always loved New York City much more than LA.) I've travelled to Mexico, Guatemala, Jamaica many times, Barbados, Haiti, England numerous times, Trinidad, Kenya, Denmark, France, Italy, Switzerland, India, Australia twice, Cuba and many more destinations. I know very well that I had one of the best jobs in the world, being exposed to numerous cultures and histories, exploring geography, meeting interesting people and sampling different cuisine. I am one of those people that has kept all of my expired passports as souvenirs of my world travels, but God only knows what the hell the unintelligible blurred stamps actually read.

Monte Carlo, Monaco was an annual destination for six years in a row where I covered the World Music Awards. The week-long assignments were intense but fun. Over those six years, some of the interviews I conducted included ones with Prince Albert, Pam Anderson, Cher, Janet

BILL WELYCHKA

Jackson, Jon Bon Jovi, Celine Dion, Tony Bennett, Bo Derek, Will Smith, Lionel Richie, Evander Holyfield, the Backstreet Boys, Shania Twain, the Bee Gees, Mariah Carey, Britney Spears, Sugar Ray's Mark McGrath, Ace of Base, Shaggy, Christina Aguilera, Mike Tyson, The Corrs, A-ha's Morten Harket, Tyra Banks, Michael Jackson, Barenaked Ladies and so many more. One particular year, I met up with Johnny Rzeznik (the Goo Goo Dolls) repeatedly at an Irish pub after the long days spent at glitzy champagne receptions. We both realized a quiet pub was much more our speed amidst the glamourous backdrops of palaces and yacht club soirées. I vividly recall one late night trying to explain to him the magic and brilliance of Canada's The Tragically Hip after he admitted that he couldn't understand their popularity. I schooled him properly.

· · · · ·

In 1999, the highly respected aid agency World Vision Canada asked me to host their 30 Hour Famine fundraising video. The video would be shown in schools across Canada to pique students' interest in raising money to support life improvement projects and fight world hunger. I had asked to see the previous years' videos and each year seemed to show the same dire conditions in numerous third world countries. I asked if we could do something different that year. My idea was let's show where the money from the previous years' fundraising efforts actually went. Let's witness the new hospitals and schools being built, let's see the farming and irrigation projects in place. Let's prove that the money raised does amazing things and saves hundreds of lives. We'll also show where the money raised this time is needed and provide the participants with assurance that their hard work is well worth their time and interest.

About a month later, I was in Kenya helping to write and produce the video that would eventually be shown in hundreds of schools across Canada. Although we were staying in Nairobi, the video I hosted featured many visits to the outlying areas around Kenya where World Vision had a solid presence. We took a small plane to some very remote areas. One air excursion had us flying past Mount Kilimanjaro. We visited and shot successful projects in the Turkana District, Mwatate, Tunyo and other locations. I was witness to life changing projects involving food, health, education, farming, water and sanitation. On one particular day that I will never forget, we spent some time with the Masai Mara people on their reserve in Narok, Kenya, along the Serengeti. World Vision had established numerous projects there, including assisting with water catchment.

Towards the end of the two-week mission, we went on a safari. At the end of the day, I excused myself from the gathering and retired to my small, bare-bones cabin. In the darkness, I noticed a large vulture in a tree eyeing me. The thing was way too close for my comfort level, and I was imagining this *monster* swooping down on me within the next few seconds. This thing was massive! I'm a dumb-ass guy from Toronto, so to me, this was a large, menacing predator sizing me up as a meal. Or at least a snack. I ran back towards our group and had one of our tour guides walk me back to my cabin. I said thanks and quickly locked the door behind me. I imagine he was shaking his head laughing at my cowardice as he returned to the party.

I am proud to say that the resulting video that was shown in schools across Canada helped raise record funds for World Vision Canada. I am *not* proud to say that I fear mammoth birds.

· · · · ·

In 2000, I travelled to the Bahamas to interview Gloria Estefan, who was releasing her record, *Alma Caribeña*. It was an easy and fun assignment. I was there for three days for a thirty-minute interview, staying at the beautiful Atlantis Resort on Paradise Island. I was seeing a new girlfriend at this time, Anna, so I flew her down after I arrived. There was a lot of extra time before my interview with Gloria.

Admittedly, I am not a beach guy. I don't like the idea of just lying down on a blanket on a sandy beach. I always feel I should be doing something constructive, not lounging. Especially when I am on a work assignment! And I hate sand. But there really was a large amount of spare time on this particular trip. My girlfriend Anna wanted to hit the beach and begged me to come with her. I reluctantly obliged. She lathered up with sunscreen and recommended I do the same. I declined, saying, "I am not going to be here too long. Just a quick jump into the ocean, then I am heading back to the room." She explained to me that the sun's intensity is stronger in the

Caribbean. It's not the same kind of sun we have in Canada. I figured that the sun is the sun. It's not a big issue, so I declined her offer of sunscreen. I stayed longer on the beach than I had originally planned. I was enjoying our time together and getting to know her in this unique and rare fun situation. Yup . . . I developed a sunburn.

The rest of the work assignment in the Bahamas went great, except for fighting through the pain of being burned during the interview with Gloria Estefan. I was also very flattered to meet a local Bahamian who recognized me, citing that he had a satellite dish and that the Canadian music TV stations were his favourite channels to watch. Cool dude! When I returned to Toronto, I had to get ready in a few days to head to Monaco to cover the World Music Awards again. By the time I arrived at the airport to leave for Monaco, my skin had started peeling from the sunburn. On the flights to Frankfurt and then on to Nice, France, I was scratching my chest. The peeling skin was causing extreme itching. Once our flight landed in Nice, I stood up from my middle seat to retrieve my bag from the overhead compartment. All that dead skin I was scratching off my chest came out in a cascade of large skin flakes from under my shirt, falling on to the shoulder of my cameraperson, who was also my seatmate. When he realized all my dead skin was falling on his shoulder and lap while he was positioned in the aisle seat, he let out a loud, "What the fuck! What is this? GROSS!" I was embarrassed but I couldn't stop laughing. I continued to scratch and laugh all the way off the plane and through the terminal in Nice. I am sure I left a healthy dose of my DNA all the way from the plane seat to baggage claim.

· · · · ·

The United Nations celebrated their fiftieth anniversary in 1995. They had approached MuchMusic with a pitch for an hour special. We agreed to a project that eventually involved travelling to three countries where they have important projects established, and while there, we would shoot some music and culturally interesting aspects. The final result would be three specials from these countries to air on MuchMusic's *ClipTrip* (a show featuring world music), and at the end, a prime time hour special on

MuchMusic showcasing the UN's endeavours to improve infrastructure and create better living opportunities around the world.

The countries we chose were Haiti, India and Trinidad. MuchMusic producer Morgen Flury, a cameraperson and I would visit each country for a week. The assignments were spread out over three months.

Haiti has such a rich and interesting history. I learned why the United Nations had a strong presence there, especially in 1995. Haiti is considered the poorest country in the western hemisphere. Many Haitians were risking their lives trying to make it to Florida for a better life, but many died when their homemade vessels sank on the Antillas Mayores route between the West Indies and Cuba. Enough Haitians would make it past Cuba and arrive at Florida's most southern tip that the Clinton Administration needed assistance from the UN. The week we were in Haiti was the same week that US military personnel sent to Haiti were being relieved of their duties to make way for UN troops to establish enforcements in order to stop refugees from attempting the dangerous journey to the USA.

During our week in Haiti, we videotaped President Clinton's speech at the Haitian President's National Palace. We also spoke to then–UN Secretary-General, Boutros Boutros-Ghali (a name that David Letterman has cited as one of his favourites on the *Late Night* show).

We travelled all over the island filming the numerous UN projects that had been established to aid in Haiti's recovery. We also interviewed many Haitian artists and musicians. I learned that art in all its forms is something people turn to, even in the direst situations. We tracked down a voodoo priest and visited his compound. The joyful and short old fellow recounted Haiti's sad history and how voodoo played into the country's culture. During the interview, he was drinking from a large bottle containing some kind of alcohol. Our Haitian French translator said it was homemade whisky. Our voodoo priest friend passed it to Tony Wannamaker, our cameraperson. Tony had a swig and passed it to me. I drank a mouthful and passed it to Morgen. She shook her head, implying, "No, thanks!" I passed it back to our lil voodoo priest friend. We eventually wrapped up the interview and drove back to our hotel in Port-au-Prince.

The next morning, Tony and I became close-to-death ill. We discovered that the both of us were getting searing pains in our stomachs and pissing out our asses with major diarrhea. Morgen said she felt fine. We blamed it on our voodoo priest friend who was now our sworn enemy. Tony and I popped some Imodium and finished the rest of our trip in Haiti. Back in Toronto, we each went to our own doctor. We both tested positive for the same parasite. Yup, I was correct in blaming our voodoo priest friend. We were both prescribed the same antibiotics, and we both started feeling better at the same time, two or so days later.

In three weeks, Morgen, cameraperson Basil Young and I travelled to India, again as part of our UN commitment. That week I developed a love for Indian food that I still carry to this day. One of the assignments that week was to visit a UN-funded jewellery project that employed many folks in Rajasthan, a state in northern India. I bought a silver ring that to this very day is still the only ring I wear.

On our way back to New Delhi, our UN driver passed a tree that was filled with monkeys. I freakin' love monkeys! I asked the driver to stop so I could look at them. He did stop but said in broken English, "Please, stay in the vehicle." I ignored his plea and took out a banana I had in my backpack. I slid open the van's side door, walked over to the tree and tossed out my banana. The damn fruit didn't have a chance to hit the ground before at least twenty monkeys charged down from the tree. They zeroed in on me as a target and began their monkey run towards me. I hightailed it back to the van, reached the open door, dove inside and slid the panel closed behind me. Our exhausted and fed up driver yelled at me, "I told you to stay in the van!"

Despite this somewhat scary encounter with the monkeys in which my face could have been ripped off, I still consider them one of my favourite animals of all time.

Closer to home, there was a lot travelling to cover music festivals. I developed a love-hate relationship with music festivals. I loved the assignments where I had to travel and visit many cities across North America, but I hated the long days waiting for interviews in the hot sun and eating crap music festival food while drinking flat, warm beer backstage.

There was Edgefest, classic rock fests, Eden Fest, blues fests, Buzzard Fest, Woodstock '94, Woodstock '99, SARSStock and many other fests and stocks. The countless music festivals, despite being featured in numerous different cities and boasting different lineups, all seemed to become one giant collective loud musical blur. The upside was always getting great interviews with the artists, capturing live performances and shooting moments with fans. All that footage would be packaged into awesome specials. The downside was the predictable downtime during those days of shooting. But, in the end, once all the elements were shot, produced, edited and ready for air, MuchMusic would usually broadcast an hour special. Even though I would play an integral role every step of the way and see everything through to the final post-production, watching it on TV like everyone else across Canada gave everything a whole new perspective. I was always proud of the final result.

In 1998, I was asked to cover Our Lady Peace's inaugural Summersault Festival at Molson Park in Barrie, Ontario. The goal was to shoot performances, interview fans and conduct interviews with the performers, including Our Lady Peace, Harvey Danger, Eve 6, Esthero, Goldfinger, The Crystal Method, I Mother Earth, Garbage and others. This was stop number one of a cross-Canada tour, and the idea was to get it on the air as soon as possible to promote the rest of the Canadian stops. I let my boss Denise Donlon know that a four-hour block showcasing the best of Summersault would air starting at noon the day after, on Monday. She didn't believe it was possible. She was hoping for the broadcast to be on Tuesday at the earliest.

It was after midnight on Monday morning when the cameraperson and I got back to the station. He handed me the box of thirty-minute Betacam tapes and I went straight to an edit bay. I stayed up all night editing all the interviews, live performances and complete highlights. I also programmed all the full-length videos and completed all the cue sheets for our crew. I was finishing the final edited segment as the broadcast went to air at noon EST. I couldn't watch the rest of the broadcast because I was at home sleeping.

The cross-Canada Edgefest tours were very memorable, especially the 1998 edition. A cameraperson and I flew to all the national stops. The bill that year featured the Foo Fighters, Green Day, The Tea Party, Econoline Crush, Matthew Good Band, Sloan, The Killjoys, Bif Naked and others. In each city we would shoot local landmarks, gather band interviews, record live music, get fan reactions and shoot other fun, scene-setting stories. The next morning, we would courier all the tapes back to Toronto so MuchMusic could air highlights and viewers could follow along with our journey.

Early in the tour in Montreal, I was sitting next to a burly biker-looking guy in catering. His name was Jack and it turned out he was the bus driver for Green Day. He had been a tour bus driver for decades, but this was his first time travelling with Green Day. I asked him who he had worked with over his lengthy career, and his list was long. One of the acts he drove for was country legend Charlie Daniels. Charlie was Jack's long-time friend and the two had worked together for many years. I recounted a story to Jack about how seven years previous, I was in Nashville to do a bunch of interviews for the then-defunct MuchMusic country show *Outlaws & Heroes*, and in one day I had interviewed Tanya Tucker, Charlie Daniels and some others. I told him of the conversation I had with Charlie's publicist who had accompanied him to the interview. Her name was Angela and after Charlie's interview, she and I spoke at length and arranged to meet for drinks later that evening. I told him how sweet and beautiful she was. When she had learned that I was sick the day before I had to return to Toronto, she had picked me up at the hotel and took me to Charlie Daniels's house where she was staying to house-sit while Charlie was away on tour. I explained to Jack how amazing and attentive Angela had been and how she had fed me chicken noodle soup. I reiterated how sweet she was in making sure that I was feeling better the next morning.

I remember feeling downright mortified when Jack told me, "I wish Angela was as amazing and sweet and attentive to me! That's my ex-wife that took care of you!" I immediately stopped eating and said, "Ummm, gotta go. Cheers, bud." I grabbed my plate that was still full of food, threw it into the garbage and walked quickly out of the catering tent.

In Edmonton at Commonwealth Stadium, I thought it was a good idea to interview Green Day while they took a golf cart ride around the grounds before their appearance. Jay, our cameraperson, sat at the front of the golf cart with his legs on either side of the steering column, facing the driver. Green Day's bassist Mike Dirnt drove, and seated next to him was drummer Tré Cool. I was positioned in the back, facing the camera, kneeling on the small flatbed while holding the wireless microphone between the two band members. The shot and ensuing interview was great! But, at some point while driving out of the stadium and into the parking lot, Mike tried to make a turn without slowing down. Apparently, Jay's foot was in the way of the pedal and the turn was fast and sharp. The centrifugal force rolled me off the cart, spilling me onto the pavement with my head hitting the asphalt. Jay's camera angle caught everything. The clip is on YouTube and looking back, I was amazed that I kept the microphone held up to avoid it hitting the pavement. I didn't want it to break. I sacrificed my body and head to avoid damaging our microphone.

Miraculously, I was OK. Mike stopped the golf cart, put it in reverse and stopped where I was lying on the ground. I stood up, climbed back onto the golf cart and resumed our interview, albeit at a slower speed, until we were back in the stadium's backstage area.

When we finished, Jay climbed off the front of the golf cart and said, "Man! Are you OK? I got everything!"

I said, "Yeah, I'm fine I think." Tré Cool got off the cart and felt my head, looking for a bump or any sign of blood. Thankfully, there was none. Both Tré and Mike asked me if I wanted to get on their bus so that they could drive me after the Edmonton concert to the next concert stop in Calgary. I thought it was kind of them to ensure that I was OK. They seemed genuinely concerned. I said, "Thanks, but no. I am fine. No worries. Jay and I have a flight tomorrow morning. We'll see ya in Calgary."

Green Day went on to do their usual blistering set, and Jay and I carried on with our Edmonton Edgefest coverage. MuchMusic would play the "Green Day Golf Cart Incident" incessantly for weeks and months to come. Looking back, yes, it was great television.

The next day in Calgary, I saw Green Day's bus driver Jack again, who I had met two weeks prior in Montreal at the Edgefest show there. Jack was Angie's ex. He had heard about the accident and asked how I was feeling. I said I felt fine, and I remarked how I appreciated the guys' concerns about my health and how they wanted me on their bus to make sure I was fine and well enough to continue for the rest of the tour.

"Bullshit," he said. "They were just covering their asses. They didn't want you to sue them!"

I think that secretly, he might have wished I had suffered more severe injuries.

BILL WELYCHKA

· · · · ·

The Edgefest concert in Barrie, Ontario at Molson Park in 1999 was brilliant. I was assigned to conduct interviews during the day-long event and the artists featured were some of Canada's biggest attractions: Moist, Matthew Good Band, Wide Mouth Mason, Big Wreck and more. Also featured was Courtney Love's band, Hole. They were soaring high internationally with the landmark release of *Celebrity Skin*. By the time of that summer's Edgefest, Hole were already three singles deep into the album's global acceptance.

For some, Courtney would only be considered as Kurt Cobain's widow. Not to me. I loved Hole's tunes and I had championed the release of the Hole single "Awful" and its message of warning young girls to not buy into the expectations established by media's standards of beauty and fame.

I interviewed the controversial Courtney Love and Hole's bass player Melissa Auf der Maur backstage after their set. Courtney could be intimidating. I had heard stories about how she had no patience for dumb questions or ignorant interviewers. I equate her reputation with Madonna's: they don't have time for stupidity. Courtney is a very strong, confident and unpredictable figure. Our interview went extremely well, and we talked a lot about Melissa's contribution to the band. Many of us Canadians were proud of Melissa and her Montreal roots.

About a year later, I was excited to see Melissa again, but not in a professional TV format. We reconnected at a concert in Toronto at the Molson Amphitheatre to see The Cure. We talked and laughed and caught up with each other's lives. We both made our way closer to the stage, forgetting how we both lost our friends in the crowd.

I have always found it interesting that my admiration and respect level for someone always rises when I find out we have similar tastes in musical acts. You love The Cure too? We will be lifelong friends. That's why going to a concert is so fulfilling and joyous! We can be surrounded by complete strangers but feel a bond and strong connection with each other. That's the power of music.

Melissa remains one of my favourite musicians, ever.

CHAPTER NINE
A COWBOY'S BULLET AND BODYGUARDS

For all of the 1990s, travelling was non-stop while I was at MuchMusic. My first trip for MuchMusic was for the inaugural Canadian Music Video Awards (later renamed the MuchMusic Video Awards). It took place in 1990 on a decked out VIA Rail train, complete with a performance car, my editing suite and everything else needed for a mobile TV studio on the rails for a three-week excursion across Canada. Bands including National Velvet, Jeff Healey, Blue Rodeo and more gave performances at various train station stops and awards were handed out during the stops on the ten-city journey, culminating in a final party in Halifax that was broadcast across Canada. In Quebec City, we watched the performance of a new rising star, Céline Dion. At this time, Céline had garnered a large francophone fan base but was still unknown to most English-speaking Canadians.

In 1995, I was sent across Canada for our MM VJ search. It was a huge promotion with record store chain HMV, involving appearances at HMV stores to explain how to submit a VJ demo tape to the gathered public. A cameraperson, a producer and I visited places like Winnipeg, Regina, Calgary, Edmonton, Whitehorse, Yellowknife, Vancouver and other cities to shoot local human-interest stories, musicians and the required HMV appearances.

There was plenty of time in each city to visit historic landmarks and shoot some fun exploring. In Regina, I spent the day at the RCMP training facility. I was shown how to load a gun and shoot it at the firing range training grounds. I drove a skid car and marched with the cadets in a parade. At the end of the day, my staff instructor presented me with an official RCMP cap, complete with an official badge. The priceless gift came with a warning though. He said I must never wear it in public as it could be confiscated and I could be charged with impersonating an officer. That cap has always remained on display wherever I have lived, but never taken outside.

That cross-Canada tour had me fishing and scuba diving in Great Slave Lake, riding a horse through the Rockies, looking down on beautiful untouched glaciers in a helicopter ride, spending a day with the Haida indigenous people on their traditional lands along BC's coast and many more experiences that only the luckiest person in the world could partake in.

While near Dawson City, Yukon, we visited a modern gold mining operation. Dawson City is considered the home of the Klondike Gold Rush of the 1890s, but unlike old-timey visions of bearded, toothless old men panning for gold in rivers, the current methods for extracting gold from the ground involve large, heavy machinery. On the particular day we visited, an excavator had hit an old, abandoned underground mine and was pulling up wooden tracks, railway ties and other debris. A huge bucket was sweeping over the site and depositing its contents onto the ground, forming a large mound. During the workers' break, I walked over to the huge pile of dirt and saw the remnants of an old rail track. There were some unspent bullets I also found and an old pair of denim overalls I pulled out from between some rocks. I imagined some old miner from the 1890s removing them after nearly sweating to death and never returning to retrieve them. Looking back, I wish I had kept them! In October 2022, a news story stated that an old pair of Levi's jeans recovered from an old California gold mine fetched over $87,000 at auction. Damn!

During our interview with the site manager, I asked if the old railway ties, overalls, or bullets I found were worth anything. I offered that many museums would be interested in the old artifacts they dug up from deep in the ground. He said, "Nah. We don't care about that stuff. It's all garbage. We just want the gold."

After our interview, I walked over to the large pile of dirt. I bent down and picked up an unfired Smith & Wesson branded bullet. I imagined an old cowboy down in the mine losing it while looking for gold in the 1890s. I put it in my pocket. I still have that bullet in my collection of trinkets and treasures I have kept over the years. I have often wondered if that bullet belonged to the same poor bastard who lost his overalls.

By the time we arrived in Vancouver for our appearance at HMV during that cross-Canada trek in 1995, there was some concern from the bosses in Toronto. A that point, I had been receiving some disturbing letters from a viewer in BC for about two years. Her letters would be handwritten, single-spaced and about seven to ten pages in length. They would come addressed to me at the station at least twice a month. I recognized that they were coming from someone dealing with severe mental health issues as the letters were psycho-sexual in nature. She would vividly describe how she wanted to be sexually assaulted by me. She would write at great length about dreams she had that involved me. She explained that when she watched MuchMusic, it didn't matter who I was interviewing or what music video I was throwing to or introducing, all she would hear through her TV speakers was, "This is Bill. Move to Toronto. I want to rape you." She said this repeatedly to me in her long letters and told me how we were destined to be together. It got to the point where I stopped opening her letters and would hand them to our station lawyer instead.

I received a phone call one afternoon from a concerned viewer. Somehow, the woman in Vancouver had gotten a hold of an old Toronto phone book that had my name in it along with an older published number. The number had since been recycled and the new holder of this particular phone number called me to say that she was getting death threats from someone who demanded that she stay away from Bill Welychka. The frightened viewer explained that the woman on the other end of the line said that I lived there and that she wasn't going to stand for another woman in my house. I explained as best I could that she was in no way in danger. The threats were coming from someone very far away who dealt with severe delusions.

Somehow, our station lawyer did some research, and I was told that he learned from police officials and the woman's doctor that her relationship with me was only through the TV screen. She would most likely not show up at my Vancouver HMV appearance, and if she did, she would stay in the background, unnoticed.

I really wasn't concerned for my safety at all. I was embarrassed to learn that MuchMusic had hired some bodyguards for my appearance at the Vancouver HMV store. I was told it was simply a precautionary measure. We met two very large men at one of the mall entrances. They escorted us to the record store and were also assigned to be with me for the duration of the day. I explained to them that I appreciated their task, but that it really wasn't necessary. I asked them to always stay well behind me. I didn't want anyone to think I travelled with security or bodyguards.

Our crew arrived at the mall's HMV ahead of schedule. The store had set up a small stage with a table to sign autographs and a long line of eager viewers had already formed. There were many cheers as our cameraperson, production assistant, office manager, two huge bodyguards and I entered the store. After a few minutes, I wanted a coffee and needed to find the food court. I asked our crew who wanted coffees and took orders. As I walked quickly out of the store, I looked behind me and laughed as I saw the two large bodyguards running after me. I explained again that they didn't have to be so visible and obvious.

A few minutes later I had returned to the record store and distributed the coffees. Eventually, I was introduced and explained to the large crowd what MuchMusic was looking for in terms of VJs. After the presentation, I took a seat at the table to sign autographs and take pictures.

I had totally forgotten about the assigned bodyguards at this point. I sat in my chair at the table and met viewer after viewer for about an hour. I answered every question asked and posed for many pictures. I have always enjoyed meeting viewers, and I always have time for anyone who wants to spend a few minutes conversing. At some point, a young viewer of about twelve years old stood on her toes at the table across from me saying, "I love you! Can I have a picture? And a hug?"

"Absolutely!" I spoke. "Thanks for being here. A pleasure to meet ya! Come around the table to this side." I invited her closer so that her parents could take the picture.

A HAPPY HAS-BEEN

As I stood up to greet this great kid maneuvering her way around the table, I noticed the two big bodyguards rushing over to the table to get a closer look. They resembled two gargantuan football players running onto the field. I motioned to them to back off, that all was fine. Kneeling down, I took some pictures with my new friend. Both her and her parents thanked me, and I thanked them for coming.

I can only imagine how bored the bodyguards were at the uneventful afternoon, wanting to protect me from an excited twelve-year-old.

In time, the letters from the Vancouver viewer stopped. I will never know what happened to her. I can only hope that she found a doctor who prescribed the proper meds for her to get along with her life. I hope that was the case.

While I was sent out on numerous assignments to cover music festivals, I had noticed that concertgoers (our viewers) had changed. When I was an editor for MuchMusic in the late '80s and early '90s, I would get the raw footage and put together specials for broadcast of early Lollapalooza festivals, Glastonbury and other large concert events. I felt bad for our reporters and VJs then, having to deal with hostile young people hurling profanities while our on-air team tried to shoot segments in the crowd. Fans of the early '90s music scene were often described as disgruntled and angry. It was not uncommon for a VJ to do three or four or ten takes before getting a solid throw recorded without some ass yelling, "You SUCK!" a foot away from their face.

By the time I was doing music festival coverage in the mid to late '90s, the young people in the audience were actually very sweet! What a difference a few years made. I had witnessed very negative reactions to our crew and thankfully, by the time I was covering music festivals, I was being met with requests for pictures and autographs and being offered kind receptions. Perhaps it was a reflection of the times, with pop music taking over from the angry alt music revolution of the early '90s?

I had also noticed a big difference between Canadian audiences and American music festival attendees. A great example was Woodstock '99. Looking back, I am embarrassed to have played a small roll in our coverage.

I was part of the MuchMusic crew that covered Woodstock '94. The festival was to commemorate the twenty-fifth anniversary of the original

Woodstock festival of 1969. The three-day 1994 installment was hyped as being an extension of even more days of peace, love and music. It was a noble effort on paper, but the execution was disappointing to many. The 1994 edition of Woodstock was held near Saugerties, New York, about 100 km northeast of Bethel, the site of Woodstock '69.

The crowd at Woodstock '94 was estimated at 350,000, and the festival had its share of problems. There were security issues as a non-stop barrage of fans broke through the fencing to attend for free, and many brought in banned items. It really wasn't the peaceful re-creation of 1969 the organizers had hoped for.

A vivid memory for me was stepping down from the tour bus I was working in, which was parked directly backstage. I had a video-editing station set up on the bus and was editing stories throughout the weekend, sending them back to Toronto via satellite so MuchMusic could broadcast the coverage to all of Canada. It was early Sunday morning at about 3 a.m., and Aerosmith was performing just a few metres away on the other side of the giant stage. (An interesting side note, Aerosmith's Steven Tyler and Joe Perry attended the original Woodstock '69 festival, a year before forming Aerosmith.) I was all alone backstage, enjoying the solitude but feeling tired, and doing some stretches while having a cigarette. It was surreal to hear "What It Takes" live—it was a song that reminded me of breaking up with Ronna. I was alone, yet I knew that on the other side of the enormous five-story stage were maybe 250,000 people rocking out to and loving Aerosmith's performance. It was amazing to me that a barrier and a few metres could create two wildly different experiences.

Sadly, five years later, the organizers of Woodstock '69 and '94 tried to recreate peace, love and music again for the thirtieth anniversary in 1999.

There were a couple of Woodstock '99 televised documentary series in 2021 and 2022. I heard the same reaction to these from many: "I saw you!" The production companies for these docs had acquired MuchMusic footage from Bell Media, the current owners and proprietors of the extensive MuchMusic videotape library.

We had a big crew broadcasting from Woodstock '99 in Rome, New York. A lot has already been written about, reported, recounted and retold about the three-day disaster. I had arrived on-site with many from MuchMusic on Wednesday, July 21. We established a control room and office in a trailer backstage, led by our bosses David Kines and Denise Donlon. Many of our crew had access to an abandoned subdivision adjacent to the decommissioned air force base that would be the site for Woodstock '99.

After several of us had unpacked our bags in an empty house in the subdivision, we explored the rest of our surreal "neighborhood." A cameraperson and I found a big party happening a few doors down. The house was filled with Woodstock '99 volunteers and this was their night to let loose before their long days of volunteering began.

As we entered the house, we were immediately recognized by many young Canadians who had found their way to the event as unpaid volunteers. They had met some American volunteers and established great friendships. The house was filled with jubilant partiers who I quickly surmised as being responsible but who were having fun. After we all introduced ourselves, I set into motion a fun shoot that would set the scene for our coverage.

The viewers back in Canada would see our edited story the next day. It involved me explaining where we were and walking up to a noisy house party. We conducted a lot of interviews with everyone gathered in the house—a varied collection of Canadians and Americans. I set the scene for viewers, citing how many volunteers were gathered at Woodstock '99 to take care of over 220,000 attendees. Once we deduced who was Canadian, large joyous yells and hugs followed. When we discovered who was American, they were escorted out of the house. For me, the humour lay in the fact that us sweet lovable Canadians were kicking out our American hosts on their turf. Eventually, the party escalated to a large ruckus, with me crowd-surfing in the living room, held up by dozens of Canadian partiers screaming excitedly. The next shot was from outside, looking in through the window at the out-of-control party, then panning over to our American friends yelling "USA! USA!" The HBO 2021 doc, *Woodstock 99: Peace, Love and Rage*, opened with parts of that story.

Early in the weekend, I ventured around the grounds with fellow Much VJ Rick Campanelli. We shot many fun segments overnight with those wandering around at 2 a.m. Woodstock attendees were a subculture, and those meandering about the grounds at 2 a.m. at Woodstock were a subculture of the subculture.

I had asked my boss Denise Donlon if I could only do artist interviews. At this point in my career, I was suffering from festival-fatigue. Or music festival-itis. She agreed and let me handle most of the responsibility in the artist compound area, where we had a tent and camerapeople waiting to tape interviews.

I spent much of my weekend backstage taping interviews with Red Hot Chili Peppers, Korn, The Tragically Hip, Kid Rock, The Offspring, John Entwistle Band, Bush and many others.

On the Saturday afternoon, during a break, I was asked to get up on stage and make some announcements. On the main stage. In front of 220,000 people. YIKES! I said yes and proceeded to walk up the stairs onto the side of the stage, where I was given a live mic before walking out onto the stage. It hit me in a quick moment . . . these rowdy, sunburnt, tired and anxious American music fans had no clue who the fuck I was and I am sure they didn't really care to *want* to know who the fuck I was. As I walked to centre stage, I saw many Canadian flags rise up and heard cheers from a large Canadian contingent of MuchMusic viewers, interspersed among the crowd. It was an easy four to five minutes of talking, tossing out t-shirts Denise had given me, tossing out bottles of water and reminding everyone to take care of each other. Thankfully, I wasn't hated, nor did anyone toss anything at me. It was the only time in my life that I saw what over 200,000 people looking at me looked like. It was bodies stretched out as far as the horizon.

At that exact moment, MuchMusic was broadcasting live. MuchMusic "personality" Ed the Sock was on the air while I was on stage. The shot that people saw at home was an aerial view of me on stage, zooming out to show the enormous crowd while viewers heard Ed's live commentary: "Ed the Sock here at Woodstock '99. That's our own Bill Welychka on stage. The way he's doing these announcements, he may have a future on the loudspeaker at K-Mart. Can you imagine what's going through the minds of the audience right now? 'Who's this knob and where is Limp Bizkit? I didn't pay $180 to see this idiot stand up there with those shorts!'"

When I saw the clip back, I howled with laughter. If one is going to be insulted, it's best if it's coming from a sock puppet. Hilarious!

It was a truly odd work assignment. I was proud of my involvement with the weekend's great interviews but was disappointed after the fact. I was ashamed, shocked and disgusted to later hear about the rampant fires, looting, rioting, assaults and rapes. There were many stories of girls crowd-surfing while ass-faced, loutish males were reaching up to try and feel their breasts. I only found out about the shit-show that evolved after returning home to Toronto and reading the headlines like everyone else.

I have been asked a lot about what I witnessed at Woodstock '99 and if it was as bad as several documentaries released in 2021 and 2022 have shown. To me, one single assault on any female is tragic, maddening and one too many. My anger at hearing about the assaults against women stemmed from a cause I had become active in a few years earlier. Much of my time and attention therefore then turned to this cause that I still believe in: the call-out to all men to help end men's violence against women.

CHAPTER TEN
ELEVATING WOMEN AND A WHITE RIBBON

My first involvement with trying to end male violence against women came by joining the White Ribbon Campaign. The WRC is the world's largest movement of males working to end violence against women and girls. It assists in promoting gender equity and healthy relationships, and it seeks to establish a new vision of masculinity. It started in 1991 in Toronto as a response to the École Polytechnique massacre in Montreal, when on December 6, 1989, fourteen women were targeted and killed.

The world already recognizes November 25 as the International Day for the Elimination of Violence Against Women. In Canada, December 6 is our National Day of Remembrance and Action on Violence Against Women. It is commemorated by the wearing of a white ribbon.

The WRC asks men to wear white ribbons as a pledge to never commit, condone or remain silent about violence against women. Since its inception, the WRC has spread to more than seventy countries around the world. Some of these countries still battle with women's rights.

I first heard about the White Ribbon Campaign in 1997. I was honoured to be asked to emcee the White Ribbon Campaign benefit concert in Toronto, spearheaded by Canadian rock band The Tea Party and their management SRO (who also managed Rush). SRO Management's (the late and very missed) Steve Hoffman worked closely with The Tea Party's Jeff Martin to bring this concert to fruition during Toronto's Canada Music

Week. I would emcee the following four years' annual concerts as well. It was a beautiful concept: some of Canada's best male vocalists would put egos aside and sing only covers with the help of a house band led by Rush's Alex Lifeson. I also donated many cool autographs and bits of memorabilia to the silent auctions. Participants that came on board were Moist's David Usher, Matthew Good, I Mother Earth's Edwin, Todd Kerns, members of Billy Talent, members of Barenaked Ladies, Snow, The Tragically Hip and many others.

The proceeds of the Tea Party's 1998 hit single "Release" went to the WRC. Jeff Martin wrote the words for the song after watching a documentary about the state of women's rights worldwide. The song acts as a sort of apology to women.

One of my favourite quotes by Jeff Martin comes from an interview we did in 2000, and I echo his thoughts when he says, "Women are the better half of our species. The violence has to stop."

The White Ribbon Campaign's initiatives have raised funds for women's shelters and brought about much awareness about ending violence towards women. The WRC has also conducted seminars globally, and I have attended some of these seminars in schools. They have led to much dialogue between guys. To me, that is a crucial step in ending men's violence towards women. Males must engage other males!

Most of my closest friends have always been female. I never fit into the macho male dominant role. I played hockey and football growing up, but I am proudly in touch with my feminine side. I believe that sensitivity, nurturance and empathy are largely positive feminine qualities, and all males should strive to achieve these traits. I have been asked if my own mother, Barb, was abused. Is this why I carry a flag to end violence against women? No, Barb was never physically abused during her marriage to my dad. I did, however, find out many years later that she was sexually abused as a child by a relative. But, my need to speak out about violence against women comes mainly from being raised mostly by a single mother from about the age of ten. I was witness to her strong work ethic and her need to donate to many charities. Barb was a devout Catholic, and she prayed on her rosary daily. She always had compassion for others, and I am grateful she instilled in me some of her attributes.

I was working in Ottawa at the CHUM Limited TV station A-Channel from 2006 to 2011. We were reporting many stories about how Ottawa area women's shelters were underfunded and overflowing. Many of the shelters were getting hotel rooms for women looking to flee abusive situations, often with kids in tow. I felt that something needed to be done, so I organized a benefit concert with my friend and A-Channel office manager Tina Cerilli. I called the show, "Men Rocking for Women." It was pulled together in a month and featured several Ottawa bands with all proceeds going to four Ottawa area women's shelters and the White Ribbon Campaign. Two of the bands eager to participate were Loudlove and Sojourn (later renamed The Goodluck Assembly). I had become a big fan of these two indie Ottawa bands, and they were easy to love. I wished they had gained bigger national followings.

Leading up to the November 29, 2008 concert at the historic Barrymore's Music Hall, I was getting emails at work from many guys who were denouncing my efforts to shine a spotlight on women's issues. They had cited that many men's charities needed assistance. I agreed, but I told them that this was not a battle of the sexes. All I could really say to them was that the issue of helping women was important to me. I also reassured them that I gave privately to many charities involving men, women, kids and animals. I also told them how a retired Ottawa cop sent me a cheque to put towards the concert because he had been to too many domestic abuse calls and witnessed up close how a man can inflict pain and injuries onto a woman. I certainly didn't require proof that battered women existed at the hands of men, but I kept thinking of all those women that were in desperate need to flee abusive situations.

Despite hearing from some angry males, I also heard from a specific male who wanted to help. Glass Tiger's Alan Frew reached out to me asking if he could come to the show and perhaps sing a song. He had heard about the show and the issue of men ending violence towards women sparked an interest in him as he was writing about the exact same topic in his autobiography. He told me it was destiny to read about my initiative at the same time that he was writing about the same topic. All I could think was, *Well . . . we have a headliner!*

A HAPPY HAS-BEEN

Alan said he would come on and do one song. He didn't want it to be an Alan Frew concert, he was simply eager to lend his name to the event. He requested one keyboard player to accompany him for a performance of John Lennon's "Imagine." Ottawa's Dan McNeil happily obliged as he would be present with one of the bands anyway. During the soundcheck in the afternoon, before Alan arrived, I asked the bands if anyone knew Glass Tiger's "Diamond Sun." I explained that Alan didn't know I would ask him to do the song, and if he knew the assembled players could do it, he might sing it! The bands divided up and offered Dan on keys, a drummer, a guitar player and a bassist. When Alan arrived for the soundcheck, I asked him to do "Diamond Sun" and told him the band was waiting. They went through the song once and even Alan was surprised at how great it sounded.

Momentum was building towards the night. Tickets were selling and there was a sense of love and community throughout the venue that evening. I pulled some favours from record company friends and acquired donations of signed merchandise from ZZ Top, Coldplay and many others for the silent auction.

There was some radio, TV and print interviews leading up to the concert, but the standout article for me came from Kristy Kirkup, written for one of Ottawa's newspapers.

> **Male Musicians Jam for a Good Cause**
>
> A number of male musicians hit the stage at Barrymore's on Saturday night in support of ending violence against women.
>
> The event, called Men Rocking for Women, wasn't a paid gig for bands Loudlove, Sojourn, Heroes Offer Her or Glass Tiger's Alan Frew. Instead, the performers donated their time and support.
>
> Frew says it's important for men to speak out against violence perpetuated by men.
>
> "There are some days when I wake up and I'm actually ashamed to be part of the club," says Frew. "But I have to

be part of the club, so I try to want to try and educate, work with and guide younger males around me."

The man who organized the event, Bill Welychka, isn't a rocker himself. He's the longest-running MuchMusic VJ who now works at A-News in Ottawa.

Back in his days at Much, Welychka was heavily involved in the White Ribbon Campaign, an initiative led by men working to end violence against women. When he saw the campaign lacked a presence in Ottawa, Welychka decided to organize the benefit concert.

"This isn't a battle of the sexes night," says Welychka. "It's for guys to admit we're at fault for a lot of things."

Proceeds of the concert will be donated to four women's shelters in Ottawa. Women's shelters across the city are over flooded and often have to turn people away because they do not have enough room.

Welychka hopes the event will not only raise funds for shelters but will send a strong message to other men.

"If guys hear enough guys denounce any acts of violence against women, hopefully there won't be a need for a concert like this."

I recently watched the DVD of the concert and remembered how I almost couldn't get through my remarks on stage during the show because tears were welling up during my unscripted, impromptu delivery. Here is what I said to the concert attendees:

> This night is about music. It's about how music inspires. And about how music heals and how music is a friend. This night is also about elevating women and helping women. It saddens me that we even have to do an evening like this!

> I find it funny that many have thanked me and Tina for organizing this night. I want to say to you . . . thank you for being here!
>
> Every time I read about sexual assaults on Ottawa campuses, it tears away at my spirit. Each time I hear about date rape drugs being used in our bars, that tears away at my spirit. This week, reading about female teachers on their way to work in Afghanistan having acid thrown in their faces by disapproving males, tore away at my spirit.
>
> I am sometimes ashamed of my own sex, but I am seeing a lot of guys here tonight who want to help.
>
> So, all of you being here tonight is healing for me and all males who wish to do something. So, thanks for giving me some of my spirit back!

We raised thousands of dollars for four Ottawa area women's shelters.

In the past five years or so, social media has reignited the conversation and has played a big role in bringing awareness to ending violence towards women and creating much more equitable conditions for women. We all know about the #MeToo social movement against sexual abuse, harassment and rape culture in the US, but here in Canada, we were witness to the heavily reported case against Canadian broadcaster Jian Ghomeshi in 2016. In 2022, Hedley frontman Jacob Hoggard was found guilty of taking advantage of younger fans and sentenced to five years in prison.

During the heightened activity of each case, a multitude of brave female victims came forward, stating their individual experiences.

Even more hashtags were shared: #BeenRapedNeverReported and #rapedneverreported trended on social media platforms with many women sharing stories and recognizing that there are many others that have experienced the same frustration and abuse.

This discussion is not about kinky adults having consensual fun behind their closed doors. I don't judge. I certainly don't judge that. This is about violence. According to victims coming forward in some of these cases, there was slapping, choking and punching without consent.

The lesson learned is if you feel threatened or were in any way abused, emotionally or physically, at work or anywhere, it is your right to make a complaint. Do not be afraid to come forward.

Clay Jones, the communications manager for the WRC was quoted as saying, "We have definitely noticed an increase in people talking about [this] on Twitter, and many women have chosen to disclose their own experiences with harassment and violence. We also noted many people, mostly men but not only, who felt that Ghomeshi was due his day in court and that too many people were jumping to conclusions. This became harder to defend as more people came forward about Ghomeshi and their own experiences."

If any positive can be extracted from this, it is the dialogue now happening online. The White Ribbon Campaign has started a social media movement called #webelieveyou as a way to express its support for anyone coming forward with stories of harassment and abuse. There is strength in numbers and social media can be a great purveyor in getting guys on board to learn more and share their thoughts. Guys are reading what other guys are posting online.

The paradigm has truly shifted. Many more males are realizing that there is no room in our world for violence against women on any level. I and every man should do what we can to be vocal and use social media to further the message and show that we stand together.

At the point of writing these words, my wish is for this book to sell many copies. Partial proceeds that come to me will be donated to the White Ribbon Campaign and various women's shelters across Canada.

Thank you to Jeff Martin and his The Tea Party brothers, Stuart Chatwood and Jeff Burrows, for opening my eyes to the movement of guys talking to guys about joining together to end men's violence towards women.

CHAPTER ELEVEN
MADONNA'S MONITOR

Most days at MuchMusic were spent doing live four-hour shifts providing commentary, introducing music videos and conducting live interviews. I never took it for granted that I had one of the best jobs in the world. I was literally bonding with every single one of my music heroes on a weekly basis.

One of the unexpected by-products of being on TV for a lengthy time is having to adjust to being elevated to some strange level of celebrity status. I never thought of TV personalities as *celebrities*. I of course interviewed celebrities, but I never thought of myself as one.

I first noticed the "fame" aspect of what I did when I was hosting MuchMusic's ninety-minute weekly country show *Outlaws & Heroes*. People would stop me on the street to say hi, or drinks would be on the house at bars. (By the way, I don't believe in free drinks. I always left generous tips.) When I shifted to being a regular flow Much VJ, the notoriety level increased enormously. Giggling girls would wait outside the station on Queen Street for me to leave, then try to follow me home. I would eventually stop and engage them in a friendly chat, perhaps sign something, and then in a polite and gentle way tell them it was time for them to go home.

I reserved about an hour each day to read viewer mail, and I responded to each letter with a postcard. MuchMusic had started printing personalized postcards to be signed at appearances and to be sent out in response to viewer letters. Many years later, I would receive emails or social media messages from viewers with pictures of the signed postcards. If they weren't thrown out, they were found in storage boxes or gathered with other meaningless papers from twenty years prior. Man, my handwriting was embarrassingly messy!

One summer evening at Toronto's large concert venue, Molson Amphitheatre (now The Budweiser Stage), I was swarmed by dozens of screaming girls. It started with four or five girls rushing over to take pictures with their disposable cameras and it quickly escalated. It was strange, being grabbed at and hearing shouts of, "Bill! I love you!" Eventually, security broke through the large throng and escorted me out. Although I never really ever felt truly threatened, I did realize that I stood out when I was in public. My poor dear mother Barb would often tell me weekly that she had received yet more calls from girls asking for me. Her number was listed in the phone book (the only listed Welychka in the GTA at the time), and so on a regular basis, she would get calls from strangers asking for me. She was very polite and explained to the callers that yes, she was my mother, but no, I did not live there. I begged her to stop being so generous with her time and requested that she simply say, "Sorry, wrong number. Please don't call here." But Barb was a saint and she said she couldn't be so cold to a random phone caller.

Some would consider fame to bothersome. I never had an issue with it and always accepted that it was part of the job. I was especially grateful for the chance to follow up on many requests to visit younger viewers at the hospital, even once a terminally ill girl. I will never forget that particular visit to Sick Kids Hospital in Toronto for as long as I live. It brings a lot of perspective in knowing a child's dying wish was to meet *me*. Many years later, her mother got in touch with me to say thanks again for bringing joy to her child. She even sent me pictures of the visit and a picture of the large scrapbook her child had made of the time we had spent together, complete with a poem she had written. It was truly a wonderful and cherished experience that will be with me forever.

· · · · ·

The national and international travelling for taped interviews was a huge perk of the job, but nothing beat the fun, frantic and exciting energy of a live presentation, especially with viewers in the studio and a band performing.

It was a regular day for Much to host big-name musicians and even A-list actors, many of them being my favourite recording artists of all time. Occasionally, I also conducted live interviews with artists that I personally wouldn't listen to when I would go home, but it didn't matter. It was live television, and it was engaging and fun and creative. Some stand-out live interviews for me where the artist had a great time and the interview resulted in compelling live television include Mel Gibson, Harrison Ford, Denis Leary, Oasis's Noel Gallagher a couple of times, Liz Phair, Hanson, Cher, Ricky Martin, Van Halen, Dwayne "The Rock" Johnson, Sean Lennon, The Offspring, Bryan Adams, Stone Temple Pilots, Blind Melon, Weezer, Kevin Bacon, Aerosmith, The Cure, Mel C from the Spice Girls, David Bowie, Mike Ness from Social Distortion and many more.

Occasionally, MuchMusic would air live *Intimate and Interactive* ninety-minute prime-time specials. These broadcasts would involve a big name being interviewed in the Much environment, interspersed with live performances and questions coming not just from me, but from fans live in the studio. Sometimes viewer questions were also faxed or emailed in. I was fortunate enough to host some great *I&I* presentations with Silverchair, The Tea Party, Live, Tom Cochrane, Alanis Morissette and many others.

I often wished I had saved many of these priceless moments. I did save some on VHS tapes and years later digitized a few and posted them on my YouTube channel, but most of these groundbreaking exclusive shows are gone and lost forever. Some viewers had also saved some broadcasts and I have seen some of my work show up on others' YouTube channels in later years. I love getting a random email or direct message from a Facebook follower posting a link from an interview I did saying, "Hey, it's you!"

A special moment for me was interviewing the legendary Chuck D and Flavor Flav from the highly influential hip hop group Public Enemy. It was live on MuchMusic in 1999 and we were discussing their prominent status in the hip hop world. I let them know we had a short video clip on standby and asked them to look at the monitor. I had interviewed the Beastie Boys a few days prior in New York City and I knew I'd be interviewing Public

Enemy later in the week. I asked The Beasties about Public Enemy's influence on their music and Mike D, Adam "MCA" Yauch and Adam "Ad-Rock" Horovitz all shared beautiful sentiments about Public Enemy and why they loved the band. I asked them if they had ever expressed those thoughts to Public Enemy before and they said, "No, we haven't." I replied, "Well, you just did." After the clip was played, the crew cheered loudly as we returned live to a normally serious, stoic and intense Chuck D, who had broken out into a huge smile. His reaction proved it was great television.

One of my favourite things about working at MuchMusic was the boundless energy and creativity required to pull off engaging and compelling television. One of our producers, Craig Halket, was a genius at coming up with theme weekends. One of the most exciting and successful theme weekends he developed was the '80s weekend, hosted by Rick "The Temp" Campanelli and me. For two straight days, we played nothing but music videos from the '80s, featured archived interview clips from the '80s and even had '80s-era musician live guests drop by. Rick was an awesome co-host and some of my favourite times at Much included being paired up with Rick on some assignments. Hands down, of all the VJs I worked with, the biggest laughs always came when Rick and I were together.

During VJ shifts, I was always forthright with the audience, often expressing my crushes on the air. It was always a treat to interview, meet and bond with some of the females I was not only a fan of, but in awe of. Often when we cite *crushes*, we refer to physical beauty, but to me, having a crush on someone could also refer to their inner strength, character, positive outlook, talent, wisdom and conviction. I have met and interviewed most of my life's crushes: Liz Phair, Lisa Marie Presley, Jennifer Love Hewitt, Britney Spears, Avril Lavigne, Mel C of the Spice Girls, Tiffany, Poe, Sarah Harmer, Natalie Merchant, Traci Lords, Kinnie Starr, Grace Slick from Jefferson Airplane, Metric's Emily Haines, Veruca Salt's Nina Gordon, Feist and so many more.

It's an odd question that I have been asked many times: "Have you ever dated anyone famous?" Besides my relationship with Ronna Reeves, there has been more than a few, but I certainly don't want this book to come off as a tawdry tell-all. I know full well that many love to read and hear about *the dirt*, but I never let gossip into my life, so I don't want to share gossip. But I will offer a story about a date I had with another crush, pop star Debbie Gibson.

Debbie Gibson remains the youngest female artist to write, produce and perform a Billboard number one single. "Only in My Dreams" from her debut album *Out of The Blue* was a huge smash for Debbie in 1987. MuchMusic played Debbie's videos incessantly in those days, and I couldn't help becoming a fan of those catchy pop hooks, even though my taste in music was a million miles away.

Fast forward to 1997 when I interviewed Debbie at MuchMusic for her new album entitled *Deborah*. It was a great time and we both laughed and enjoyed each other's company. Yup, my crush on her was still there.

We didn't see each other until she came back to Toronto in 2001 to star in the National Theatre tour of *Cinderella*. I was sent out on assignment to tape an interview with her at the Pantages Theatre in the afternoon. It was an amazing time and a great interview. We continued to talk well after the interview, and I gave her my card. When I returned to the station and came back to my desk, I had a voicemail from Debbie. "Hi, Bill. It's Debbie. Nice to see you again. Let's go out tonight! Call my assistant and we'll have fun! Here's her number . . ."

I thought, *Cool! Debbie Gibson. Wow.* To borrow from her song, a date with Debbie was "only in my dreams." But this wasn't a dream. I called her assistant back later and made arrangements to see Debbie after her performance. I was told to meet Debbie at the stage door of the theatre after the show.

I am early for everything. I arrived at the door well ahead of time. There were many Debbie Gibson fans gathered and many recognized me. "Bill Welychka!? Can I get a picture with you? Are you going in? Are you seeing Debbie?"

Debbie's assistant eventually opened the door and pulled me in. She escorted me to Debbie's dressing room. She then said, "Debbie's getting changed. Hang out here on the couch." She also said to me, "Take her to a nice restaurant, but whatever you do, don't smoke around her."

I sat and waited in Deb's dressing room on the couch. She eventually emerged looking beautiful and showing no signs of having just been on stage performing to thousands. We made small talk while leaving the theatre, and both of us signed and posed for pictures. I felt like I was on TMZ or some other lame-ass entertainment TV show. I eventually hailed a cab. I directed the driver to one of my favourite restaurants on Front Street.

I escorted her to the table while we continued talking. This was at a time in Toronto when smoking was allowed in public places. Yes, I was a smoker at the time.

After having some drinks and sharing some fun moments at our table, I excused myself, went to the bar and proceeded to have a cigarette well away from our spot. I returned to the table to a very disappointed and angry person who expressed, "I am done. Please drop me off at my hotel." Wow.

I did as directed and didn't ask questions while making sure Debbie was dropped off safe at her hotel entrance. I felt bad that I disappointed someone. Never mind who she was. I felt awful.

Four years later, Debbie posed nude for *Playboy* magazine. In some corner in my mind, I imagined a parallel universe where she was thinking, "Bill. You're an ass-face. I hope you're seeing these awesome photos. Here's what you're missing!"

Yes, smoking is very, *very* bad.

· · · · ·

In 1998, Steve Waxman from Warner Music Canada escorted cameraperson Steve Gelder and I to LA for a few days for some memorable assignments. The first was videotaping pop music icon Madonna accepting a MuchMusic Video Award for Best International Video. Madonna could not make it to Toronto for the live national broadcast, so we would tape her at her house, which was in a private gated community in the Hollywood Hills. Let us remember that Madonna was the single biggest star on earth, and at this time she was staging a huge comeback with her album, *Ray of Light*.

We drove up to the locked gate in our rental car and Steve pulled out some papers and proceeded to punch in the key codes. A few seconds later, we heard a woman's voice coming from the speaker saying, "Hello?"

"Hi, it's Steve Waxman with Warner Music Canada. I am here with two people from MuchMusic for a taping with Madonna." Within moments, the double gate had swung open. We drove down a long driveway and came to a beautiful, sprawling house. As we stepped out of the vehicle in front of the big doors, a woman came out to greet us. She explained that she was Madonna's assistant and that she would show us inside. I helped our cameraperson Steve Gelder by carrying his lighting kit in one hand while in my other hand was the large MuchMusic Video Awards trophy. We followed her into the house and turned right off the vestibule into what looked like a living room. Much art adorned the walls. I suppose I expected a huge portrait of Madge herself with many lit candles and a huge trophy case with dozens of music awards, but nope. Just very tasteful and uncluttered decor.

Her assistant said we could set up anywhere in the room and that Madonna would be out to join us in twenty minutes. As she left the room, I suggested to Steve where the shot should be. Steve proceeded to set up two light stands with me acting as a stand-in for Madonna.

A very prompt Madonna walked into the room twenty minutes later. Steve Waxman introduced himself and then introduced Steve Gelder as the MuchMusic cameraperson and me as the MuchMusic VJ. She looked at me and said, "*You're* a VJ? You don't *look* like a VJ." I didn't know what she had expected, but I made small talk and eventually brought her to the area we had chosen.

I handed her the MuchMusic Video Awards trophy and explained, "Please stand here and hold the trophy. Say anything you like, and the award is for Best International Video for 'Ray of Light.' Have fun with it!"

She replied, "OK. But where's the monitor? I need to see the shot first. I don't work without a monitor. Did you guys bring a monitor?"

I looked at Steve Waxman and said, "Steve, sorry. We don't travel with monitors. You didn't tell us to bring one."

Steve replied, "No one told me. Sorry."

Madonna looked at me and asked, "Can you get a monitor?"

I replied, "We *are* in Hollywood. I am sure there are plenty of production houses close by. We could rent one?"

Madonna looked frustrated. She said, "Boys, I'll give you thirty minutes. There's the phone and a phone book." She turned around and walked out of the room. I swear we looked like the Three Stooges running around, bumping into each other, trying to figure out the next move. All we needed was some wacky music to go with our fast maneuvering around each other. Madonna was kind enough to turn on some music, playing some Madonna music on shuffle.

I opened the phone book and looked under the audio-visual rentals listings. Steve Waxman apologized again and said, "Get a monitor now! Tell them it's an emergency! Warner Music will pay for it! Get it here fast!"

We got lucky and a delivery person was on his way over with a monitor within minutes. Madonna's assistant explained that we were very fortunate and that normally Madonna would have cancelled the shoot, but for some reason, she had felt sorry for us. I think it was me she felt sorry for, because I didn't *look* like a VJ, whatever the hell *that* meant!

The assistant explained that she would buzz the delivery man in at the gate, but that Steve Waxman and I had to meet him outside the house's main doors. The delivery man was not to be allowed inside and we were told to absolutely not tell him who lived at the house. Of course we agreed and formed a quick plan for me to take the monitor inside while Steve would take care of the paperwork and keep the guy outside.

The van arrived and Steve and I greeted it, with me grabbing the monitor and cables and walking back into the house quickly, right through into the living room. It was only seconds later that I heard from behind me, "Wow! Whose house is this? Are you guys shooting some porn? Can I stay and watch?"

What the fuck!? The guy had given the forms to Steve to sign and while Steve was distracted, the guy had followed me into the house. In the living room, I turned around and said, "Sorry man. You can't be in here. Please leave and wait outside by your van. We'll be done shortly."

Cameraperson Steve Gelder took the monitor from me and proceeded to attach the cables and cords to his camera and the wall plug. Madonna entered the room minutes later and began directing the shot that Steve Gelder had established. I held the heavy monitor with both arms outstretched next to Steve while Madonna stood in place, trophy in hand, telling Steve to lower one light while raising the other light.

Madonna seemed happy with the shot she saw in the monitor and said, "OK, I'll start now . . . in three seconds . . ." At that point, one of the bulbs blew in the light stand, making the shot dark on one side. Madonna looked at Steve and said, "Tell me you travel with spare light bulbs!?"

Steve Gelder locked his camera on the tripod and searched his light kit for a spare bulb. He found one, unlocked the light stand clamps, lowered the stand and replaced the blown bulb with a fresh one. He raised the light again and secured the telescopic stand with its clamp.

The not-so-heavy monitor I was holding started to feel like it weighed fifty pounds. Steve said, "OK . . . We're ready to roll!"

Madonna waited a few seconds and then started her acceptance speech. She got as far as saying, "Hi, I'm Madonna! Welcome to my living room and . . ." She stopped and looked very agitated. The light stand Steve had adjusted had started to slowly lower itself. The clamp wasn't fully tightened! The light atop the stand was inching downward. Everyone in the room just stared at it and I am sure we were all thinking the same thing, which was, "Oh c'mon! What the fuck!?"

Steve relocked the camera and adjusted the light stand, again. The monitor I was holding doubled its weight. I began sweating profusely. This was beyond embarrassing.

Madonna took a deep breath and started her acceptance speech again. She knocked off a thirty second clip in one take. I was so thankful as I placed the monitor on the ground. My sore arms were trembling. I wiped my brow. I said, "Awesome! Sorry for all the troubles but great job and thanks for your patience. By the way, your real award will be given to you at a later date. I need the trophy back—it's the only one. It's a prototype."

She replied "Here ya go. No hurry, believe me! I'm not crazy about awards anyway. They're tacky."

I asked her what she had done with all her Grammys, American Music Awards and other trophies. She replied, "They're all in boxes in storage under the stairs. I don't clutter my space with shit like that. Look around. I like fine art."

Steve, Steve and I thanked her again and she left the room. I started to help pack Steve's lights and gear. As Steve was wrapping some cables, he looked at me and whispered, "Do you think I can ask her to come back and get a picture?"

"No fucking way," I said. "We over-stayed our welcome. Let's get the fuck outta here!"

I would see Madonna five years later for a great, lengthy interview at the Four Seasons Hotel in downtown Los Angeles. We exchanged pleasantries at the start of the interview, and she asked, "Why do you look familiar? I know you, I think."

I was not going to tell her that I was once at her house. That would sound too creepy and stalker-ish. I said I was a VJ with MuchMusic and MuchMoreMusic in Canada. She said, "Of course. Yes! That's why you look familiar! You look like a VJ!"

To this day, I have no clue what a VJ was supposed to look like.

The day after the fiasco at Madonna's house, Warner Music Canada took us to the next assignment. It was for yet another music icon inside yet another gated community. We visited Brian Wilson's house. The legendary Beach Boys singer, songwriter, producer and visionary was releasing his new solo album, *Imagination*.

As we were let in by security at the gates, I asked Warner Music rep Steve Waxman in a full-on sarcastic tone, "Will Brian Wilson need a monitor too?" He did not like my question and he glared at me disapprovingly. We were met at the door by Brian and his wife where we made introductions before being brought inside. We chose a nice area in his living room for the interview, his piano in the background. Most people with pianos in their living rooms arrange framed family photos on top of them. Brian and his wife had done so, and I immediately recognized Carnie Wilson and Wendy Wilson of pop group Wilson Phillips.

Admittingly, I was a tad cautious on how I approached this interview. Brian had a long history of hating interviews and hating many interviewers. There really hadn't been a large amount of *really* good Brian Wilson interviews through the years. I am proud to say, Brian was a champion and very forthright, open and honest throughout our conversation. I was very happy with the experience and so was Brian. After the interview, as cameraperson Steve Gelder was packing up his gear, Brian and I continued to talk. He got up, walked over to his piano and started playing. I sensed that he was giving me this private moment as a "thank you" for enjoying his time with us, without a camera rolling.

After Brian's private concert of ten or fifteen minutes, I stood up and graciously thanked him and his wife for their precious time. I had brought with me five Brian Wilson pictures for him to sign, with the goal of giving the pictures to people that I knew would *love* them. He was eager to sign the pictures, and then we left.

Those signed Brian Wilson pictures would prove to be a hit the next day with some well-known Canadians who were also visiting Los Angeles. That four-day trip in 1998 to Los Angeles culminated in another visit to the Hollywood Hills, this time to catch up with Canada's Barenaked Ladies.

The band had achieved major sales numbers with their album *Stunt* in both Canada and the USA. As part of our whirlwind trip to LA, we covered the band's filming of the video for their forthcoming single, "It's All Been Done." The video was directed by multimedia artist Doug Aitken.

After shooting some on-set performances and visuals, I interviewed director Doug Aitken and the Barenaked Ladies. It's always a treat to catch up with Ed Robertson, Steven Page, Jim Creeggan, Tyler Stewart and Kevin Hearn. The guys not only keep an audience entertained, but each other. After the interview, I pulled out my five autographed pictures of Brian Wilson from the night before, one signed picture for each member of the band.

The band's hit song "Brian Wilson" from their 1992 major label debut *Gordon* was a sort of tribute to the music icon. At this point in the band's career, they hadn't yet met Brian Wilson. I thought a gift from a fellow Canadian to some Canadians working in the US would be a kind gesture. The boys loved their gifts. I love seeing people happy.

CHAPTER TWELVE
A NEW YORK CITY BDSM CLUB

When an artist welcomes you onto their private turf, it's a great feeling. It's trust-based and it's a thrill to realize that only a few are welcomed into their inner sanctum, their actual home. It leaves a journalist with a feeling of extreme pride. In most cases, it becomes an "exclusive." I felt that after interviewing Eddie Van Halen and the rest of Van Halen at Eddie's house in LA in 1998. The next year, I interviewed Enrique Iglesias at his home in Miami in 1999. His backyard has a beautiful pool that looks like it drops off into the Atlantic.

An artist's inner sanctum can also mean where they are working, like at a recording studio. I interviewed Lisa Loeb live on MuchMusic in 1996. Three years later, I caught up with Lisa again as part of a trip to LA that also included an interview with the band Live, which I had become a huge supporter of. We caught up with lead singer and songwriter Ed Kowalczyk at A&M Studios while the band was recording tracks for their album, *The Distance to Here*. The next day, we were whisked to another studio to interview Lisa.

Lisa was recording a new single, and while waiting for the interview to start, our cameraperson Tim Crough and I learned that Guns N' Roses singer Axl Rose was down the hall in another studio working on his *Chinese Democracy* album. Lisa told us that she had met him a few times and that despite his reputation, he was actually very sweet. Tim asked me if he could meander down the hall and listen through the door to Axl's recordings. I was responsible and said, "No way." I envisioned the worst-case scenario where Tim was crouched down with his camera at the studio door and the notoriously private and extremely moody Axl came out, saw Tim and proceeded to kick him and his expensive camera. Lisa was daring us to do it. Alas, we didn't.

I loved the work assignments to the US. As I wrote earlier, it seemed I would be in LA or New York City every other weekend. I grew to really embrace NYC. My first work trip to the Big Apple was in 1995 to interview Dolores O'Riordan and The Cranberries. Other New York City assignments followed throughout the years, including spending a couple of afternoons with Peter Gabriel, interviewing Enrique Iglesias, Adam Duritz from Counting Crows, Marc Anthony, Shakira, Bon Jovi, The Cure, Jewel, Boy George and Culture Club, David Bowie and many more.

MuchMusic had gained some international momentum in the late '90s, launching several incarnations around the world including MuchMusic USA in many markets through Rainbow Media. Apparently, Much USA in New York City was drawing many viewers.

I was asked to cover the 1999 New Year's Eve festivities in New York City for all of our Canadian and Much USA viewers. There would be live cut-ins from me in Times Square ringing in the new millennium airing throughout North America. I opted to drive down to Manhattan from Toronto in a MuchMusic vehicle a few days prior and had asked my best friend Jeff Parissi to accompany me. He said yes. We arrived a few days early because the hotel parking lot would be locked and sealed until January 1st.

Jeff and I spent the night before New Year's Eve (New Year's Eve Eve?) in the Chelsea District on the Hudson River, a trendy restaurant and night club area. We found our way to a bar where the patrons were walking around in almost no clothing—both men and women. Jeff and I looked at each other and wondered, "What did we stumble upon? Was this a sex club?" We sat at the bar and ordered some drinks from Linda, the bartender. Jeff asked her very shyly, "Ummm, what kind of club is this?"

She replied, "It's a BDSM club. No sex in the open, but our guests like to spank each other and engage in other kinky adult play and have fun! What are you guys into?"

Jeff answered, "Well, we're both straight. And he likes feet." Linda looked at me, smiled and asked me if I wanted to suck on her toes.

"I'm good. Thanks, though," I said. I quickly changed the subject and the three of us continued to talk while Jeff and I had drinks. Around midnight, Linda proclaimed that she was off duty and asked if she could sit with us. For the next hour or so, we got to know Linda and had a great time at the bar while the thirty or so other leather-clad, half-naked people behind us spanked, danced with and/or kissed each other.

Linda eventually said that her ride was coming to pick her up soon, and she asked us if we wanted to hang at her place for a while. Within minutes, we had walked outside and soon climbed into a dirty, messy car driven by her friend, who was also dirty and messy. We crossed the Brooklyn Bridge into a dirty and messy Brooklyn neighborhood. The three of us got out and we followed Linda upstairs to her small and (yup, you guessed it) dirty and messy apartment. Jeff dozed off on the floor while Linda and I talked until the sun rose.

I asked her to call a taxi for us. I woke Jeff from his deep slumber and as we said our thanks and goodbyes, Linda asked me to come back to the club after we were finished our New Year's Eve broadcast. She said she wanted to buy us drinks and say a proper goodbye before our trek back to Canada. I said, "We will see ya after midnight." In the taxi back over the bridge to Manhattan, Jeff noticed that the car we had been passengers in while driving to Linda's apartment had been pulled over by the police. We looked at each other and shrugged it off.

In Times Square, a five-story media tower was constructed to enable the numerous TV crews to get their coverage. We had secured our press credentials and security passes earlier in the day. I recall CNN was at the top tier, and local New York City network affiliates had positioned themselves on the other platforms. I think we occupied the third tier with some other US television stations.

Throughout the evening, we conducted live hits twice an hour and recorded some moments off-air for Much and Toronto's Citytv for broadcast later. We left our position a few times to grab interviews with the revelers on the other side of the security fencing. At one point, we saw New York City Mayor Rudy Giuliani and some handlers climb the stairs to the top tier of the broadcast tower. The host from another station next to us said that only CNN gets Rudy.

A few moments later, as we were broadcasting live, I noticed Rudy's people descending the stairs of the platform above us. I slowly maneuvered closer to the stairs while continuing my live hit, our cameraperson following me. When Rudy was next to us, continuing his walk down the stairs, I said loudly ". . . and here is the man of the hour, New York City mayor, Rudy Giuliani! Rudy, good evening. We are live right now with Canada and the US . . . do you have a moment?" Rudy looked at me and our camera and stepped away from his entourage, towards me.

"Thanks for stopping by! I'm Bill Welychka with MuchMusic. Sir, you throw a hell of a party!" Rudy proceeded to welcome us and spoke at length about what it took to pull off a millennium party in the greatest city on Earth, and he offered other great comments. I thanked him and wrapped up the live hit. Rudy and his people carried on their way down the stairs and eventually exited the media compound.

Jeff looked at me and said, "That was awesome. Fuck CNN!"

When we had finished all our live hits and post-midnight coverage, I said thanks to our crew and wished everyone around me a Happy New Year. Jeff and I walked south until we hailed a taxi and found our way back to Linda's club. I was exhausted but I was going to keep my promise and say goodbye to our new friend.

Once again, Jeff and I took some seats at the bar. Linda saw us and immediately came out from behind, rushed over to me and gave me a strong, lengthy hug. She said, "I missed you!" We exchanged our evening's fun stories. Jeff asked her about her friend that drove all of us the night prior and how we had seen his car pulled over by the police. She responded, "Oh, shit, yeah! The cops pulled him over, something about his plates. Shitty New Year's for him, he got detained. They found a gun in his back seat."

Jeff and I looked at each other and again shrugged it off. We only stayed for two drinks before standing up from the bar stools to say goodbye. Linda reached under the bar and handed me a thick envelope. She said, "Read this later. I loved meeting you."

Once Jeff and I were back in the hotel room, I opened the envelope. There was a silver ring inside and the accompanying pages described her strong feelings for me. She recounted her sad life in detail and described how she had never experienced meeting someone who didn't try to use her. She explained that after meeting me, she could finally feel what it was like to be respected. She expressed to me that she knew she was beautiful and that she attracted a lot of attention, but that she never knew how to deal with the attention. She ended the letter by thanking me and explaining that the ring was a gift to remind me of the life I had inadvertently touched.

Wow. I was extremely flattered and deeply moved. It was a very odd realization for me, and a lesson I carry with me to this very moment. No matter who we are or who we meet, we must be kind and respectful to everyone! Without even trying or knowing it, we all have the ability to elevate those that need to be elevated.

CHAPTER THIRTEEN
BOOZE CANS AND FLOOR HOCKEY

If one is old enough, I am sure they remember where their life was at as they changed their calendar to the year 2000. For me, I felt I wanted to leave MuchMusic, but not necessarily leave the building at 299 Queen Street West in Toronto.

I was very aware that my position was a great one, but if my math is correct, I was in my early thirties in 2000. I recall looking back at our recent MuchMusic ratings-winner broadcast of "Spice Girls Day," where I had to dress up as Posh Spice for a full day of Spice Girls videos and programming. (Rick Campanelli was dressed as Sporty Spice. He had better abs than me. Most likely, still does.) Yes, the Spice Girls were one of the biggest selling bands on Earth at that time, and when MuchMusic devoted an entire day to an artist, they did it with a whole lot of fun and creativity.

I have always loved creating television and all its disciplines. I still do! I love editing and producing and interviewing and hosting and even videography. But at this time with MuchMusic, I began to realize the focus wasn't necessarily on the music or the artist, but *how* it was delivered.

MuchMusic sister-station MuchMoreMusic was launched in late 1998. It was intended to be a more adult-oriented version of MuchMusic. There was no incessant VJ chatter and it focused on the *artist* and the *music*, with an emphasis on singer-songwriters who didn't fit the extremely tight demographics of MuchMusic. I embraced the concept because I was getting older and I saw the value in a cross-Canada TV music channel that could cater to an older audience that appreciated something more than discarded, beyond-their-expiry pop artists and (trending only) hits.

In mid-1999, I asked to be transferred to our newly launched music channel and was told by Denise Donlon (who had recently been elevated to the role of vice-president and general manager) that yes, I would be moved over, but in due time. I was glad it wasn't an immediate transfer because for the first year or so, MuchMoreMusic was still trying to find its focus. It was a work in progress. The channel was also extremely short staffed. Its playlist was very limited, and I thought it needed way more original programming. I envisioned a music channel that could be very successful if it just coloured outside the lines a little.

My wish was granted in May 2000. I transferred upstairs to the newly renovated fourth floor offices of MuchMoreMusic. My final VJ shift for Much was a four-hour live broadcast. It was a chance to say goodbye to the younger Much audience and let them know I wasn't exactly leaving the building, just shifting gears a little. Artists like Gob, Chantal Kreviazuk, Danko Jones, Matthew Good and others either dropped by or called in live to say farewell. We ran many taped favourite moments from my previous eight years at MuchMusic. I thanked on air notoriously shy producer Tania Natscheff for pulling the entire broadcast together. I learned a lot from Tania in my latter years at MuchMusic. She was a diligent perfectionist, and we spent many hours in edit bays together crafting amazing TV specials.

My move to MuchMoreMusic came with many meetings and boardroom strategizing on what I wanted to bring to the channel and how I could add some value to the somewhat stagnant programming that currently existed. To me, it was imperative that we widened the parameters to allow edgier artists onto the playlists.

I developed, created and hosted many new shows for MMM including *Freshly Pressed* (a weekly look at new music releases), *We're with the Band* (hanging out with an artist on the road and at a concert with exclusive access), *Backtrax* (a reborn show from MuchMusic featuring gold videos and new interviews with classic artists), *Press Day* (following an artist from morning to night while they did press in Toronto) and what would become MMM's signature series, *The Story of . . .*

A HAPPY HAS-BEEN

The Story of . . . series was a simple concept, but it would become hugely successful, even winning some international TV industry awards. I was very proud and grateful that I was given the chance to create the show and given the task to do the interviews, produce and edit the hour and direct the post-production. Each installment of the series featured a new interview I conducted with a marquee artist and incorporated past archived interviews, performances and music videos from our extensive music library.

We hit a homerun with one of the first installments, "The Story of Led Zeppelin." The hour-long special showcased my new interview with Jimmy Page in New York City and my new interview with John Paul Jones while he was in Toronto promoting a new solo disc. Both Zep members were notorious for not granting many interviews over the course of their careers, and in Jimmy Page's case, he was noted for not being a terribly forthright interview subject. I guess I caught both guys on good days because they gave me great moments, and both laughed a lot. The two Zep members truly enjoyed themselves during the interviews, and it showed.

The CHUM publicity department sent out some screening copies of the special to various Canadian press outlets before the airdate, and Canada's weekly published *TV Guide* gave it a glowing "must watch" review. I was just excited to see that MuchMoreMusic was getting some recognition. Admittedly, MMM was always in the shadow of the juggernaut MuchMusic.

Many more *The Story of* . . . features followed. A lot of the new featured interviews I conducted involved some travelling too. I also started to notice a pattern. A lot of the interviews and specials I was doing involved older artists whom I idolized and respected. These were the artists whose music I grew up to, whose artistry brought back cherished memories from many years prior or whose music touched me in some way. I formed perfect circles with Rush, The Cure, Metallica, David Bowie, The Rolling Stones, Ray Manzarek from The Doors, Kiss, Sting, Fleetwood Mac, INXS, Steve Earle, Blue Rodeo, Meat Loaf, AC/DC, REM, Carlos Santana, Duran Duran, Alice Cooper, Def Leppard, Ozzy Osbourne, The Cult, the Bee Gees, Jane's Addiction, Peter Gabriel, Aerosmith, Depeche Mode, 54-40, Triumph and many others.

I also pushed for showcasing newer artists and some acts that were experiencing a resurgence. Some of these musicians included Shaggy, The Black Crowes, Live, Avril Lavigne, Shakira, Red Hot Chili Peppers, Ricky Martin, Bon Jovi, Dave Mathews Band, Kid Rock, Jann Arden, Moby, The Cranberries, Sheryl Crow, Jewel, Coldplay, Nickelback, Pearl Jam, Counting Crows and countless more. A couple of the specials would win silver medals at the New York Festivals TV & Film Awards for best talk/entertainment programming.

One of the specials I was very proud of wasn't about a specific artist, but about an explicit topic: drugs and addiction. "The Story of Drugs and Rock" was an hour-long open and honest look at the history of drug use by musicians and its influence on their music. It featured many new interviews I had conducted and a vast number of older archived interviews from our MuchMusic library. The special also included interviews with doctors, psychotherapists and other professionals. The special ended with a look at the many noted musicians whose lives had ended because of drugs, alcohol and addiction. It was important to me to not present this hour as a giant "Just Say No" slap in the head to each viewer. I wanted it to be—and it was—an entertaining and educational television event that asked questions and allowed the viewer to consider all sides. I was honoured to find out that "The Story of Drugs and Rock" became part of the curriculum for some schoolboards across Canada. I received many emails from teachers stating that they and their classes had thoroughly enjoyed the program and that the messaging was perfectly balanced.

Putting the hour together involved many hours of screening videotapes, connecting many dots and threading a seamless flow for a well-paced hour. It was apparent to me that I had a very expansive ability to recall subject matter from so many of our catalogued interviews in the Much library. My knack for recalling artists' interviews and topics came from many years of watching interviews and producing and editing artist spotlights and specials. I took pride in the fact that if anyone asked, for example, "Who do we have archived that talks about aliens?" I could easily recall three or four catalogued interviews out of our video library of thousands of interviews.

Backtrax was a show that was resurrected from MuchMusic. The hour featured older, classic and gold music videos, but I would occasionally tape new interviews and co-host with musicians. Some of these included Pat Benatar, Sir Bob Geldof, Hall & Oates, Men at Work's Colin Hay, Jerry Lee Lewis, David Cassidy, Elvis Costello, April Wine, Richard Marx, Tiffany, Cyndi Lauper, Bryan Adams, Cheap Trick, Split Enz's Tim and Neil Finn, Run DMC, The Pretenders' Chrissie Hynde and many more. We would also produce some *Backtrax* specials from classic rock festivals and concerts. A very memorable episode was centered around Poison's sold-out "Hollyweird" 2002 concert at Toronto's Molson Amphitheatre. I was on-site for most of the afternoon conducting interviews with Poison's Bret Michaels and opening acts Faster Pussycat, Winger and one of my fave metal acts, Cinderella. Bret gives a great interview. He is energetic and very well-spoken. We talked about the resurrection of metal music. We discussed Poison's contributions to the pantheon of hard rock. We also talked about how a Poison concert is a giant party.

Bret explained, "We love going out and putting on a great show. We promise one thing: we will never go through the motions. I don't have it in me to walk through it. If you lose that, give it up because you're cheating the fans. Poison has never cheated our fans. Also, we love to blow shit up [with pyrotechnics and flames]! I hope to drag you up on stage and you can see for yourself how much fun it is!"

After the interview, Bret said to me, "I'm serious Bill! Can I get you and your camera-guy up there on to the stage?"

Without hesitation, I eagerly said, "Yes, please!"

We made arrangements to meet Poison's road manager at the soundboard at a specific time during their set. He would come and get us and bring us down to the front. Towards the end of their show, Bret announced to the sold-out crowd, "We got a little surprise for you tonight . . . I have a friend here for ya . . . from MuchMusic and MuchMoreMusic, Bill Welychka!" The thunderous cheers blew me away. Wow. The road manager said, "OK, go up." We helped our cameraperson up to the stage and I followed.

I took in the moment and smiled. I walked to Bret's mic and let him know that people from all over Canada had made their way to Toronto to catch a real rock 'n' roll sold-out show. More cheers. I thanked Bret and left the stage, leaving our cameraperson onstage to shoot the final two songs of the night. Confetti rained down. The shots he got were breathtaking.

• • • • •

MuchMoreMusic was now showcasing music video blocks that not only featured older, established artists but also newer and fresh acts. My theory has always been to be fearless with programming. When I listen to a classic rock station, I hear the same twenty songs in rotation that are thirty to forty years old. Is it that radio programmers are being lazy, or do they perhaps not know enough about music? If I programmed a classic rock station and had to come up with ten Can-con (Canadian content) acts, I wouldn't settle for just the obvious Loverboy, Bryan Adams, Trooper, April Wine, Chilliwack, Headpins and Rush I hear daily. Or if you do play Rush, there is a lot more to the band than "Closer to the Heart." Yes, these acts are great, but they also have more than their *one* song that gets played repeatedly. I would suggest to radio programmers to explore and have fun with acts like I Mother Earth, Sloan, the Headstones, Lee Aaron, Skinny Puppy, The Northern Pikes, k.d. lang, the Arkells, The Tea Party, The Pursuit of Happiness, the Killjoys, Bif Naked, Matthew Good Band, 54-40, Sarah McLachlan, The Trews, the Rheostatics, Great Big Sea, Bruce Cockburn, Robbie Robertson, the Skydiggers, Kinnie Starr, The Grapes of Wrath, Rusty, Treble Charger, Big Sugar, Ron Sexsmith, Moist and so many more.

MuchMoreMusic gave me the opportunity to also interview and spend a lot of time with, in the truest sense of the word, *legends*. Many of these artists didn't fit into the increasingly narrowed demographics of MuchMusic, so I jumped at the chance to spend a large amount of time interviewing Gordon Lightfoot, Creedence Clearwater Revival's John Fogerty, Joan Jett, The Rolling Stones' Mick Jagger and Bill Wyman, Tina Turner, Ringo Starr, Grace Slick, Steppenwolf's John Kay, Yes's Jon Anderson, Robbie Robertson, Deep Purple, Cheap Trick, Herbie Hancock, Blondie's Debbie Harry and many others.

The big difference between MuchMusic and MuchMoreMusic, besides the music content, was the ability to be *live*. Everything on MMM was taped and missing the energy of spontaneity and live guests. It was an extension of the idea that music itself came first on MMM, and not so much the *delivery* of the music. With MMM interviews, what aired was a little bit more substantial. It was all about the art and craft of an interview, but it was usually taped in a relaxed and quiet environment.

Eventually, MuchMoreMusic introduced live event specials. MuchMusic's *Intimate and Interactive* style of presentations would become *Live at MuchMoreMusic with . . .* I was stoked to go live for sixty or ninety minutes hosting amazing shows featuring Sting, Prince, The Guess Who, Sarah McLachlan, Celine Dion, Barenaked Ladies, Lisa Marie Presley, Gord Downie, Janet Jackson, Shania Twain and others. I was always proud of our live crews and our supervising producer Morgen Flury. Morgen was always open to my suggestions with our live presentations, and she trusted me enough to hand me the reins so that I had freedom for every interview's content. She let me do what I needed to do unfettered, and she rarely looked over my shoulder. Having a supervisor grant trust and faith is a great feeling and it certainly furthers morale.

· · · · ·

I was sent to New York City in the fall of 2002 to meet up with Jon Bon Jovi. He was promoting Bon Jovi's forthcoming album *Bounce*. There was a big push for this release from the record company and from Bon Jovi's management, as this disc would catapult the band to sales exceeding one hundred million albums worldwide. I had interviewed Jon a few times prior: once in Toronto, once in Monaco and once in LA. We always had a great rapport, and Jon is any interviewer's dream subject. He is very well-spoken, intelligent, forthright, giving and honest in interviews. We did the interview just outside of Times Square at the famed Sony Music Studios.

About four days after getting back to Toronto, I was told by my boss that Bon Jovi had requested me for a cool project. Their management team had devised an ingenious way to promote their new album with a TV special that was to be shown in ten different countries in different languages. The idea seemed lofty, but it turned out to be a really simple concept. It would involve me returning to New York City for a Bon Jovi concert, and to interview the band in front of a crowd of about five hundred New Yorkers at the Hammerstein Ballroom in the Manhattan Center. The shot of me asking the questions showed me at the front of the stage and a big, boisterous crowd cheering behind me. The "intimate" concert was about thirty minutes worth of music. I would crouch down during the performance but stand up to ask a question after two or three songs, and Jon would answer my question before kicking into another song. There would be five questions in all. When the concert was over and the band had left the stage, the production crew would position each of the other nine hosts in my spot with a small crowd gathered behind them and have them ask the same questions I asked but in their own language. The country's respective record company would then send the foreign TV outlet the taped live show and their host's taped questions, and that specific TV outlet would be responsible for re-editing the show for air in that particular country.

I had to send five questions in advance of the trip for approval and five back-up questions. The band OK'd my initial five questions. The final result for the band would be ten different specials, with ten different hosts asking questions during the concert and the band answering them. The production would be misleading, but no one would ever know, except the TV outlet that re-edited the broadcast for their country.

In a great negotiating tactic, my boss also requested a thirty-minute exclusive interview with the entire band prior to them taking the stage. Also, we requested that I tape bumper throws onstage with the band. Bumpers are quick, "Stay tuned, here's a commercial break," sorts of deliveries. The band's management agreed to all of my boss's requests. The MuchMoreMusic Canadian broadcast of *Bon Jovi: Live in New York City* concert special was a ratings smash. It was also the only special of the concert that featured a bonus interview of the band interspersed throughout the broadcast.

I admit that I was a tad intimated to host the actual live taping. New Yorkers can be a tough crowd. But the nice kick for me was speaking to many of Bon Jovi's fans following the show. Much USA had ceased to exist at this point, so I was surrounded by people asking, "Where are you from?" and telling me, "You did great!" or, "You should move here! We have awful TV music hosts!" I went back to Toronto feeling pretty good about the whole thing.

A HAPPY HAS-BEEN

When I learned that Jon Bon Jovi requested me to be the primary host for the concert, I was extremely flattered. I went from being a casual fan of Bon Jovi to being a huge supporter!

As 2002 was winding down, things were looking amazing for MuchMoreMusic. About two months following the Bon Jovi special, our *MuchMoreMusic Live: Shania Twain* special aired prime time on November 11. The same day, a few hours earlier, Shania was live on Canada's national CMT. Both networks had Shania promoting her new release *Up!*. What a treat it was the next day to read the *Toronto Sun*'s review of both shows entitled, "Much Wins by a Country Mile." TV critic Bill Brioux cited that the MMM broadcast was a no-contest. He wrote that everything from host, to set design, to conversation, to audience involvement was collectively what a live music show should be. It also helped that we peppered the show with many older interviews of Shania with me, dating back to 1993. I didn't need to read a glowing critique to know what our people were capable of, but it sure validated the creativity put forth.

· · · · ·

I have referred to the perfect circles in my life where I had listened to an artist's music at a young age and eventually met them, interviewed them, spent some quality time with them and ultimately bonded with them. It has happened countless times.

When I was in high school, Duran Duran owned the music charts and magazine covers. I wasn't a huge fan, but their music was everywhere. Even while at the roller rink with friends, the music of Duran Duran was omnipresent. Almost every girl I knew in high school was in love with Simon Le Bon, Nick Rhodes or John Taylor. Or all three or any combination of them. I did learn to appreciate their music and craft years later, but only after having done interviews with them and working on some Duran Duran specials.

I actually became friends and shared many laughs with the band before I would play their music at home. It's a good gauge for me to know if I really like an artist: do I make the effort to play them in the confines of my own space and on my own time? Over the many years at Much and MuchMore, there were a lot of acts I would interview that I respected but wouldn't necessarily listen to at home. Duran Duran CDs would eventually come out and I learned to love their tunes! It was catchy synth-pop with sometimes funky bass jazz overtones sung by a passionate vocalist who sometimes wrote very introspective lyrics. I have interviewed Simon, Nick and Andy Taylor from Duran Duran many times in Toronto and in LA.

In 2000, I caught up with Simon, Nick and newest Duran Duran guitarist Warren Cuccurullo in Toronto. It was another lengthy, detailed and fun interview. This particular interview would be used for *The Story of . . .* series. The next day, I was told by Liz Doyle at MCA Records Canada that Duran Duran expressed to her that my interview was the best time they'd had doing press in their entire career. Wow. Thanks, guys.

I had become a fan of Georgia's Collective Soul the first time I heard their 1994 single "Shine." I interviewed the band a few times and hosted a live Collective Soul televised concert in the CHUM-City/MuchMusic parking lot at 299 Queen Street West in Toronto in 1995. While at MuchMoreMusic, I caught up with the guys again and interviewed the band's Ed Roland and Dean Roland in 2004. After the interview, they asked if I was coming to their show in Toronto later that night. I told them I was, and they asked me to come back to their bus after the show to have some beers. After a blistering concert at The Docks, I met the boys on their bus to chat and drink. Ed asked me if I could take him and some of the band out to some clubs, as they didn't have to pull out of Toronto until 2 or 3 a.m. I called for a taxi and just before leaving, I was told by their Warner Music Canada rep to make sure the guys were back to the bus by 2 a.m. as they had to be back on the road to get to the next city on their tour.

I took the guys to the Bovine Sex Club first for last call. The Queen Street West club has nothing to do with cows or sex. It is a fun rock club, and the guys loved it. I then took them to an overnight booze-can off Spadina Ave. In the late '80s into the 2000s, Toronto booze-cans would pop up periodically in numerous downtown areas. They were after-hours drinking establishments that would go until noon the next day. The *better* booze-cans offered full bar service and some even featured live music. These well-run places with bouncers and respectful clientele were never advertised and patrons would find out about them through word-of-mouth amongst late night revelers. Most of the guests were bar workers who wanted some place to go after their late-night shifts ended. Sometimes guests at the tables were smoking pot or doing lines of cocaine. I don't judge, as long as everyone maintains a sense of responsibility, shows respect for others and takes care of each other, and the attendees always did. The boys from Collective Soul had a great time. I sent them off in a taxi back to The Docks to board their bus at about 5 a.m.

On the following Monday, I was told by my boss that the band was late getting to the next city on their tour. The record company blamed me, and I was told I was never to interview their artists ever again. I defended myself by saying that I took care of the band. I showed them a good time at their request, and I made sure they got back to their bus safely. I also stated that they were big boys who knew their schedule better than I did. I also said I was sure that they let their parent company in the US know that the Canadian label rocked and that they loved Canada.

My ban on interviewing Warner Music Canada artists lasted about sixteen seconds.

· · · · ·

When I think of my favourite bands of all time, there is a long list. And Blue Rodeo is always close to the top. Blue Rodeo's music is something a lot of us listen to on long drives. It is music we hear coming across lakes and rivers at the cottage. It is music that is comforting and is a friend during joyous times, sad times and also horrible times. Jim Cuddy, Greg Keelor and Bazil Donovan, the mainstays and original members of Blue Rodeo, are people I have enormous respect for and are people I consider friends.

An awesome assignment I will never forget happened in 2002. I was flown to Saskatoon with cameraperson Dave Hurlbut to join Blue Rodeo for a few dates on the road. We spent time with the band at hotels, on their bus and at venues. We were there for soundchecks, live shows, post-show meet-and-greets and other private, exclusive moments. The Blue Rodeo guys and their crew figured out many years prior that after a big concert, they needed to disconnect from *the party*—they needed to find a way to shut down the adrenaline racing through their bodies. Every touring band wrestles with the idea of keeping the party going after a live show. Blue

Rodeo does it very well in typical Canadian fashion. The band and their crew wind down after their gigs with a ball hockey game.

Our first night with the band on the road after their sold-out show in Saskatoon involved hitting up a local community centre previously secured for the band. They showed up with hockey sticks and played hockey until 1 or 2 a.m.

On this particular tour, their opponents were their opening act on their cross-Canada tour, The Sadies. I can testify that playing ball hockey in a gym well after midnight will wipe anyone out. I consider myself an average to above average hockey player, but seeing Jim Cuddy run around, pass the ball, set up shots and make plays made me realize that singing, songwriting, performing and producing are just a fraction of his talents. Boarding the bus and retiring to the bunk made sleep come fast. The cycle would repeat for the rest of their tour. I must declare, Blue Rodeo drummer Glenn Milchem is a goalie any team would be grateful to have! Even he admits to not knowing where his skills come from, but he has accepted the fact that he might have a ball hockey career if the whole music thing doesn't work out.

• • • • •

I referenced The Cure early in this book. The band, led by Robert Smith, and their music were life savers to me in my teen years. Music was always important to me, but discovering that *one* artist that inspired me and spoke to me was monumental to my outlook on life. Robert Smith's music, songwriting and persona instilled in me a sense of individuality and cultivated a confidence to stand proud in not following the path that others might follow.

My first interview with Robert Smith was in New York City at the Paramount Hotel in 1996. I had just finished a week's assignment in Monte Carlo, Monaco for the World Music Awards and was told that before heading back home to Toronto, I would have to go to New York City for a few days to spend some time with The Cure. The band was in NYC for a few days before their appearance on Saturday Night Live.

After I checked into the Paramount Hotel, I looked around to find a suitable location for the interview with Robert Smith. I hated doing interviews in hotel rooms with their boring decor and prerequisite chairs and plants. I stumbled into the kids' playroom, a colourful space with chairs made from plush toys and odd wall hangings. I thought, *Perfect!*

I brought cameraperson Steve Gelder to the room, and he agreed. It was the perfect whimsical and odd flavour to fit Robert's personality. Steve set up some lights and positioned his camera for the interview. I had made contact with The Cure's road manager prior, and he walked in with keyboardist Roger O'Donnell and new drummer Jason Cooper. I imagine I looked a little disappointed because he rushed over to say, "Robert will be here later. Here's a couple other Cure guys first."

I have always taken pride and pleasure in not panicking when plans fall apart. I relish the times when I have to respond quickly to unexpected changes. The three of us went on to have a lengthy conversation about being in The Cure, music and other interesting topics that made the interview an awesome experience for all involved.

Roger and Jason left the room and three minutes later, Robert came in and sat down looking tired but ready to do some press. I welcomed him with some small talk, made the introductions and started speaking. Our interview lasted about forty-five minutes. It wasn't really an interview but more of a conversation between two guys who quickly bonded over talking about music. I maintained an air of utmost professionalism during the interview, despite the few memories I had recalling the period in my life when I had posters of The Cure hung in my bedroom and pictures in my school locker. It was another perfect circle moment for me.

Robert asked me if I wanted to hang out with him and his band while they toured around New York for the afternoon. Steve and I said yes. We acquired other great moments and more interviews. I couldn't have scripted a better day with one of my idols. I would turn my interview into an hour special on MuchMusic.

Later that year, The Cure returned to Toronto. The band performed live on MuchMusic, and I was asked to host/interview them for the hour special. It would become brilliant live national television.

Years later while on MuchMoreMusic, I had more interviews with Robert Smith. Each interview resulted in new one-hour specials featuring The Cure. I conducted my last interview with Robert Smith during The

Cure's Curiosa Festival in 2004 at the Molson Amphitheatre (now, The Budweiser Stage). MuchMusic reporters interviewed the opening acts, Interpol, The Rapture and Mogwai. I was granted the task of securing a Robert Smith interview for Much and MuchMore. There was no word from The Cure's record label the day of the show. Could the festival's headliner be unavailable?

I decided to head to the venue with cameraperson Tim Crough. I had worked with Tim since I had started at MuchMusic in 1988 when he was a tape operator. Tim was also a big Cure fan. We arrived at the venue and I told security that we had no secured time with The Cure and no record label presentation would be present. I asked if I could speak to the band's road manager.

The security officer told us to stay put and he left his post to find out what the next move might be. He returned twenty minutes later stating, "I have never seen this before. Yes, you can come in. But please, next time, secure your appointment."

Tim and I were let into the backstage area. I was very familiar with the rooms at the venue, and I saw a cool space with some road cases labeled "The Cure." I said to Tim, "Set up here. I'll be back."

I eventually located The Cure's tour manager and told him where we were set up. Within minutes, Robert Smith came to us and sat down on one of the cases we had organized for the shoot. We proceeded to launch into another great exchange that lasted about thirty minutes.

The resulting 2004 special on MuchMoreMusic, "The Story of The Cure" remains one of my favourite projects I have been involved with. It features great storytelling and editing and contains unforgettable moments of my many interviews with one of my idols, Robert Smith.

I actually got a little choked up to see The Cure being inducted into the Rock and Roll Hall of Fame in 2019. To this day, I cherish Robert Smith and The Cure, and I express a huge amount of gratitude to Robert for providing the soundtrack to my life in those years where I needed great music as an escape and a brave figurehead to inspire and teach me to fearlessly forge ahead.

• • • • •

Another perfect circle moment happened in October of 2001. I was invited to hang out with Ozzy Osbourne and his wife Sharon for a few days on the road in the US. I had interviewed Ozzy a couple of times for MuchMusic, but this assignment was very special due to the length of time I would have with the legend.

The assignment was a circle moment for me because I saw Ozzy live in Toronto at Maple Leaf Gardens when I was in grade nine. It was my first *real* rock concert, seeing Ozzy on his 1991 Diary of a Madman Tour.

The task involved flying into Long Island with cameraperson Jamie Corbett and meeting Ozzy, Sharon and Robert "Bobby" Thomson, long-time tour manager for Ozzy Osbourne. We shot the very long meet-and-greet with fans gathered at a Long Island record store. After interviewing many fans, we got into a van with our hosts and drove to the airport. In the evening, we boarded Ozzy's private Cessna Citation to Philadelphia. After checking into our hotel, I caught Ozzy's taped appearance on *Late Night with Conan O'Brien*. The next day, we were part of his entourage, shooting all his radio appearances. We conducted our lengthy interview with Ozzy the next day in his hotel room and flew home later that afternoon. During our time with Ozzy, we also recorded interviews in the van, in elevators and in other places that we travelled with him. The end result would be MuchMoreMusic's award-winning episode, "The Story of Ozzy Osbourne."

At the start of the assignment, I got to know Bobby the road manager quite well. Bobby had been with Ozzy for twenty-three years. He let me know that conversing with Ozzy was taxing at times. Bobby said Ozzy would sometimes walk away in the middle of a conversation, and at any given point a day or two or sometimes more later, Ozzy would resume the conversation as if no time had passed. He explained that after many years of drug abuse, Ozzy's brain worked in fractured thought processes. Ozzy would abandon a conversation and return to it days later as if it was still a linear thought. It happened once on the trip. While we were on his plane talking about smoking and quitting, he sort of dozed off. He didn't really fall asleep (thankfully! I'd have assumed I was very boring!), it was as if he had mentally shut down. The next day while in his van, he asked me out of the blue how my new condo smelled without smoking in it.

I was somewhat confused and thought I had missed something. I looked at Bobby and he smiled at me and gave me a wink. Ozzy and I finished our conversation about smoking twenty hours after initially starting it. In Ozzy's mind, the conversation was about five minutes long.

Sadly, two years later, Ozzy's longtime Scottish friend and road manager Bobby Thomson died from throat cancer. He was discovered in his Detroit hotel room while on tour with Ozzy. He was only fifty years old.

· · · · ·

When record companies brought in big stars to Toronto to do press, it was sometimes easiest for them to get a nice hotel room and book thirty-minute intervals for assorted press opportunities. The problem with this was that often the shot looked boring, with the usual generic hotel wallpaper, chairs, lamp, curtains, plants and couch in it. Also, with sometimes four or more TV outlets conducting interviews, all the station's shots would look the same. There was not much room for creativity or separating *your* look from the next outlet.

I interviewed ex-Genesis drummer and vocalist Phil Collins in a Toronto hotel room in 2002 for his album *Testify*. I knew the record company had set up many interviews with Phil in that hotel room. To liven it up, I asked Phil, "Hey! Can we sit on the bed? It'll be a fun shot!"

Phil replied, "This is the first time an interviewer has asked me to bed! Let's do it!" A great interview ensued.

Jann Arden's record company scheduled a press day for her at the Four Seasons Hotel in Toronto to promote her 2003 release, *Love Is the Only Soldier*. I had interviewed Jann before, and *any* Canadian journalist that has interviewed Jann knows that she has a great sense of humour and likes to have fun. I asked her if she wanted to do the interview in bed. She asked, "Under the covers? Sure! But Welychka, the clothes stay on!" she joked.

About five minutes into the interview, we could smell something burning. One of the gels (colour correction plastic filter sheets) on the light stand had started to burn and smoke. This could happen if the gel was touching the light, or if there was too much dust on the metal doors of the light's housing. Within moments, the smoke detector in the room started its loud beeping. Very soon after, there was a knock on the hotel room door. The record company rep let two very concerned hotel maintenance workers into the room.

The workers looked around, noticing the two people in bed and a cameraperson standing at the foot of the bed with a large video camera on a tripod. Jann spoke up and offered, "Hi guys. Sorry for the disturbance. You might know me? I'm a big pop star. I'm Jann Arden in bed here with television's Bill Welychka. We were just filming a pornographic film and I guess things were heating up! Sorry, we'll be done in a few minutes. You're more than welcome to stay and watch. Have a great afternoon!"

Jann Arden is easily the funniest person in all of the Canadian music industry.

CHAPTER FOURTEEN
A SAD BORDER CROSSING

I had absolutely no reason to feel like life was anything but glorious in 2001. I had been granted my request to transfer to MuchMoreMusic and work was fabulous. But I was dealing with a nagging and uncomfortable feeling. Despite a very long list of romantic relationships I had been in and out of, I wasn't emotionally happy. Since my breakup with Ronna in 1994, I became what many would consider somewhat of a tramp. I am ashamed now to admit that I indulged in many loveless temporary liaisons. I often thought about Ronna and how she was doing. It had been seven years since we had spoken, but I couldn't shake the curiosity of where her life had taken her. Did she still think of me? Internally, I admitted that I still loved her.

Around the summer of 2001, I was told that plans were being made to send me on assignment to interview Steve Earle in Nashville. It would be in about a month's time. It would be my first time back to Music City, USA since the demise of *Outlaws & Heroes* in 1994. I couldn't return to Nashville without at least trying to make an effort to contact Ronna. I didn't have her phone number anymore, so I tracked down the number of her past publicist. I left a message that went something like this: "Hello! Sorry to disturb you. My name is Bill Welychka, calling from Toronto. I work at MuchMusic here in Canada and I am wondering how to get in touch with one of your former clients, Ronna Reeves. We used to be friends, and I'd like to get in touch to say hi. Thanks. Cheers!"

I gave my work email address at the end of the voicemail message. About two weeks later, I received an email from Ronna. "Hey! I heard you were trying to get a hold of me. What's up?" I didn't blame her for the somewhat detached and cold tone emanating from her message. In fact, I was grateful she made the effort to reach back.

I followed up with my phone number. We spent the next two days talking and catching up. Ronna didn't have a record deal anymore, but she had secured a songwriting/publishing deal. I told her when I was going to be in Nashville and asked her if she wanted to grab dinner. She said she would like to.

The interview with Steve Earle went very well. Even before the interview with Steve, we spoke at length, catching up. I had met and interviewed Steve countless times since I had started at MuchMusic. Spending time with Steve certainly met my perfect circle criteria. I let him know I was going to see someone special after our interview. He asked me if I was nervous about seeing this specific girl after so much time had passed. I said, "Absolutely!"

He told me, in his good ole boy Texan accent, "That means ya still like her."

Later that evening, I called Ronna from my hotel room to meet her for dinner. We had a beautiful time getting reacquainted face to face. The odd part was that it hadn't seemed like seven years had passed. She looked as gorgeous as I remembered. Even *more* so. After dinner, we sat in her car while she let me listen to some music demos of songs she had written that her publishers were pitching to other artists. The night ended with Ronna driving me to my hotel. We both got out of the car and hugged each other. We agreed to speak a lot more in the coming days.

During the following week, we spoke on the phone for hours each day. We made plans for me to come back and spend a weekend at her place. The time together solidified our thoughts about each other. She expressed that we shouldn't only get back together, but that we should get married. She offered that she would move to Toronto. Ronna didn't have an artist deal anymore, but because of her songwriting/publishing deal, she could write songs from anywhere. She wasn't tied physically to Nashville anymore.

We spent the remainder of the summer and fall of 2001 visiting each other between Toronto and Nashville. We eventually made plans for a wedding in Las Vegas in November. Due to travel restrictions following the tragedy of 9/11, our Las Vegas wedding wasn't a huge spectacle. My brother Ed and his wife Jan attended, and some friends from Toronto too, but it was mostly Ronna's friends and family that filled the chapel at the Monte Carlo Resort and Casino.

Following our wedding in Las Vegas, Ronna returned to Nashville and I returned to Toronto. I was in the process of selling my one-bedroom condo and buying a two-bedroom condo in the same building on King Street West in Toronto. The new space was on the top floor of the twenty-story condo complex facing south and west. It had a wood burning fireplace and floor-to-ceiling windows with a view of Lake Ontario. Ronna and I loved our new space, and I even upgraded the decor by buying some new furniture and painting the entire unit with colours chosen by Ronna.

I spent Christmas 2001 with Ronna at her parents' place in Nashville, and we drove to Toronto in a one-way rental truck with her boxes and furniture on December 27. We didn't have the correct papers for transporting Ronna's contents when we crossed the border in Windsor, Ontario, but thankfully the border agent recognized me and said she was a big viewer of my work. She expedited the border crossing process without any issue.

Ronna and I settled into my new condo nicely. MuchMusic/MuchMoreMusic publicists went into high gear in early 2002 doing a publicity splash for my ten-year on-air anniversary with the stations. Many articles printed across Canada picked up the story, and most of the subsequent articles concentrated on my new marriage.

Within five months of marriage, I started to think the union was a bad idea. I don't blame Ronna at all for the failed marriage. I put it all on me. I had been alone and single for so long that I really wasn't ready to move in with someone, let alone enter into a marriage. By the end of the year, we separated, and our divorce became official in 2003. I knew I loved her very much, but I also knew I wasn't capable of living with someone, nor was I ready for a marriage commitment. I took the responsibility of renting a one-way truck to drive Ronna and her furniture back to Nashville in late 2002. The year had started with the highest of highs and ended with the lowest of lows.

I agreed to give her enough money to buy a car and secure an apartment in Nashville for about six months' worth of rent. My lawyer who drew up the divorce papers said it was way too much money to give for an uncontested divorce. I said it was the least I could do for disrupting her life.

I drove the rented van to the border in Windsor. The boarder guard came to the driver's side window and asked our nationalities. I replied, "Canadian. Ronna here is American. Here are our passports."

After the driver examined the passports, he handed them back and asked, "Purpose of your visit to the US?"

I explained that Ronna and I were married and lived in Toronto. I told him that we were separating and soon getting a divorce. I expressed that I was driving her back to Nashville, where she had lived prior to moving to Toronto. The rental cube van was filled with her furniture and all her personal belongings. I would return to Canada after I helped her unload the contents at her new apartment.

The guard listened intently, nodding as I told him the story. He asked, "This is your ex?"

"Yes," I responded.

"You're driving, what, ten or twelve hours with her to Nashville?"

"Yes."

"And this is all her stuff?"

"Yes."

"I see." He paused for a moment, deep in thought. He then asked, "There's no guns or anything illegal in the rental, is there?"

"No, sir."

"OK, then. Ummm, have a safe trip," he leaned closer to the open window and whispered to me, "and good luck."

After a hotel room stay in Kentucky, I resumed the drive. I had driven to Nashville so many times that Kentucky seemed *almost there* to me.

Ronna had some friends meet us at her new apartment. The unloading of the truck went quickly. Eventually, after returning the rental truck to the company's compound, I made my way to the bus station in downtown Nashville with my one small bag I brought with me. I boarded a one-way bus from Nashville to Toronto. There were two or three city stops and transfers en route back to the Windsor border, where I had to transfer onto yet still another bus home to Toronto. The long ride home was easily one of the most introspective and saddest times in my life.

Back in Toronto, I was alone again, but not necessarily *lonely*. I have always found some semblance of comfort in solitude, but I couldn't shake the sense of despair, regret, sorrow, shame, remorse and guilt. It was the start of a very dark and lengthy time period for me. Thoughts of suicide were rare, but admittedly I did develop some scary thoughts. The only joy I experienced in late 2002 and for much of 2003 was throwing myself into work. And alcohol.

For someone that had dealt with depression for a long time, I recognized the deep paralyzing anxiety I was feeling. But it was darker and deeper than what I had ever experienced. A friend recommended seeking some help, perhaps a psychiatrist.

I started seeing a professional on a steady schedule for about six months. Early on in my sessions, we talked about antidepressants. I had never used them before, but after his recommendations and some of my own research, I agreed to go on venlafaxine. It took about a month before I noticed its effects. They didn't elevate me through the roof with feelings of happiness and joy—they aren't supposed to. To me, antidepressants simply removed the black cloud that continually existed over me.

The message of depression awareness needs to be dealt with. I am an eager advocate for talking openly about depression and helping demystify any concepts. I have publicly admitted many times over many years that I deal with depression, and I benefit greatly from prescription medication. The more dialogue, the better. There is absolutely no shame in admitting depression and sharing one's thoughts.

I explain it to people this way: a dark cloud visits. This heavy darkness comes with negativity and a lack of energy and strangles all desire to be social. Many that describe the same scenario will often admit utter despair and suicidal thoughts. It affects energy, sleep, emotions, thoughts, social ability and a drive to carry on.

Antidepressants simply bring you up a level to exist "normally" without the negative thoughts you would experience otherwise. Prescription medication has helped me very much. For those new to finding the proper prescription medication, I admit there is a minor hill to climb. Talk to your doctor. You will eventually find what works for you. Allow the time for it to work. It might take a few weeks, but it can really make a big difference.

Once I started circumventing depression with a prescription medication, I finally felt like I was back to functioning normally again. This has just been my experience. Again, please speak to your doctor.

After being on meds and noticing a huge difference, there were two times when I thought, *I feel normal! I will stop taking them.* Within a week, I noticed something was not quite right. The black cloud over my head materialized once again for no reason. That's when I realized that taking one little prescribed pill would be a daily regimen for the rest of my life.

Many friends, family and co-workers will never know your "little secret" unless you tell them. And there is no embarrassment in that. I am proud to say I am now doing extremely well.

I have recognized the signs of depression in some friends and have spoken and been there with them through the process, sharing my experiences. They all admit that talking to their doctor made a huge difference in their lives.

Music was and always will be the best escape for me. I found myself listening to a lot of music that related to what I was dealing with. It's a huge comfort in realizing you are not alone. I have also read that many public figures we all relate to and enjoy also deal or have dealt with major depressive disorders. In doing research, I learned Sheryl Crow, Bruce Springsteen, Joni Mitchell, Billy Corgan, Harrison Ford, Bret Hart, Sting, Bill Murray, Stephen King, Lady Gaga, Eddie Vedder, Brad Pitt, Oprah Winfrey, Janet Jackson and Peter Gabriel have all admitted to depression.

If reading my words registers with you on any level and you are seeking further assistance, know that there is help. Please see your doctor. You are not alone.

During therapy in 2003, my psychiatrist offered that my fear of relationships, my commitment issues and my desire to seek one-night stands could be based on sex addiction. What? That was an actual, *real* affliction? I didn't think I suffered from it, but I reluctantly agreed to spend three days visiting a specialized clinic in Toronto on his referral. After two days of extensive psychological testing and interviews; having heartrate monitors attached; and having to watch numerous images of trees, skylines, naked men and women; and having to listen to erotic voice recordings of men and women, I returned on the third day for the analysis results. I was told by the resident doctor and researcher that I was deemed a regular heterosexual with a healthy libido. All he could determine was that I had a fear of commitment. No fucking kidding! Why did I spend three days subjected to uncomfortable testing when I could have just said that? I asked him what the tests were supposed to reveal and whether I should have even been subjected to his examinations. He answered, "I don't think you should have been here. I only followed up on your doctor's recommendations. You are quite normal."

I could have told him that from day one! As we were wrapping up my evaluation in his office, I did ask him about the voice recordings I had to listen to. I remarked that the woman's voice was quite fetching. He laughed and said, "Really? I must tell her you said that. That was my girlfriend's voice."

• • • • •

Around late summer of 2003, I met up with a friend at one of my local neighborhood pubs. He knew I had been feeling down for a long while. I couldn't shake the black cloud that was always with me. Over drinks, he asked me point-blank, "What would make you happy?"

I said, "It's not that easy. That is a loaded question that I can't answer. It doesn't work that way. I love my job and to me, that's all that matters right now."

I did go on to tell him some ideas I had for TV shows that I thought were worth pursuing. I knew I couldn't interview rock stars forever, and I was starting to feel that entertainment wasn't the focus I wanted anymore. But, I also knew that whatever I did in the future must involve television production. It was all I'd ever known.

One specific idea I had for a TV series was a reality-based dating show. Perhaps not so much dating, but examining individuals' attempts at finding love (or no-strings-attached hookups) while on vacation.

The premise was unique. It was about showcasing the geography and history of an exotic locale, but also attempting to feature vacationers showing another side of themselves, a side that *only* comes out on vacation. I imagined a mix of *Wild On!*, *Love Connection* and a bit of Lonely Planet guides thrown into a big pot, stirred and seasoned with a tiny smidgen of

Love Island. The fast-moving, voyeur-based show would be served up to an adult audience, hosted by a curious, fun and adventurous personality who was also exploring the region's places of interest. The process involved finding vacationing singles and adventurous couples and getting them to let a camera follow their search for new friends with visits to the beach, the clubs, the hot tubs and perhaps, if they got lucky, their rooms.

My friend listened intently and we eventually switched topics, drank some more and said our good-byes. About two months later, I got a call from him saying that he wanted me to meet another friend of his. His friend apparently loved my concept and wanted to have a meeting.

I met John Temou about a month later. Johnny owned Culture Shock TV, a video production company. We talked about the show's concept and kicked around some ideas. I had another meeting with John about a month later at his place. It turned out we were neighbours, living two blocks from each other. Johnny and I agreed that if this pilot episode was going to happen, he would direct, edit and co-produce with me, while I hosted and co-produced. We also agreed that I didn't want to come off like a lecherous host looking to take advantage of my position. I wanted to ensure my presence as host reflected my personality: welcoming and somewhat naive but adventurous, gracious and trusted by the viewer to lead them on a fun excursion.

Although my idea was just that, a mere idea, Johnny showed huge initiative and got back to me saying that he had secured a week-long shoot at a resort in Jamaica with flights for us and a two-person production crew. Everything was comped. I took a week off from work in January of 2004 to shoot the TV pilot for *Taking Off*.

John and I continued to have meetings right up until our flights departed from Toronto to arrive at Hedonism II Resort in Negril, Jamaica. Our destination was world-renowned for its liberal sexual lifestyles and open swinging on the nude side of the resort, as opposed to the *prude* side. In one of our meetings, I made it clear that the show was not going to be sleazy, trashy or smutty. John and I had the same vision, and it was imperative to both of us that we were respectful of our environment and that we treated everyone we met with the utmost dignity. We were there to work and not vacation. Our directives were made very clear to our other team members.

Johnny and I chose the title *Taking Off* because it implied taking off on vacation. It also implied taking off clothes. Johnny liked it because the graphics he designed of the *TO* logo and placed on the mic flag and handheld microphone could also imply that we were from Toronto.

I bonded with Johnny during our meetings back in Toronto, but I really felt this dude could be a true friend on our two-hour ride from the airport in Montego Bay to the resort in Negril. We had very similar eclectic tastes in music and film, and his presence was comforting to me. I had told him of my diagnosis with depression prior to our trip, and I sensed he was watching out for me.

At some point during our week at Hedo II shooting the TV pilot for *Taking Off*, John Temou and I became best friends. Johnny is easily the funniest person I have ever met. He has a knack for being at the centre of the party. Even though we met a lot of great people from around the world, we both realized that the vision for our pilot episode could not be realized because swingers generally do not want their judgmental hometown neighbours to know that they occasionally indulged in open-minded adult play, or what is referred to as "the lifestyle."

It was a fun week and I witnessed a lot, but alas, the pilot would never be shopped around to any network. The final product looked like an infomercial for Hedonism II, with segments showing me water skiing, cliff diving, scuba diving or learning to trapeze on high wires at the resort. Despite what I considered to be a failed attempt at a TV pilot, I walked away from that week with a great new friend that elevated my spirit when I needed it most in my life. To this very day, I consider John Temou a lifesaver.

I still believe in the concept of a TV show that explores why people become someone else on vacation. It's an extension of why we tune into TV shows where strangers are looking for love, or a strictly physical relationship. I offer that it's like watching a car crash. It's ugly, scary and horrible, but you can't pull your eyes off of the scene. It stirs the voyeur inside of us.

If one dating show gets ratings, expect clones of the formula to pop up. There will be slight variations, but the concept will remain the same:

A HAPPY HAS-BEEN

let's all live vicariously through these strangers trying to find love. Even "losing" contestants on dating shows still have hope. Candidates that don't win on The Bachelor or The Bachelorette come back and are given a second chance.

There was a time when I wished Debbie Gibson had given me a second chance.

But as far as me finding love was concerned, it would only happen unexpectedly about thirteen years later.

· · · · ·

I was grateful for John Temou's presence in my life from late 2003 onward. Despite many laughs and a return to a fun social life, I remained aware of my strict daily regimen of antidepressants. Also helping my spirit was a very busy period for MuchMoreMusic. I was constantly travelling for work to conduct interviews and I was producing, editing and hosting some cool *The Story of . . .* hour specials. Johnny even accompanied me on a 2004 interview with Aerosmith to shoot second camera. That was a memorable interview because Steven Tyler wrapped up the interview by saying to me, "I love your questions, man!" He then turned towards our camera and said, "You see Bill? This is not *Kill Bill*, this is not 'don't mess with Bill,' this is not 'does he fit the bill?' This is Wild Bill!"

In May 2005, I was sent to Los Angeles for what would become one of my favourite assignments of all time. Dave Grohl and his Foo Fighters band were about to release the mammoth, two-album project, Grammy-winning *In Your Honor*. The album was recorded in Dave's new studio near San Bernardino, which also contained his offices and storage facilities for all of the band's gear and tour equipment. The long hallways were lined with dozens of gold and platinum record awards for Nirvana and Foo Fighters. The resulting interview, conducted at this new building, was used for MuchMoreMusic's *The Story of . . .* series.

The interview with the Foos was broken down into two lengthy tapings with the first being with Nate Mendel and Chris Shiflett and the second with Taylor Hawkins and Dave Grohl. A few weeks prior, I had been on the road with Motörhead shooting a special for MMM, and Dave wanted to hear all about my time hanging out with Lemmy. It was a great afternoon

115

talking with Dave and the band. Dave was very forthright about his time in Nirvana and went places in our interview I had never seen him go before in any other interview. To me, Dave has always been one of the brightest, most intelligent, passionate, funny and honest musicians I have ever met. He is always honest and his high energy is infectious. Even though Dave Grohl is one of the biggest rock stars in the world, his attitude is very much the antithesis of the widely accepted notion of what a rock star is. The following is an exchange from my interview with Dave and Taylor in 2005:

> ME: People try to put you up on a pedestal and they try to paint you as a celebrity, and as much as people are trying to build up this thing, you're more about the *anti* that.
>
> DAVE GROHL: Most musicians have had a love of music their whole life and would listen to and play music whether it was in the basement or at the superdome down the street. But then there's some musicians that really ache to be stars, *rock stars*. And usually when they become rock stars, they make the best rock stars in the world. They're perfect, they're like superheroes and they do crazy shit . . . and they live in a mansion and they marry a model and they become an asshole.
>
> If you really come from a place where you have an obsessive, compulsive desire to play music, and that's your main attention and main focus, that's kind of the healthiest way to go.
>
> TAYLOR HAWKINS: The rock star aspirations are usually [from being] fairly insecure people looking to fill some sort of hole or void that will probably inevitably never be filled.
>
> DG: It's so great and so flattering to be appreciated by a lot of people and have the opportunity to do something like talk to a huge TV station about your new record that you made in a studio that you built by yourself. It's really great! But at the end of the day, music should be its own reward,

whether you're doing it in this situation or you're doing it on stage or in your pal's basement. If that's not enough, don't do it.

After saying goodbye to Dave and the band, cameraperson Dave Harnden and I got into our rental and drove back to our hotel in downtown LA. I distincly remember saying to him in the car, "Don't ask me why, but I have a feeling that this is my last time in LA for this company."

He disagreed. "What? Get out. You're crazy."

"No, I'm serious! I can't shake the thought. I've had it all week. This is the final time I see LA in this capacity."

My hunch would be proven correct a few short months later.

CHAPTER FIFTEEN
POOPING ALPACAS

I have written before that Denise Donlon was one of the best bosses I ever had the pleasure to work for. She understood TV and its power to not just entertain, but to inform and bring good. Many of us at Much and MuchMore were saddened to see her leave when she took on a position heading up Sony Music Canada in 2000. Denise loved music and knew the music industry implicitly. Her decision to leave the music empire she helped shape came a few months following my move to MuchMoreMusic. Her replacement did not have as much experience as Denise. Understand, I am not insulting her replacement. Denise could never be replaced. The new head of CHUM's specialty music channels simply did not have the same knowledge of music as Denise, nor were they as passionate about music, nor were they as creative.

There was soon a big shift to air not just a lesser number of interviews, but to air shorter interviews. I remember being asked, after a long sit-down interview with music icon David Bowie, if my interview would even warrant an hour special and whether it would get ratings. I just about had a heart attack. Really? The person asking me these questions is overseeing our national music channels? They are asking me if David Bowie is worthy of airtime? I have learned to never challenge my superiors, but sometimes, superiors are *not* superior.

There were new standards implemented for all interviews conducted. Interview clips could be no longer than ten to fifteen seconds. The style of music television we were presenting began to have less to do with music, storytelling, art and creativity, and was focused more on a tabloid style of entertainment, reporting on gossip, rumours and who was dating who, who was in rehab, who had cellulite etc. I always disliked this approach to music television. I felt it was cheap, crass and a disservice to fans of music and especially to artists. The writing was on the wall for me to leave as I sensed my style and approach to music journalism was not aligned with the new way the entertainment world was being showcased.

By 2005, I became very disillusioned with where our music services were heading and where I was or wasn't fitting in. I put out some feelers in the spring and I heard back from a few TV newsrooms across the country. The move would mean taking a pay cut and moving to a smaller market, but this pattern began to emerge in my life's work decisions from then on. I realized that making less money but being happy meant more to me than making a whole lot of money but being frustrated and living with discontent. I took on a new position in the summer of 2005. Canadian rock legend Tom Cochrane was the first person to email me at MuchMoreMusic expressing how he was going to miss me and my interviews. I had interviewed Tom many times. I'd always loved Tom, and after that I loved him even more.

I said yes to joining a revamped Citytv in Edmonton to host a morning show. It seemed like an exciting opportunity. I had visited Edmonton enough over the years while at MuchMusic to know that I loved the city. Seasoned news director Chris Duncan expressed that he had watched me for years and thought I'd be an excellent fit for the launch of their new *Breakfast Television* program. I became a co-host with the station's high-energy reporter Stacey Brotzel. I quickly became enamoured with our team in Edmonton of Rob Hislop, Bridget Ryan and Wendy Sandwith. We offered up a live, three-hour serving of news, sports, guests and lifestyle/general interest chats. It was a great team on air and off air. To me, it was a great transition from being a music and entertainment personality to *something else*.

My new boss Chris Duncan was ecstatic to inform me that the *Edmonton Journal* wanted to do a story on my arrival to Edmonton. He claimed that the highly respected daily newspaper had always ignored his station. The resulting article focused on the bewildering choice I had made to step down from a national position where I had recently spent a huge amount of time with Led Zeppelin's Robert Plant in Toronto and on the road with Motörhead just weeks prior. Basically, the writer's tone for the article was, "Why the hell does he want to be in Edmonton?"

I told the writer that for me, it was a welcomed change and an exciting chance to do something new. I explained that our Edmonton morning show guests had important things to say with just as important messaging to convey as any rock star did. In my first week on the show, I learned how to properly stain a patio deck from a home reno expert and was given the chance to promote many local charities. To me, these voices had an integral place in our viewers' lives.

Around the second week of me doing the show, the CFL's Grey Cup visited the set with an interview with the treasured trophy's handlers. During the same week, I interviewed the organizers and some participants of a remote-control racer convention that was coming to Edmonton. The interview was done in front of our street-front station on Jasper Avenue. These RC racers were extreme enthusiasts, spending hundreds and sometimes thousands of dollars building their customized, high-end racers. During the interview, I asked if I could drive one of the cars. One of the racers handed me his RC unit and gave me some quick instructions on how to drive his car. Without really knowing how to use the unit, I started to press some buttons and my car immediately sped down the sidewalk, flew over the curb and out into the street, almost being run over by busy morning commuters. My reaction was one of panic of course, and without thinking I said quietly, "Ohhhhh shiiiit!" Even speaking quietly, the mic clipped to my jacket collar picked up every single word. Oops!. I just swore on live television. Not cool. My words could be easily heard by anyone watching the show. Obviously, "shit" is not a word that is accepted on any morning show. Or any live local daytime show.

After the show, I was fearful that I would be fired in only my second week for saying "shit" on air. In my post-show meeting with Chris, he reassured me that there shouldn't be a problem. We both reviewed the tape. The camera wasn't on me when I swore, as the shot was following my out-of-control racer, and the audio could have come from anyone off camera.

Most important, the expensive RC race car was *not* run over, and it was eventually retrieved and brought back to the owner.

I loved my time in Edmonton. It was fun following the 2006 Oilers' run to the Stanley Cup finals (sadly losing to the Carolina Hurricanes in seven games). I was very proud to be asked to emcee many charity benefits. I had established many new friendships. I was even nominated for an Alberta Motion Picture Industry Award in my first five months there. There were work assignments to go skiing in nearby Jasper National Park, and my best friend from Toronto, John Temou, even joined me on one ski excursion. I was asked to host all the live concerts at Edmonton's Capital Ex midway. I was told the morning show ratings had hit peaks never previously seen. It was a highly enjoyable existence for much of that first year. But, I started to develop panic attacks. Even though I was taking my antidepressants faithfully, I couldn't shake the feeling of despair and loneliness. I figured it was normal to miss family and friends since I had moved there, but about nine months in, the notion that I was cut off from everything I deemed familiar became terrifying.

I called my boss Chris Duncan during a difficult afternoon where I couldn't stop crying and shaking. He came right over to my condo, which was about three blocks from the TV station. We talked for a lengthy period, and I was grateful that he listened to my concerns. He told me that he understood what I was going through. He lent me an empathetic ear as I expressed how I had tried to create a new life in Edmonton but felt that I was failing. I told him I felt too far away from the comfortable life I knew. I let him know that the person he had hired seemed like a million miles away and that I was sorry I might have let him down. I expressed to him that I felt detached from everything and everyone I knew. It was a horrible feeling to admit defeat against one's hope and intentions. Chris assured me it would be OK and encouraged me to have faith that life would get better.

Chris was absolutely correct. Towards the end of my one-year contract in Edmonton, I received a phone call from someone named Peter Angione in Ottawa. He asked me if I was interested in becoming a weather presenter in the nation's capital.

In Edmonton, I had some lengthy phone conversations with Peter, who was Ottawa's A-Channel news director. Peter had followed my career and was looking for a weather presenter for his newly revamped 6 p.m. evening news. He let me know that the weather anchor position he needed to fill didn't necessarily require someone with a meteorology degree, but someone who could give the high and low temperatures of the day and be fun. He was looking for a likable personality to join the on-air team of news anchor Sandra Blaikie and sports anchor (and ex-CFL star) Ken Evraire.

I had never considered being a weather specialist before but was fascinated by the idea. I watched a lot of The Weather Network like some people, but I didn't particularly like most meteorologists' delivery of the weather. Most people watching weather forecasts are asking, what will the daytime's high temperature be? Will it rain? Will it snow? How much? When? What are the high temperatures expected for the weekend? What are the overnight lows? These simple questions should result in simple answers. However, most of the time the information conveyed is accompanied with numerous weather maps showing warm fronts, cold fronts, arrows and red and blue lines. The maps also show possible precipitation patterns using satellite and doppler radar images.

Some meteorologists will get excited talking about the weather, using jargon like "jet streams," "crepuscular rays," "stratocumulus and nimbostratus clouds," "Colorado lows" and "barometric pressure."

My approach to weather presenting is to get in and get out. Especially in the morning. I concentrate on what you need to know to begin your day. Do you need an umbrella or not? How hot will it get? I was very encouraged by Peter's plan for a fresh news team in Ottawa. I was also very grateful that he wanted me to be a part of this newly created collection of anchors.

While I put my Edmonton condo up for sale, Peter flew me to Ottawa for a few days to meet my new co-workers and to visit the station located in Ottawa's famed ByWard Market. I was lucky enough to buy a condo the first day I was there.

My Edmonton condo sold quickly, so after returning to Edmonton to pack up all my contents and ship them to Ottawa, I stayed in an Edmonton hotel for about a week before flying one-way to Ottawa. While in the hotel, I bought several books detailing the science of weather and studied them intently. The thought of reinventing myself as a weather specialist excited me! Also exciting was the idea that I'd be moving back to Ontario. I wasn't returning to Toronto, but at least I'd be closer. It was less than a three-hour drive from Ottawa, not three provinces away.

There were a couple times in Edmonton where I did live weather presenting with our live-eye host, Bridget Ryan. One assignment involved going live from a water park and another going live from Edmonton City Hall's fountain. Both live sequences had me drenched, running away from the camera. For the latter shoot, I hadn't been wearing a bathing suit, so I had stripped down to my boxer-briefs live on TV. I had then jumped into the water fountain and yes, run away from the camera as the shot went back to the studio. For my final shift in Edmonton, the cast and crew reminisced about how I had a penchant for taking off my clothes on camera. A few days later, as I was off to the airport to move to Ottawa, I asked my cab driver to stop at the station first. I proceeded to take off all of my clothes except for my underwear in the back of the cab. I timed it so I knew when they were live with the studio camera facing the street. I jumped out of the cab, ran to the street-front studio window and banged on the glass. I saw the hosts turn around to see me, laughing and pointing. I waved bye and jumped back into the cab. A fun and fitting way to bid adieu to the City of Champions.

I situated myself in Ottawa rather seamlessly. I made instant bonds with the news team, the reporters and the other staff at Ottawa's A-Channel TV station. I established close friendships with office manager (and soon-to-be producer) Tina Cerilli and our 6 p.m. news anchor Sandra Blaikie.

News director Peter Angione introduced several brilliant ideas for his news team and for me. We brought the news live to various locations across the region in a semi-regular delivery called *Live from Where You Live*. Peter also introduced the idea of kidcasters. Twice a year, we held auditions at various locations around Ottawa for younger viewers to assist me in presenting the weather. The broadcasts with the kidcasters featured fun graphic elements like a sun with a smiling face or a frowning rain cloud holding up an umbrella. Each round of auditions got bigger and bigger. At one afternoon of auditions at Gloucester Centre Mall, the numbers were enormous. We heard from parents throughout the afternoon saying, "We only watch your news broadcasts now!"

As Tina and I were heading into the mall to meet up with our crew, a family stopped us to say hello. The young boy said to me, "Are you here for all the children? I see you on TV with all the children."

I smiled and replied yes. I asked him if he was auditioning to be a kidcaster.

The young boy was excited. "Yes! I want to be on TV with you, like all the children!"

I said, "Good luck to ya, buddy! We'll see ya in there!" A few moments later, as Tina and I went inside the mall, she excused herself to go to the women's washroom. We had been joking about the cute kid and how he kept referring to the kidcasters as "all the children."

Tina took a long time in the bathroom. I was getting impatient, so I opened up the bathroom door a crack and said loudly, "Hurry up! I am here for *all* the children! I don't want to miss the children."

Seconds later, an elderly woman walked out of the bathroom glaring at me with disgust. Tina exited right behind, barely able to contain a bellowing laugh. She whispered through her laughter, "You should really keep your intentions about *all* the children to yourself!"

In 2008, Peter Angione introduced *Bill's Block Party*. Throughout the summer, we would go live from a neighbourhood park with a pizza party, bands, attractions, bouncy castles and celebrities. For the July 1st *Bill's Block Party*, we featured the Ottawa Roller Derby girls performing stunts in our parking lot and Randy and Mr. Lahey of TV's *Trailer Park Boys* dropped by to help me present the weather. The broadcasts were a huge hit with neighbourhood families coming out to say hi and have a great time. Our final block party of the summer occurred at Ottawa's City Hall, and Mayor Larry O'Brien joined in on the live broadcast. He brought with him a framed document officially declaring August 29, 2008 as Bill Welychka Day. I was very close to tears. What a huge honour! But sadly, it isn't an *official* city holiday in Ottawa. Everyone still must work.

Early after my move to Ottawa, Peter wanted to introduce a new weekly feature, *Bill's Excellent Adventures*. These explorative vignettes showcased fun and interesting locations, attractions and characters around Ottawa and eastern Ontario. Some of these adventures included skydiving, skating with the Ottawa Roller Derby girls, learning to play the carillon in the Peace Tower on Parliament Hill, performing in a rock band, doing a stand-up set at a comedy club, taking acting classes with kids, being a nude model in an art class (although, I kept my underwear on—it was for TV, after all), polar-dipping into the Ottawa River in January, learning to rappel at CFB Petawawa, training with the Ottawa Police Service and being pepper sprayed *and* tasered in the same hour, learning to drive a bus, speed dating, driving in a demolition derby, playing the new 2010 Wii NHL Slapshot video game with Ottawa Senators legend Chris Phillips, learning to salsa dance, learning to pole dance, learning to Scottish dance, taking ballet lessons, learning to be a ski patrol aid at Mont-Tremblant, learning gymnastics, ice fishing on the Ottawa River, white water rafting and dozens of other awesome assignments.

I took my weather deliveries very seriously, but I would have fun with the adventures. Many were silly and humorous. In 2010, it was an honour receiving Ottawa's Favourite Comedian award through a city-wide poll. I don't do stand-up comedy, but I suppose *Bill's Excellent Adventures* were funny enough to garner some attention as an entertaining host.

I felt blessed to be in Ottawa and loved every single day. One particular year, some of us at the station received invitations to attend Prime Minister Stephen Harper's spring garden party at 24 Sussex Drive, the official residence of the Prime Minister of Canada. My boss, Peter Angione, attended with his wife and two young daughters.

At one point during the afternoon, I noticed one of Peter's daughters standing at my table. Hannah was maybe seven or eight years old. As I finished my drink, I pretended to hide the empty glass inside my blazer and said, "Hannah, don't tell anyone, but I'm stealing all of the Prime Minister's glasses. Shhhh!"

She nodded and walked away. A few minutes later, Tina approached me laughing, asking what I told Hannah. I asked why. She said, "Hannah is walking around telling people that you are stealing Stephen Harper's glasses."

I explained that I was just joking. I thought it was funny.

At the end of the party, as guests were leaving, there was a photo opportunity with the Prime Minister. I had one taken with Tina and then we left on our way to hit some pubs in the ByWard Market.

The following Monday at work, Peter told me how embarrassed he was when his time came for the photo op with Prime Minister Stephen Harper. "As we were standing there getting ready for the picture, Hannah tugged on Stephen Harper's pant leg. He looked down and she whispered, 'Bill is stealing all your glasses!' Mr. Harper then looked at *me* confusedly and I said, 'I'm not Bill. I don't know what she means!'"

· · · · ·

I have always endeavoured to make very strong connections to viewers. I joked one time on air, leading up to my first Thanksgiving in Ottawa, that I was alone and if anyone wanted to have me over for Thanksgiving dinner, I'd accept. I heard from many families and actually chose one, graciously accepting their invite. I brought a small video camera with me and shot some fun highlights. I aired the footage during the next broadcast. This became a pattern for many Thanksgivings to follow. I have always loved meeting viewers.

During December, viewers sent us pictures of their brightly lit and decorated houses. We would choose some homes and for a week or so, go live with the weather from these homes. These were generous and friendly viewers, and I would comment on how amazing each family was, coming out and giving us cookies and hot chocolate. With each night's broadcast, each family would try and out-do the previous night's family with treats and goodies for us. By the end of the week, there would be full-on five course meals waiting for us! I had learned about establishing a strong connection to viewers from my early days at MuchMusic hosting *Outlaws & Heroes*. I was so grateful to anyone that watched and would do what I could to further deepen connections with as many viewers as possible. To me, it was a vital part of the job, and one that is never considered or discussed.

One year, I was asked to be the parade marshal for the annual Navan Fair. Navan was about thirty minutes east of Ottawa, and I knew there was an alpaca farm there. I accepted the offer, and asked if I could walk with a couple of alpacas. The answer was yes! I was proud to lead the parade with a leash on each hand, walking these two gorgeous animals. At one point, both alpacas stopped. They decided to crap, right there in the middle of the street, with onlookers on each side of the road pointing and laughing.

A HAPPY HAS-BEEN

I couldn't help but laugh too. When they were done their business, we carried on walking. I looked back and saw the marching band behind me separate in perfect synchronicity around the two piles of alpaca shit and join up again after the messy piles on the road.

· · · · ·

Ottawa meant reinvention for me. I wanted to downplay my music past and concentrate on being a weather specialist. I was pleased to learn that many older viewers gravitated towards my weather delivery while having no clue of my music journalism past. To me, I was successful in not just being known as someone who interviewed rock stars. In Ottawa, I proved I could interview anyone, from local politicians and community leaders to those that headed up charitable organizations.

There was a small party one afternoon in the newsroom when ratings had come out. After my first year there and Peter's introduction of several new looks and concepts to his 6 and 11 p.m. news broadcasts, the ratings for A-Channel News showed that we were about to eclipse Ottawa's heritage station CJOH's long-held dominance in the Ottawa region. It was a big victory for all who worked at A-Channel. It was a short celebration though as within months, A-Channel's newscasts were cancelled.

In 2006, CHUM Limited's radio and TV interests were sold off to Rogers Media Inc. and CTV/Bell Media. Basically, A-Channel in Ottawa was now owned by their once-rival local TV station's parent company. The popular rumour in Ottawa was that heritage station CJOH-TV shouldn't have to compete with an upstart TV news outlet that was closing in on their ratings, especially when both were owned by the same broadcast company.

Sadly, many talented people from our station were laid off. Some staff were kept and transferred to our newly revamped A-Channel morning show, including news anchor Sandra Blaikie, producer Tina Cerilli and myself. I was grateful to still be employed, but it was a difficult transition seeing our 6 and 11 p.m. news shows obliterated and burst asunder.

The newly tweaked show, 'A'-Morning, was much like the live morning show I did in Edmonton. After several years of some great shows, Sandra Blaikie eventually exited. I started to see many bright and awesome people being given packages. Our best producer, Tina Cerilli, was eventually given a package. At some point, I took some concerns I had to the station's VP/GM. I complained about bullying in the newsroom. I expressed concerns about sexist insults I had witnessed. I explained that a toxic environment was running rampant, and I even offered suggestions on how to improve falling morale.

I will never know the reason why, but I can only suspect that for my efforts in trying to better the work environment, I was terminated. My dismissal came only minutes after the morning show had ended on August 9, 2011. I was asked to come to the VP/GM's office. I noticed a small video camera on a tripod, recording the enormous office. The VP/GM was present, as was our supervising producer, our HR person and two local union representatives. One union rep next to me was doodling on a pad of paper as I was told, "Bill, your services are no longer required." I was then handed a large envelope.

All I could say was "Ummm, wow. Thanks. Best of luck with the show." I was escorted to my desk to grab some things and was told I could make arrangements to come back at a later date to grab the rest of my personal belongings. I was then walked to the reception doors.

I was stunned. When I got home, I had about ten messages from my co-workers (I guess now, former co-workers) asking what the fuck happened. I began a lengthy drinking session that didn't stop for a few days. I was shattered. For the first time in my life, I wasn't working. Work was all I loved doing! I eventually rummaged through the papers that had been handed to me. There was a lot of legalese terminology, but essentially, in order to get the money owed to me, I had to sign some documents stating that I wouldn't disclose the terms and conditions of my dismissal. Nor was I allowed to work in Canada for a very lengthy period of time.

I was told that the next day, the *'A'-Morning* social media pages lit up with comments from confused and irate viewers. Hundreds of people said they would never watch the station again. I was told by some friends who still worked there that producers were assigned to constantly delete the negative comments and feedback the station was getting on their social media. It went on for many months. I was told reception was also kept busy for months taking calls from concerned and angry viewers. Apparently, a protest was being formed to picket the station. The backlash the station experienced lasted close to a year. I was inundated with comments on my Facebook page from complete strangers asking me what had happened, telling me they missed me and saying they would never watch the channel again. Despite it being a very dark time for me, I could feel the huge amount of love and support and I was very grateful for it.

About two days following my dismissal (termination? ass being canned?) I received a message from one of the local popular radio stations in Ottawa asking me if I wanted to come on the air to co-host one morning. I accepted because I never did get a chance to say goodbye properly to our viewers. I notified Facebook followers and viewers that I missed them, and I let them know when I was going to be on the radio. Later that afternoon, a courier came to my door and hand-delivered a letter to me from my former station's VP/GM. It was a one-page letter stating that if I was to say anything disparaging about the station or disclose any details of my dismissal, then there would be "dire and severe consequences" for me.

I would never do such a thing, but *really*? They were *threatening* me? *They* took away my livelihood and my career. What else could they do to me? Should I have lied there on my condo floor so they could kick me in the crotch too?

The radio broadcast was therapeutic for me. I was given the chance to speak about how grateful I was for all the viewer support. In no way did I divulge anything that would bring "dire and severe consequences" to my life. I'm not the kind of vindictive person that would do that anyway. I believe in karma, and I do believe things happen for a reason, although you never see it that way at the time.

Was I bitter about the way I was treated? Hell yeah! I had broken bones for this company (well, I had fractured a rib in a charity hockey game). I had represented them proudly with charity appearances at least once a week, sometimes twice or three times a week. I had been at work early every day. I had never called in sick. I had helped increase ratings to record levels. Peter had referred to me as a "great influence" and a "spark plug" for the newsroom. I had been proud of my work and proud of *where* I had worked. All that didn't matter though. To this very day, all I can deduce is that I challenged a higher authority to do better, and this figure in their high position did not like to be challenged.

I was entering another very dark period. I would say it was one of the worst years of my life. During the year I was told I couldn't work, I had also found out that my mom was dying of cancer. I used my time off to drive back and forth to Barrie, ON to visit her in the hospital. I also used my year not working in Ottawa to spend some time volunteering. I joined The Good Companions, a service that helps elderly and mobility-challenged people do their groceries. I needed to be kept busy.

In the spring of 2012, as I was approaching my one-year anniversary of not working and after attending my mom's funeral, I got a phone call that put me on the path to experiencing a happy life once again. A very happy life!

Three years old in Welland, ON...already displaying hints of being a poser

First year at Seneca College in 1986...complete with eyeliner, black overcoat and caught in a brooding, pensive moment

Hangin' with the perennially cool Dwight Yoakam in 1992

A true original, Johnny Cash. Pic taken in 1993 after a lengthy interview with The Man in Black. (I kept the glass he was drinking water from during the interview.)

A night out in Toronto with Slash - 1993

One of my fave music artists ever, Bob Seger.
After a 1994 interview, live on MuchMusic

Garth presented me with a double-platinum sales award after our live Much interview in 1994

Meeting a big crush! Gillian Anderson in Vancouver at the 1997 'X-Files' wrap party.

Chillin' with rapper/ actor Ice-T in 1997

A moment from MuchMusic's 1998 live interview
with Dwayne 'The Rock' Johnson

A cool pic taken during the 1998 live broadcast of 'Intimate & Interactive with Alanis Morissette'

Presenting Britney Spears with an award at the live 1999 MMVAs

Poison's Bret Michaels calls me up on stage in Toronto in 2002.
Quick! Be witty, fun, cool and engaging!

It's a good thing I was there to elevate Bret Michaels.
He has no clue how to whip a crowd of thousands into a frenzy.
Seriously, the guy is one of the best frontmen in rock.

Somewhere over Pennsylvania with Ozzy on his private jet in 2002

With Madonna in LA in 2003

Remaining focused during live coverage of Molson Canadian Rocks for Toronto (SarsStock) benefit concert - July 30, 2003.

Interviewing Fleetwood Mac's Lindsey Buckingham in 2003

A moment I will never forget...a smooch during 'MuchMoreMusic Live with Lisa Marie Presley' in 2004

Hosting 'MuchMoreMusic Live with Janet Jackson' in 2004

A great time with one of my heroes, an interview backstage with The Cure's Robert Smith in 2004

A moment with Led Zeppelin's Robert Plant in Toronto, prior to a lengthy interview in 2005

Interviewing Dave Grohl and Taylor Hawkins at the Foo Fighters' offices and studio north of LA in 2005. I love Dave and The Foos!

2007 in Ottawa, interviewing Spice Girl Melanie C before showtime
(Mel C is another huge crush)

Another band I love, Blue Rodeo. Interviewing Jim Cuddy
and Greg Keelor in Kingston (2013)

A fun moment with The Tragically Hip's Gord Downie,
during a 2014 post-show party in Kingston

An aerial view of 2016's 'The Tragically Hip: A National Celebration' live public screening in Kingston. That tiny speck on stage? Me. (Credit: SkEye Stream)

What an honour hosting thousands for 2016's
'The Tragically Hip: A National Celebration' live public screening in Kingston.

Hangin' with The Hip's Paul Langlois, after hosting the 2017 unveiling of The Hip Brick in Kingston's Springer Market Square

Kingstonians are very friendly! A kind greeting from The Hip's Rob Baker during a party in Kingston in 2018.

My fave pro-wrestler, The Honky Tonk Man raises my arm in victory following an attack by CJ Felony during Chinlock Wrestling's Bill Welychka Appreciation night in Kingston in 2018. HTM chased CJ out of the ring after he gave me two DDTs.

Beating up on my wrestling nemesis CJ Felony. He would eventually win the 2019 match at The Leon's Centre in Kingston after smashing a metal garbage can on my head.

A refreshing dip into Lake Ontario off the Gord Edgar Downie Pier at Breakwater Park in Kingston (2019)

Visiting Toronto to watch my beloved Chicago Blackhawks take on The Leafs in 2021

Bill and long-time bud Jeff Parissi at The Cure in Toronto June 2023

Bill with Amanda

CHAPTER SIXTEEN
A BOW FROM PRINCE AND A HUG FROM LIAM

Before we resume with the timeline of my life and my various stories (are you still here reading? Awesome. I wish I could give you a hug!), I'd like to address the art of interviewing.

For decades, I have heard from many who expressed, "I love your interviews!" It has always been an endless source of joy and pride when I get that feedback. I take the craft very seriously. I have been conducting broadcast interviews since 1990. Winning awards is very nice, but the true satisfaction of a job well done comes from co-workers, people on the street, or comments on social media or YouTube.

I have had some great teachers. I don't necessarily mean being taught directly by someone, but by watching what works and what doesn't. Former co-workers like Denise Donlon, Christopher Ward, Steve Anthony, Erica Ehm, Michael Williams, Terry David Mulligan and Laurie Brown were masters at their craft. I learned by osmosis what makes a great interview. I realized early on that interviewing is truly an art form, whether live or taped.

In 1995, I was honoured to be asked to give media training lessons to MCA/Universal's newly signed country artists. One of the tips I offered was to be aware of interviewers who are not prepared. In that case, the artist will have to take control and steer the conversation towards topics and subjects *they* want to discuss.

During an interview, I rarely look at notes. While watching interviews, I find it distracting to see an interviewer with large sheets of paper or note pads on their laps. For the person being interviewed, it's also distracting to speak to someone who is constantly looking down at notes and not listening. If I must use notes, I prefer to use small index cards with brief points on subjects I'd like to hit or some specifics about tour dates perhaps. The very best interviews for me are conversations that flow and not interrogations with awkward back and forth choppy exchanges.

I have had the huge pleasure of speaking with various guests over the years where the conversation involved diving deep into sometimes personal subject matter. I have always found it a privilege to have an artist get comfortable enough with me to *let me in* and to have them share personal stories about their lives and art. I can recall on several occasions, including times with Tori Amos, Tanya Tucker, Garth Brooks and Triumph's Rik Emmett, when I'd have conversations that would lead to moments when my guest's eyes would well up with tears. No interviewer wants to make their guest cry, but it does show a sort of bond for an artist to allow themselves to be brought to a deeply emotional state with someone they trust and hopefully like and respect. Yes, tears do make great television, but to me, that's not what it's about. It is about providing a platform for a guest to be themselves and express what they need to, hopefully in a way they haven't before.

Extrapolating a thought from someone when they have put into words a meaningful, heartfelt, powerful and memorable statement can sometimes be tricky. An interviewer tries to capture the essence of what the interviewee wants to express. In journalism, the resulting interview clip is called a "sound bite." My internal reaction to hearing a great nugget is, *Yes! Nailed it!* It's a wonderful feeling all journalists share.

A great sound bite should draw the viewer in at the start of an hour special. A great sound bite should end the hour special, encapsulating many emotions and showcasing the essential reflections desired in a few words or sentences.

There are integral elements required in conducting interviews. One must have the ability to improvise. The most important element is to always do research. Know your subject well. Know what they want to talk about, why it's important to them and how it relates to the audience. The interviewer is simply the conduit between the always-important audience and the interview subject.

Whether interviewing Madonna or a local real estate agent, I like to believe I have treated all interview subjects the same. I show respect and let the conversation flow. Every interview subject has something to offer. The interviewer has been trusted to offer the subject a platform to showcase their message. I have always maintained that the interviewer is providing a spotlight for the guest. The interviewer should let the guest have their time to shine and elevate them, and the interview should be about the guest, not the interviewer. We have all been subjected to interviewers who compete for airtime with their guest. I have worked with some people who believed that *they* were a star interviewing another star.

The biggest treat for any interviewer is to be requested by an artist. This has happened to me many times over the years. There have been occasions where I was told I'd be doing a specific interview because I had been asked for by the artist. It's a very satisfying feeling to know that Alanis Morissette, Aerosmith's Steven Tyler, Garth Brooks, The Tragically Hip's Gord Downie and many others wanted *me*, knowing they were going to get a comfortable, intelligent and memorable experience.

There have been countless times that I have interviewed musical acts whose patches and buttons I wore on my jean jacket many years previous. I have spent great times with artists whose posters hung in my room or in my school locker, or whose band logos I would doodle on my school notebooks. There have been numerous times that I have interviewed musicians whose music I woke up to or went to sleep to, or whose music accompanied me on long drives. I never grew bored of interviewing artists whose concerts I attended during my formative teen years or in college. Earlier in this book, I referred to these priceless moments as perfect circles.

When interviewing an artist, I want them to feel comfortable and like they are in a professional environment. There have been times where I have wondered if it was OK to ask for an autograph or a picture. It all depends on the situation and every scenario is different. There have been a few times where I did ask for an autograph for myself, but only after analyzing the situation and understanding that it was fine to do so. But there have been many times where I didn't ask for an autograph or picture because I forgot to or because I was distracted. There were also many times I acquired an autograph for the sole purpose of donating it to a charity auction. I would be asked a lot for items to donate, and so I always stockpiled cool items for distribution to many very worthwhile causes.

Admittedly, my walls at home do have some hangings of items and memorabilia that I am proud of. Along with numerous Chicago Blackhawks items and memorabilia and pictures of family, friends and past pets, I have many entertainment-related items. Actually, many work-oriented projects were given to me as gifts from assorted record companies or film studios for projects I was involved with. Sometimes these entertainment companies felt like I had championed a certain artist or project or album. I occasionally stop and look at these things on my walls and think, *Nice, but maybe kinda tacky?* Not all are tacky though. I have some paintings and art proudly displayed from numerous world travels.

One of my favourite things that hangs on my walls is a cool Led Zeppelin photo that was personally signed to me by Robert Plant, John Paul Jones and Jimmy Page. These autographs were acquired separately from different assignments but form a complete set of signatures from the remaining living members of the greatest rock band that ever existed.

I had an assignment in 2005 where I visited the Metalworks recording studio outside of Toronto to shoot an interview with Rush, Ed Robertson (Barenaked Ladies) and Bubbles (*Trailer Park Boys*). They had re-recorded Rush's "Closer to the Heart" for the national telethon *Canada For Asia* to bring relief to tsunami-stricken Sri Lanka, India and Thailand. A photo hangs on my wall at home from that evening with Ed and the members of Rush signing sweet, beautiful sentiments. Also on the framed picture, Bubbles wrote, "Bill, go fuck yourself." Bahahaha! I love it!

I also love the hand-drawn portrait of me pencilled by Tony Bennett in 2003. I suggested to the legendary crooner prior to our interview that he do his famous pencil work while talking. I expected a sketch of the view outside the large hotel window that was in front of us. Instead of the obvious Toronto skyline, he drew *me*. He signs his art as "Benedetto." I treasure that drawing so much.

A HAPPY HAS-BEEN

I have a framed Rush program signed by all three guys; they gave it to me as a gift in 2011.

I have a Steve Earle double-platinum award on my wall for the *Copperhead Road* album.

I have also proudly hung other gold or platinum award presentations featuring album sales awards for Matt Good, Live, Blue Rodeo, Garth Brooks and many others.

Paramount Pictures presented me with elaborately framed and signed pictures of some of their actors after their live interviews. These include Harrison Ford, the *Kids in the Hall* cast and Mel Gibson.

My most prized possession is a Fender Stratocaster guitar played by Rob Baker and signed by all the guys from The Tragically Hip. I acquired it at a charity auction when I first moved to Kingston in 2012. I have been blessed to interview The Hip boys many times, but never collected their autographs.

I never asked for an autograph or picture from Prince when I interviewed him in 2004. Prince was a very memorable experience for me, not only because I was a fan of the legendary artist but because he rarely did interviews. The Oscar-winning and Grammy-winning Prince Rogers Nelson and his music have always been there, it seems. Who didn't grow up in the 1980s loving the *Purple Rain* album?

But Prince refused to be stuck in the '80s, like so many of his contemporaries had been, locked into that decade. He would be very prolific, and his album releases came at a pace never before witnessed by the music industry. Prince sometimes put forth two or three albums a year. Even in death his album sales soared. In the first five days after his passing on April 21, 2016, Prince songs made up twenty-five per cent of the Top 40.

For two days following his death, radio and TV outlets around the world rolled out any Prince pundits they could find. Music journalists were needed to fill four minutes of airtime, highlighting Prince's genius and contributions to music. Fans were rounded up and scurried to the cameras. Everyone offered great insights. That's all any media outlet can do.

Despite this, no new *real* revelations were offered. No one really knew Prince. I certainly don't claim to have known him, but I can offer insight into some of our moments together from an exclusive live TV event at

MuchMoreMusic from the summer of 2004 to promote his disc *Musicology*. It was also the same year Prince was inducted into the Rock and Roll Hall of Fame. He was notoriously guarded and rarely granted interviews for print or TV. A live ninety-minute TV presentation with Prince during which he talked openly and played live had never been conducted before in Canada or anywhere else globally.

My favourite memory from that day actually happened hours before the live broadcast. Earlier in the day, I was walking out from the studio after doing microphone checks. Prince was coming into the studio followed by his band to do a sound check. In the doorway, I stepped aside to let him and his entourage through. He stopped, looked at me, bowed his head and said, "Bill . . . I'm a big fan." I knew he lived in Toronto part-time, but it never registered that he might have watched MuchMusic and MuchMoreMusic and that he might have seen some of my work.

I replied, "Thanks! I'm a fan of yours. It's going to be a great show!"

He remarked, "Yes, it will be."

It was indeed a great show. What followed was live TV that was both magical and rare. Prince was polite, thoughtful, gracious, spontaneous, funny and possessed no affectations or quirks that many expected. During our time, Prince sensed that he had this live, ninety-minute platform in front of an intimate gathering of about a hundred fans to offer his many opinions, unencumbered by preconceived notions.

Prince was at times very serious, yet he displayed his humorous side during the telecast too. A fan in the studio asked, "What is real music?" Prince paused, then looked right into the camera lens and said, "Come to the concert. You'll see." The studio audience erupted into wild cheering.

A Prince concert wasn't just Prince playing live. I remarked that it was an evangelical experience and that his live shows were visibly inclusive. Black and white, young and old, his music was the common denominator. Prince responded by making the correlation between music, talent and faith. "Ultimately, the music does show that we are one people. I don't like divisions."

He went on to say, "A lot of the music now is prepackaged pop with computers. Kids need to hear live music and pick up an instrument. If kids don't learn the craft of songwriting or learn to play an instrument, we'll lose this art form. It will become technology-based and there is no heart in that."

Prince explained the power of live music... "Anytime you get people together, like in *this* situation, we see we're all one people. I study the scriptures as deep as I can. I advise anybody, if you want to feel hope, pick up the Book and read it."

Always a groundbreaker, Prince was the first artist to publicly shine a light on some unfair music industry practices and how some music labels mistreated their artists. His goal in the mid-'90s was to reclaim ownership of the art.

Prince has been described as a "visionary." We explored this lofty word during the broadcast. Prince explained, "Ultimately, I think [the word "visionary"] applies to all of us. If you asked anybody in this room, if they had their way, how they would reshape their life and the world, they could give you a wonderful scenario. So, the idea is to just try to live that." The studio audience let his thoughts sink in. There was silence for about three seconds and then thunderous applause. A cherished and inspirational connection was made.

It hit me then during the live broadcast, and I am reminded now while recalling my memories of Prince, why he was so gifted and special. He was all about connecting. He was an excellent conduit, connecting people to music. Connecting people to creativity. Connecting cultures and races. Connecting an audience to positivity. Connecting people to God.

I have a very long list of favourite interview moments and sound bites. My memories could easily fill another book. What follows is just a fraction of some of my favourite sound bites and experiences from select interviews.

- I have interviewed the boys from Kiss a few times. One particular interview with Gene Simmons, Paul Stanley, Ace Frehley and Peter Criss happened on set for the filming of the Kiss movie, *Detroit Rock City*. We were on set a few times, gathering footage and interviews for a thirty-minute special I was assigned to, to be aired on MuchMusic to coincide with the 1999 film release. During one evening of filming in November 1998, I befriended film producer and former Kiss official photographer Barry Levine. Barry asked me if I wanted to portray him in the film. The role was only as an extra where I would appear in a scene at a backstage party for a '70s Kiss concert. The scene would have me in a hot tub with several topless women. I declined, saying, "Sounds fun, but not exactly a wholesome look for a VJ." He then told me I could just be an extra walking around with a girl on my arm during the big backstage party instead. I agreed. In the film's scene, I am barely recognizable as I was sporting a '70s-style long-haired wig.

During the interview with Kiss a few days later, I asked them if there was indeed a hot tub backstage on their 1977 Love Gun tour. Paul answered, "I think there was at some shows . . . we were always looking for a *warm* and *wet* place to jump in." In my mind, I heard a drum's rimshot sting: *ba-dum tshh!* He explained further, "Rock 'n' roll backstage is everything anybody could imagine and then some. It's no coincidence that politicians, actors, everybody wants to be a rock star. We have a president in the US right now who wants to be a rock star [Bill Clinton]. He's tried the lifestyle too. We get paid for it. He gets in trouble."

I asked, "What do you think of my performance as an extra? Should I get an Oscar?"

Paul Stanley quipped, "You get an Oscar Mayer wiener. That's all."

By the way, I am credited as "Man Backstage" in the film for a one second shot.

I met up with Gene Simmons again in 2002. He was in Toronto to promote his autobiography *KISS and Make-Up*. We did the lengthy interview at Filmores Gentlemen's Club (a fancy title meaning strip joint). At the very start of the interview, two exotic dancers came by the table and Gene positioned each girl on his lap. It made it difficult to shoot close-ups of Gene's face, because on either side of his head were the girls' boobs. Yes, one wore a bikini and the other was bra-less and wearing a tight t-shirt, but the shot's framing did look a little distracting. Gene proceeded to tell me what it was like to be Gene Simmons. "My job? It beats working for a living. I haven't had a bad day in my life. My worst day would be anyone else's best day. Honest!"

At some point during the interview, Gene motioned to one of the girls to position her outstretched leg on my left shoulder across from him. I said, "Gene, what are you doing? I just got married!"

He replied, "You're an idiot. You're a moron." We laughed and he proceeded to elaborate on his relationship with long-time partner Shannon Tweed. "I'm crazy about Shannon and we have two kids together, but the notion that any human being, including the one who gave birth to your children, is ever going to have anything to say about what you do as a human being is lunacy. The only one who should ever have the right to ask you anything is the one who gave you birth. She earned the right—it's your mom. Listen, I love women. I love how they're built. God gave you a day above ground. Figure out what makes you happy. If what makes you happy is different than mine, I'm sorry . . . I believe that marriage is archaic and wrong. The only thing wrong with marriage is that usually one of the two getting married is a man."

After a twenty-eight-year relationship, Gene eventually married Shannon on October 1, 2011.

- I spent an hour with Johnny Cash in 1994 when he came to Toronto to promote his album, *American Recordings*. We spoke at length about his addictions. He disclosed, "I can't close the door on those addictions because there are times when I'll be compulsive and impulsive. That beast is caged inside of me. But the beast is caged by frail and fragile bars. And every morning I wake up, that beast is in there howling, wanting out. And I pray and dedicate that day to God. And the beast lays low."

  Damn, I miss Johnny!

- Steve Earle (2001 in Nashville) on kicking a long-time drug addiction: "I had to quit. It was a matter of life or death. I realized there are people that I love, and they love me. Once you're a pickle, you can't become a cucumber again."

- I interviewed Robert Smith from The Cure numerous times and each was always a lengthy and amazing conversation. My first interview with him was in New York City in 1996, and then I interviewed him again a few months later, live on MuchMusic. I also interviewed Robert in 2000, and our final interview was in 2005. One of my favourite sound bites from Robert came in our very first interview, when he tried to explain the band's never-ending support from legions of fans worldwide: "It's more than the music and the tunes. People that I talk to that like the group, often just like the idea of a group like The Cure being there. It shows that you can do things *your* way and still be successful. Although it wasn't the point of the group to be successful, the point of the group was to be able to do what I want. And people like that! People who are fans of the group like it, but the people who don't like it are journalists. They resent that I can do what I want, while other people like that. In a strange way, people want us to continue to exist, which is sort of worrying. They think if we stop, we're the last band of their generation. A lot of our older fans want us to keep going at all costs."

I remarked, "That seems like a lot of pressure."

Robert smiled and answered, "Yeah, but that's not why I keep going."

- Madonna (2003 in Los Angeles) on what is important in life: "Who better to say that fame, fortune and beauty doesn't bring you happiness than someone who's been through all those things? We're all focusing on the wrong things. The real heroes are schoolteachers, science researchers and spiritual leaders. What I care about is making the world a better place."

It was a lengthy amount of time spent with Madonna. We covered a lot of topics, including her use of sexual imagery in music videos and in lyrics. Despite a long career of repeating the mantra *No regrets*, I asked her if she ever reconsidered being so fearless with her body…

Madonna: "Well, maybe. I mean there's a difference between saying I made a mistake and I'm going to learn from that mistake and saying I regret something. I don't regret anything. At the end of the day I would say that I have a different point of view of what sex is in the world and in my life and what I did 10 years ago. I was wrestling with a lot of my own demons and a lot of repression that I felt and guilt about sex and things like that. I felt like I was going to liberate myself and all of the woman in the world at the same time, by serving up my own version of a sexual revolution so to speak or liberation. At the end of the day, I do think that sex is a very sacred thing. I would have presented it in a different way, I think now versus then. If I think sex is a sacred thing then I probably wouldn't have been so frivolous about it."

- Hot on the heels of the Madonna interview, I interviewed Vanilla Ice (real name Rob Van Winkle) in London, ON in 2003. Some of this interview was used for my national Madonna special I was producing. It had been thirteen years since his debut album *To the Extreme* became the fastest selling hip-hop album of all time, and he was suffering from a career slow-down. There was no interest in him anymore from the mainstream press. An old high school friend from Barrie, Sherri Pascoe got in touch with me in 2003. She said that she had become close to Vanilla Ice, and she wanted to know if I wanted to interview him for Much and MuchMore. He was performing in a small club in London, ON. Sherri told me following my interview with Vanilla Ice (which aired on Much/ MuchMore and in the Madonna special) that he admitted my interview helped him get back into the spotlight again. He said when no one cared, I did.

    The Vanilla Ice interview was used in my Madonna special because the two dated in 1990. He even appears in photographs in her 1992 'Sex' book. I asked him while flipping through the book, looking at the pictures of him and Madonna in various stages of undress: "Rob...what's going on here?"

    He replied "These pictures? Oh man! I didn't even know there was going to be a book. This was done without any permission from me at all or anything, for real! And she threw me into her whole slutty package, man and I wasn't digging it! It just wasn't her, you know. I see her differently. She was sweet to me and then all of a sudden this popped up and I was like *whaaaaat?*"

- Ozzy Osbourne (2001, somewhere over Pennsylvania on his private jet) on signing autographs: "I get embarrassed. I'm just a guy, you know? But there's people we call 'the professionals.' I'll sign something and see it on eBay the next day. If someone said to me, 'Please, Ozzy, I'm out of work. Sign this and I can sell it. I need the dough!' I can see that! But they tell you a load of crap! Don't lie to me! The stupid thing is, I don't play guitar, but they'll ask me to sign one and sell it! If they ask me to sign a microphone, I get that! I'm waiting for the day some guy will ask me to sign his double bass drum set. Or a clarinet!"

- It was a bucket-list wish to interview Lisa Marie Presley. We are close to the same age, so I developed a wee crush on her after seeing pictures of her in the tabloids. My crush on her developed around the same time as the one I had on Linda Belcastro in grade three (I heard she married an NHL hockey player) and Sharon Gazeley in grade four (she became a doctor).

I was blown away by Lisa Marie's debut album in 2003, *To Whom It May Concern*. I was told that MuchMoreMusic secured her for Canada's only live prime time interview, and I was to host. I was giddy and stoked until I learned that she had cancelled all Canadian press because of the SARS outbreak that took place at that time. I was hugely disappointed, but I understood.

Two years later in 2005, Lisa Marie released her second album, *Now What*, and plans were back on for a Canadian prime time special. It was a sixty-minute broadcast that would feature my live interview, a live studio audience and two live performances with Lisa Marie and her band. I knew it was going to be a great experience when, after my live introduction of her, she came out with a huge smile to roaring applause. Normally, from what I'd seen in most pictures, she had a poker face and carried a serious presence. But on this night, her smile lit up the large studio. I showed her to her chair and there was a moment where she leaned in to give me a kiss, so I leaned in too and gave her a kiss on her cheek. It was a beautiful moment. That split second was captured in a picture and sent to me a couple days after the broadcast. I set it as my screen saver at work and at home. It is still my screen saver.

Interviewing Lisa Marie Presley was difficult, in terms of trying to please everybody. I most certainly did not want to take the tabloid and trashy approach, bringing up her failed marriages to Michael Jackson and actor Nicholas Cage. Nor did I want to keep the interview focused on her being Elvis's only child. It would have been easy to regurgitate tabloid headlines, but I wanted to stand out as not being crass, nor disrespectful. But most importantly, I wanted Lisa Marie to walk away from the broadcast after having a great time and appreciating her experience with me.

I was told before the broadcast that VH1 was visiting from New York City, documenting her North American press tour. The resulting footage would be used for a one-hour TV special for the US, painting most interviewers as ignorant, awkward and lacking couth. I am proud to say I did not make their broadcast.

I did want to talk about tabloids though, and the enormous feeling of invasion that being under a microscope for her entire life had caused her. She explained, "[Entertainment coverage] is crap. It's all about sensationalism. It's truly amazing but it's the nature of the beast. It's like spitting against a tidal wave. But I'm spitting! I don't think it'll ever be the case when stuff is gone and forgotten. If it keeps going, I might just have to move to an island somewhere. But it's different here [in Canada] than the US side."

I asked her if she could trust easily. Was she guarded? "I am not that guarded. I might come across that way, but I am not. I do genuinely appreciate people and especially their sincerity. I am very moved by people when they're being sincere. If you're sincere and straight up with me, there is no problem. But if you're full of it, we might have a problem."

The topic of reality shows came up. Would she ever do one? "You'd have to kill me and film my corpse. Which they would do, I am sure! Film me dead and you can have a reality show."

Very sadly, Lisa Marie Presley passed away on January 12, 2023, nineteen days shy of her fifty-fifth birthday. The picture of us sharing a kiss remains my screen saver picture to this very day.

- Aerosmith's Steven Tyler (2004 in Boston) on the band's long-time drug abuse and kicking their bad habits: "We've learned all the right things the wrong way. We went public with our own addictions. If you ever get out as far as we did, there *is* hope to come back. Sex, drugs and rock 'n' roll . . . take out drugs and there's a lot more room for the other two! There is nothing that will get you more intoxicated than an Aerosmith song!"

- The Rolling Stones' Mick Jagger (2002 in Los Angeles) on being Mick: "Most of the time it's fun. There's ups and downs. I can't be private too much. I expect the paparazzi to be there when I go out. Most people would become reclusive. I can't do that. It's not healthy. I don't cultivate a mystique. [Mick Jagger] still gets a cold! Hahaha." We talked about his social life and I asked him how big his address book was. He responded, "It's thick enough. It gets me through!"

- Not a lot of people can claim that they have met a Beatle. Even more rare, interviewed a Beatle. I've had the enormous pleasure of interviewing The Beatles' original drummer Pete Best in 1997 and Ringo Starr in 2001. I have also interviewed the unofficial fifth Beatle, John Lennon's wife Yoko Ono, and John's kids, Sean Lennon and Julian Lennon.

  Around the time I interviewed Pete Best, he had been paid an estimated $2 million for his involvement in early The Beatles recordings released on 1995's *Anthology 1*. Legend has it that several never-heard-before recordings featuring Pete on drums were found in boxes in someone's attic. The unearthed tapes were cleaned up and released. Pete and I talked about his great fortune in finally being paid for being in The Beatles. I asked him what was in *his* attic? Were there any other long-lost treasures? He replied, "I wish I had some stuff. The only thing in my attic is a lot of dust." For the ten songs he played on, it is estimated that he has earned $8 million thanks to the release of *Anthology 1*.

  When I interviewed Pete's replacement, Ringo Starr, we talked about Beatlemania and the noise levels of screaming girls during The Beatles' concerts. I remarked that monitors weren't that great back then. As the drummer and timekeeper, how could the band hear each other while playing live? Ringo explained, "We didn't hear each other. We vaguely knew where we were at [in the song]. I'd be watching the guys in front of me and their feet and the nodding of their heads and watching their bums. I'd think, 'Oh, that's where we're at!'"

- I love AC/DC and have had the honour and privilege of interviewing Angus Young, Brian Johnson and Malcolm Young several times. On one occasion in 2000, I spoke with the band while they were in Toronto promoting the disc *Stiff Upper Lip*. We talked about how they still considered themselves a blue-collar rock band, even though they had sold in excess of one hundred million albums. Malcolm explained, "We're still working class. We're not lavish. Yeah, we buy gadgets, but that's all they are. It's a waste of money. Yes, we have nice homes and nice beds, but we still sleep on the couch!"

- David Bowie is another artist I love and respect and consider myself a big fan of. I am lucky enough to have interviewed David a number of times. It's tricky interviewing David as he likes to downplay his contributions to music, art and fashion. He also has a reputation for not having a lot of patience for bad interviewers. I can look back and be proud that all our interviews were absolute gold. The last time we spoke was in 2002 while he was in Toronto, touring to support his album *Heathen*. It was another amazing time with him. He summed up his career to me in a very thoughtful way: "The subject matter that I write about has been fairly consistent over the years. It's always about the same thing . . . a separateness, isolation, a sense of anguish, there's some fear in there, a little bit of misery . . . and it's been really consistent for thirty, thirty-five years. It's just the way I approach it changes from year to year. I try to approach the same questions in a different way each time . . . I have to do it for my own amusement. I can't possibly begin to think that there are people out there that know or like what I do. So, it's always a treasure when people like what I do. It's very rewarding. I think, 'Cool!' That's very good! They really like it. I won't repeat it then! Hahahaha!"

- On the band's legacy and longevity, Def Leppard's Joe Elliott said in 2002, "We are getting a lot of that legacy thing happening to us now, while we're still alive, which is cool!"

    Phil Collen agreed, "It is cool! You hope to get that legacy thing and to have an effect. It's neat to have it come to fruition. The fact that you've worked your balls off and people appreciate it is cool."

    Joe continued, "You don't get into it to pass the torch. That's something you develop as you go along. It happens over time. It's really nice when someone comes up and says, 'I picked up a guitar because of you.' It's very weird but very cool!"

    Joe explained that despite all the amazing success the band had experienced since 1980, there had been some tragedies. But they carried on. "Anything now just doesn't faze us anymore. What the hell can anybody throw at us that hasn't been thrown at us already? During these life-changing experiences, we've been there for each other! Through accidents, deaths, marriages, divorces, childbirth, we've been there and done it all. It's part of life. It's a family. You get on, you get up the next day and figure out what do we do today? We don't look back at what we've achieved. That's for other people to do. Our thing is to achieve more to give them more stuff to talk about."

- Admittedly, I am a latecomer to loving and appreciating Mike Ness's contributions to rock 'n' roll. Mike Ness formed Fullerton, California's punk band Social Distortion in 1978. His love of punk *and* country music is evident in his solo albums. I interviewed Mike live on MuchMusic in 1999 while he was in town supporting his solo disc *Cheating at Solitaire*. The album was his jacked-up take on folk, roots and country songs, and featured special guests Bruce Springsteen and Brian Setzer. After Mike performed live on Much, we sat and talked about his career and love of country music. Mike said, "I hate labels. But I brought elements of American roots music to punk music with Social Distortion, and with this record, I felt I brought elements of punk music to roots music. The attitude, the honesty, the emotion. It's stuff that I learned from punk music. It was full circle."

    I then asked him if there were a lot of similarities between classic Americana roots music and punk. Mike elaborated, "I saw the connection very early on. People seem to forget that roots music was the first voice of rebellion. Not the hippy-dippy stuff of the '60s but way before that, when immigrants first started arriving and writing and singing about class issues. As long as it's honest and heartfelt, it's true."

    I reminded him Hank Williams Sr. and those cats that were part of the outlaw movement in country music, did more drugs and drank more booze and shagged more groupies than most rock stars.

    Mike said, "Yeah, I know. They made Mötley Crüe look like boy scouts."

- Led Zeppelin was truly the first rock band that I really became enamoured with. I delved into their music and history in the ninth grade. I spent every dollar I had buying their entire album catalogue and purchasing any music magazine that featured articles on Zep. I listened intently to the bombastic sounds and magical musicianship and vocal intricacies. To me, Robert Plant, Jimmy Page, John Paul Jones and John Bonham were superheroes. Led Zeppelin broke up in 1980 following the death of drummer John Bonham. Everything I learned and loved about Led Zep happened following their breakup. Zeppelin's music has been omnipresent in my life since then. One of the biggest collections of perfect circles for me was interviewing Jimmy Page in New York City in March 2000 and again in NYC in May 2003. I interviewed John Paul Jones in Toronto in April 2000 and finally Robert Plant in Toronto in 2005. In November of 2002, I even interviewed John Bonham's son Jason in Toronto. Jason had grown up to also be a very accomplished and respected drummer.

All these interviews were used for MuchMoreMusic's "The Story of Led Zeppelin" specials in 2000 and 2003. My moments with all the remaining members of Zep will be cherished memories for the rest of my life. All the interviews were extraordinary. The following quotes are just some of my favourite moments garnered from my interviews with the members of Led Zeppelin.

Jimmy Page on Zep's hedonistic reputation in the '70s: "I'm not going to rebut that at all. All those stories, you know, there's no smoke without fire. But I've calmed down quite a lot. I'm older and wiser." Jimmy's huge grin after saying that brought a huge grin to my face.

Robert Plant on Led Zeppelin's early days: "I was very fortunate. I was just trying to keep my head above water in those days, playing with three of the most dramatic and most dynamic musicians on the scene. I really didn't have a lot of room to move. I had verses and lines of songs to fit in between this musical deluge ... To me, it worked at that time, in that format. But the music has gone somewhere else. It's gone."

I asked Robert about how pride for a project can diminish over time. Robert responded, "It's all about stumbling around. I used to think 'That's good!' and then years later you go, 'Ugghh.' There are moments in Zep where I think, 'That's naive.' I hate 'Livin' Lovin' Maid.' But I was twenty! There are some moments that are really alive for me, and some that aren't, in everything I've done. [With Zep] there are things that leave me very emotional, when I see just how good it was. And there were times when it was prickly and narcissistic and a bit of a yawn. The benefit of hindsight is a bastard."

Robert's desire to not look back was evident. He told me how crucial it was for him to find exciting new sounds and to travel the world in search of undiscovered music and rhythms in isolated areas. "I could sit at home and get really circumspect about my life in music and say, 'I've done everything I could ever do.' But I see how music exists in other environments . . . no stages, no lights, no PA, no revenue, no CDs. It's like the old troubadour form of music. And it's still going on. It sounds like John Lee Hooker's great-great-granddad. It's all coming from the desert and Africa!"

John Paul Jones never did a lot of interviews over the years. I found him to be very honest and passionate when the conversation turned towards persistent rumours of a Led Zeppelin reunion: "When we first got together and started playing, it was electrifying. It exploded from the word go. It was fantastic. Led Zeppelin was all about the four individual members. If one person isn't there, Led Zeppelin doesn't exist. It's like a house of cards, it'll come down. No John Bonham, no Led Zeppelin. So, no reunion."

Led Zeppelin eventually reunited with Jason Bonham on drums in December 2007 at The O2 Arena in London, England. Recordings of the monumental show were finally released in 2012.

- I have been blessed to have interviewed the boys from The Tragically Hip many times. So many times, I have lost count. It is safe to say that no other journalist in the world has spent as much time with and interviewed Paul Langlois, Gord Downie, Rob Baker, Johnny Fay and Gord Sinclair as much as I have. It is a badge I wear with huge pride and joy. All the guys are seasoned pros when it comes to being interviewed. They are a bit of an anomaly because they really haven't over-saturated the music market with interviews since 1984. They pick and choose when and where to be interviewed, and when interviewed, they are generous, thoughtful and giving.

No one forgets their first time, whether it's their first kiss, their first car, their first job, their first apartment, their first pet or if playing

A HAPPY HAS-BEEN

hockey, their first goal. My first time actually interviewing anybody from The Hip for assignment was just outside of Cleveland for a big music festival called Buzzard Fest. The date was Saturday, May 18, 1996, and I was at the Blossom Music Amphitheater in Cuyahoga Falls, Ohio. The Hip shared the bill with 311, No Doubt, Goldfinger, Candlebox and many others. They had just released the landmark album *Trouble at the Henhouse*. Our interview was backstage after their evening performance and featured Gord Downie and Johnny Fay. The lengthy interview was used for a MuchMusic special to promote the band's new disc.

One of my favourite succinct sound bites I ever heard from a band came from Gord Downie during our interview. He was explaining how he and the rest of the band took great joy in doing things their way, in a spirit that made them happy. He said, "We are playing the music we want to play and we're making the music we want to make. We are making a career out of our imaginations. We're having a great time!"

- I didn't like Rush as much as some friends did in high school. I knew some guys who were obsessed with Rush, and an ex-girlfriend in grade nine, Bev Tanquiy, was a ginormous fan. I liked Rush but I didn't have their patches on my jean jacket. I started to become a big fan of Rush only after interviewing Geddy Lee and Alex Lifeson a few times. While putting together an hour special for MuchMoreMusic, I became reacquainted with their music. I was listening to many of their songs I knew but hearing them differently somehow. I started to fall in love with Rush and finally understood what my friends in high school were freaking out about. A lot of my love and respect for Rush came from spending time with the guys and interviewing them. One must love a band whose guitarist and singer greet you with big smiles and hugs. Especially when the guitarist is considered one of the best in the world, and the singer is one of the best bassists on Earth too. I have spent many nights alone at home listening to Rush and playing air-drums, air-guitar and air-bass—often during the same song! It was a huge thrill to learn my 2002 interview with the boys wound up as a bonus extra on their 2005 DVD release *R30: 30th Anniversary World Tour*. Maybe it's a Canadian thing? They are very down to earth and lack dangerous egos. Quite simply, they are sweet and humble.

That 2002 interview was done at their management offices in Toronto. Some standout moments include when Alex Lifeson said, "I think we recognize that there is respect for the band and a lot of that comes from the fact that we've been together since 1968. We've managed in a business where it's notoriously short-lived. We've managed to maintain our beliefs and standards throughout this whole period. We've worked very hard to do things the way we believe they should be done. We've been loyal and true to our music and to our art and that's a very difficult thing to do in the music business."

Geddy Lee continued, "We've failed a lot in public too. Not all our experiments worked. Part of what was so great about the era we came through was that we had the latitude to fail in public. Not all our records were successful. Not all of them achieved what we wanted them to achieve, but for some reason, whether it was our insistence or our recording lives, we were able to learn a lot. And you learn way more from your failures than you ever do from your successes."

And Alex summed up, "It's about where we come from. We are very normal middle-class guys. We have middle-class values and good worth ethic. What we do is not that special. Isn't that such a nice typical Canadian attitude?"

- England's Motörhead was always a band that confounded critics and musicologists. They played a music that was hard, heavy, fast and thrashy, but the members always maintained they simply played rock 'n' roll. Motörhead's Lemmy Kilmister (vocals and bass) gave one of the best interviews. In 2005, I interviewed the band on the road a few times as part of the MuchMoreMusic special series, *We're with the Band*. A cameraperson and I spent time with them on their tour bus, at their soundchecks and backstage at their sold-out shows in Toronto and Montreal. Besides Lemmy, drummer Mikkey Dee and guitarist Phil Campbell, I also interviewed fans, the band's crew and their opening acts.

  A moment I will never forget happened in Montreal. I followed the band from their dressing room and up some stairs to the stage, shooting with a small video camera. We paused side-stage while the lights were turned down, and I captured them walking out on stage to thunderous applause and cheers. In Toronto, I asked Lemmy about his legacy and what he thought the band brought to rock 'n' roll. "It's not a legacy. We're just a rock 'n' roll band, that's it. I don't think, 'Oh wow, we've been going thirty years.' All I think about is, 'What do we have going on next year?' You see, idiocy really helps you last thirty years. You have no conception of anything when you're an idiot. Thirty years is nothing. It'd be big if we lasted a hundred years."

Mikkey added, "We've lasted so long because of our loyal fan base. These guys that follow us around, we're their lives and souls. They appreciate what we do. We never gave up or gave in. And we're honest and real. What you see is what you get. We've never compromised the pureness we have. There's nothing fake about this band. Well, except my hairdo."

Lemmy elaborates, "The sad thing is that it's so unusual, to be honest. Our rule is no rules."

I asked Lemmy and Mikkey about the pretty girls I saw backstage. Mikkey explained, "Thank God some of the girls want to hang out with us before a show. We hang out with some guys too, but it's better than some guy yelling an inch from your ear, 'Heeeey! Motörhead!' Girls are more fun to hang out with."

Lemmy offered, "Some say 'groupies.' What a stupid word. There's girls that like guys in bands and why not? [Motörhead] is mostly quite attractive and we're egomaniacs so we're interesting. We treat women well! There are a few bands who shouldn't be allowed to even hang out with them. I know worse ways to go if you're a girl. You could go after a plumber. Going after a band is a good thing for a woman to do. I highly advise it. They get to hang out with us in limos and have a good time and we take them to our hotel room."

I told Lemmy, "That sounds better than a free Motörhead t-shirt!"

He replied "Yeah! They get a t-shirt as well!"

We ended our final interview with some shots of Jack Daniel's. Lemmy poured some for me in a glass and asked if I wanted ice. I replied, "No bud, straight up. Thanks." We toasted each other and said, "Cheers."

On December 28, 2015, Lemmy died at his home in Los Angeles from prostate cancer, cardiac arrhythmia and congestive heart failure. It was four days after his seventieth birthday.

- Any fan of harder-edged rock music loves Metallica. What's not to love? The groundbreaking rockers first began their climb to the top of the metal mountain in 1981 in Los Angeles. I spent the day with James Hetfield, Lars Ulrich, Kirk Hammett and Robert Trujillo in 2003 at the Silverdome in Pontiac, Michigan for the start of their Summer Sanitarium tour. The interviews occurred in their spacious backstage rooms.

  Three years prior, Metallica made headlines worldwide in their efforts to shut down the Internet's file-sharing platform, Napster. Music could be uploaded there and shared for free. Musicians lost billions of dollars in revenue. Lars spearheaded the successful effort to close Napster, despite backlash from many fans. Sadly, the band was painted as greedy, but they insisted they weren't against the technology, they simply wanted control of their music and their art. I agreed with Lars and many music industry folks in citing that the 'net was responsible for many artists' demise and for ending the system of record companies signing new talent. Yes, the Internet is a great resource to find new music and discover new talent, but the trade-off is that a lot of music is available for free. It's a losing battle for a lot of talented musicians.

  I asked Lars if the fight was worth it. He said, "This was never about money, but no one believed me. When we make a record, it's a record of songs sequenced, and somewhere in there, in our selfishness, we like to think these songs play off each other in a particular way. So, if you're interested in acquiring these songs, they all come together in a nifty little package. The idea of taking song seven and isolating that as a downloadable track, that's not where our heads were at. If we wanted song number seven to be its own thing, we would have made it available to be its own thing. If you took out one of these songs, it might get lonely and miss the other ten songs."

  I joked, "That poor song! That makes me sad!"

  Kirk added, "Right!? Who would want to upset the song?"

  I asked if people secretly thanked them for stepping up to the plate to make a difference, and Kirk responded, "Yeah! There was a lot of behind-the-scenes hand shaking. And a lot of artists coming up to us saying, 'Good job! I fully agree [with] and support you!' And I say, 'That's great!' But we need more than a handshake and a pat on the back. That's great that we had their support but damn it, c'mon! Make a stand! Help us!"

I told them they're seeing that now. Lars replied, "Only after we're over it. We're over it now, but it took two years of therapy getting over all the shots we took and all the hatred thrown our way. I'm just finally only now able to walk outside and not have to worry if someone is going to say something bad about me."

- In my career, I have been asked quite often who was one of my favourite interviewees. I always cite Manchester, England band Oasis. The reaction I get to my answer is usually one of surprise and disappointment. "Eww! Really? Why Oasis? They seem like assholes," I am told. Not to me. I fuckin' love Oasis.

Oasis blew me away when they came on the scene. I loved their tunes and their swagger. If you didn't believe they were the biggest band in the world for a while in the '90s, ask them. They would tell you they were. Music fans globally (me included) saw it to be true. Their album sales and concert attendance numbers broke several UK records, and their presence on music magazine covers lasted a long time.

The Gallagher brothers were always entertaining on stage and off. I loved their story about how older brother Noel Gallagher (guitarist and songwriter) took over younger brother (lead vocalist) Liam's newly formed band. It became apparent in the early days that despite the huge talents they shared, they didn't get along. They stopped being interviewed together very early on because fights would ensue between the two.

Interviewing Liam and Noel (always separately) many times proved to be entertaining television. I appreciated their honesty and ability to deliver brilliant answers to any question posed.

In the British press, Liam had a reputation for being a bit of a hooligan. I can honestly say that during the times I interviewed Liam, he was friendly and very giving. In fact, the last time I interviewed him in Toronto in 2005, he rushed over to me at the start of the interview to give me a hug.

The following are numerous sound bites garnered from my many interviews with Oasis.

Noel Gallagher (1996 in Barrie, Ontario, backstage at Molson Park): "We're from Manchester. It's an industrial city that has had the heart ripped out of it. There's lot of factories that are empty and derelict. It's a rough city and there's nothing to do there. There's a big problem with gangs and drugs. If you want to get out of there, there's only three things to do: become a footballer or soccer player, become a drug dealer or become a musician. We're not that good at football. We're not very good to buy drugs from. And so, we chose the third option. It's as simple as that."

Liam Gallagher (1997 in Oakland, California, backstage at The Coliseum): "Our record deal came because of confidence and talent. Noel says it was a bit of luck. He's wrong. There are shit bands that got to where they are because of luck. We got to where we did because we're good."

Noel (1998, live on MuchMusic): "That's one side of the band that never gets written about . . . our sense of humour. This is no word of a lie, but I could easily have a career as a stand-up comedian! 'Cause I'm really funny, man. We're taken as being this serious, arrogant and rude band." I offered, "I find that really endearing about the band, though," and Noel responded, "I find it endearing too! But it's not quite the true picture, is it?"

Liam on techno music and electronica (1997): "Ahhh, fuck! That's shite! I've never let that into my world." I then asked him what he thought of electronica duo The Chemical Brothers' work with older brother Noel on the number one single, "Setting Sun." Liam replied, "Oh, that's our kid. He's great. I hear [The Chemical Brothers] are nice lads and all but I don't like their music. I'm a rock 'n' roll man."

Liam on his persona in the UK versus North America (1997): "I don't think many people get me. I think they get me. I dunno. I don't get me-self. Hey, listen, in England, they don't even fuckin' get me, so fuck it. And the day they do get me is the day I'll start worryin'. Because I'm not doing my job proper."

Noel on Liam's persona (1997 in Oakland, California, backstage at The Coliseum): "Liam doesn't even get Liam. Who would want him? People don't like him because he's confrontational. It must be boring to be that confrontational all the time. He'd pick a fight with his own toenails! Well, he's always claiming to be picking a fight with someone, but he's a pussycat really."

Liam on reading his own press (1997): "I love reading about me in the papers. I'm mad fer it! Because I'll read it and go, 'I'll sue you and I'll sue you,' because you got it wrong. That's the only reason why I read it, so I can say, 'Thank you very much . . . a couple thousand pounds off you, a couple thousand pounds off of you and a couple thousand pounds off of you!'"

Noel (2002 in Toronto): "I'm the brother of the prince of darkness!"

Noel on his drug abuse (2001): "You can't hang anything on me from the years '94 to '98. I was on drugs. I started getting really bad panic attacks. In the beginning, I'd literally party for days. Then maybe two days after the party there was a bit of a come down but it wasn't too bad. And then the come downs began to get unbearable, to the point where I thought I was going to get really sick. So, I stopped. I went home, shut the front door, took the phone off the hook, and about six weeks later I was fine." I asked him if he had ever heard the theory that some drugs could lend themselves to creativity. Noel continued, "It didn't work for me. I got into [drugs] to get totally fucked up. I couldn't physically hold a pen to be creative. I can't play guitar unless I'm 100% straight. It's as simple as that. It never enhanced *my* creativity. It stopped it."

Noel (1999, live on MuchMusic): "There was a six-month period leading up to playing Knebworth in England where we were the biggest band in the world. We were selling the most records and playing to the most people. We were the biggest band in the world. But when you're in the biggest band in the world, you also get the biggest tax bill in the world."

Noel (2001 in Toronto): "I think, undeniably, we'll go down as one of the best British bands of all time. If we don't, then it's an absolute outrage. I'm in the best band in the world."

Liam (2005 in Toronto): "I'm proud that we're still here. And we'll remain still here, as long as we're healthy. I don't see why we can't make another ten records. Six [records] isn't enough. I want to be remembered as a band that made some fuckin' great records!"

Yes, Oasis will be remembered as a band that did make some great records, but sadly, Oasis broke up in 2009. Legions of fans worldwide (yes, me included) hope that the Gallagher brothers will put aside their differences and one day reunite.

- In 2003, I had a great interview with Alice Cooper on his tour bus in Toronto. He spoke at length about the image of Alice: "I treat Alice as a third person. He's a separate character. But what got Alice here were the songs and the songwriting. It wasn't just about image and the look and the stage antics. Shock rock? We just saw a real war on TV, with real people, real time, real blood and real death. It's hard to shock people by putting your head in a guillotine on stage where everyone knows it's a trick. To me, it's pure entertainment, it's all theatrics. There's nothing shocking anymore. Unless Marilyn Manson goes up on stage and cuts his arm off for real. OK, I'll give you that one!"

- In 2000, I was fortunate enough to be given a tour of the Bee Gees' studio in Miami by the Gibb brothers, Barry, Maurice and Robin. We talked about their iconic 1977 *Saturday Night Fever* soundtrack.

  Barry Gibb: "Many people hold that record in high regard, and so do we. But people don't say, 'Tell us about *Fever*.' They say, "Tell us about what happened *after* Fever." We don't want to talk about the backlash."

  Maurice Gibb: "It brings back great memories of the '70s and people love dancing to it. It's come full circle. It's amazing how young people are experiencing it now because they only heard about it. And older people that do remember it, like going back to it."

  Barry: "We were slapped around for having that very successful record, and we didn't like it, and it made us unhappy for a very long time. We've outgrown that now. We're like everybody else now, we look back at *Fever* now with reverence. We're proud of it now."

Robin Gibb: "*Fever* is beyond us! You can go to any dance club in the world and hear a modern dance track and hear something from *Fever* right after."

Barry added, "Or, you can stand outside any nightclub in the world, and stand in line, and not be able to get in, like I have done, but still hear my music inside!"

- In 2004, I spent the afternoon with ex-Guns N' Roses members Slash, Duff McKagan, and Matt Sorum, and ex-Stone Temple Pilots vocalist Scott Weiland in LA. I interviewed them at the Chateau Marmont in West Hollywood, in the private area of the hotel's luxurious bungalows. We were steps away from the bungalow where comedian John Belushi had died from a drug overdose. Our conversation turned towards their partying days.

  Slash: "[Guns N' Roses] was a very entertaining band outside the music! The weirdest thing I have ever heard about myself is that I was dead. It happened a couple times. I once had a message on my answering machine from a friend: 'Dude, you alright? I heard you were dead!?' I know about *not* pacing myself now. I really have to give myself a lot of credit for getting this far. You learn after a while about what your limitations are. A man has got to learn his limitations."

  Scott Weiland: "It's not live fast and die young anymore. It's live fast and live long."

  Very sadly, in December 2015, Scott died of an accidental drug overdose on his tour bus in Minnesota at the age of forty-eight.

- I interviewed Fleetwood Mac's Mick Fleetwood and Lindsey Buckingham in Toronto in 2003. We spoke about Lindsey's desire to experiment musically and take chances, despite selling millions.

  Mick Fleetwood: "Going back to 1967 when the band was first formed under Peter Green, he had a lot of those similarities. He and Lindsey had those same creative smarts."

  Lindsey Buckingham: "It's an irony because without the success we experienced, we would not have the financial freedom or the political freedom to make that choice. It takes being on a mega-selling machine in order to reject what is *not* valid about that. It's not an easy path to walk. People who are interested in only what sells will not validate what the critics may love. It can make people lose their confidence in what's important. You *have* to do it for yourself."

- I was MuchMusic's resident pro wrestling fan, so I was assigned to interview many wrestlers that visited the Much environment. In November 1999, WWE World Heavyweight Champion Dwayne "The Rock" Johnson spent thirty minutes with me live on Much in front of a large and boisterous audience in the studio and outside on Queen Street. Prior to the broadcast, we chatted at length in the makeup room about some of the questions I was going to ask. I expressed that I wanted to end the segment with him laying into me with a typical Rock insult. He was a master on the mic for his promos and his insults were brilliant! After the awesome broadcast, I said, "Before we wrap things up here, give me a Rock insult."

    He didn't hold back, "Insult you? That's easy! A jabroni like you, sitting there with your little pearly whites and your two-dollar sweater . . . The Rock says this: I'll take that little microphone you like talking into, shine it up real nice, turn that son of a bitch sideways and stick it straight up your candy ass!"

    Wow. What a big honour! The moment was captured for posterity and the picture was printed in 2000 in The Rock's first memoir, *The Rock Says . . .*

CHAPTER SEVENTEEN
KINGSTON'S SADDEST DAY

As I wrote earlier, in 2011, I was let go from a major Ottawa TV station despite solid ratings. I believe it was due to a combination of politics and cost-cutting measures. I was a victim of downsizing. There have been waves of cuts in Canadian media since 2005. I've seen many friends let go from media jobs in Vancouver all the way to Halifax. In Ottawa, several waves of cuts occurred, and I dodged more than a few bullets, but eventually, a bullet found me.

For the first time in my adult life, I was not working. I had gone from putting myself through college and graduating to my first full-time job at CHUM Limited's MuchMusic in the same week. Years later, CHUM was sold and absorbed by a couple of large Canadian media companies. In that business transition, I witnessed dozens of friends and former co-workers lose their jobs in both TV and radio. This was in a span of less than five to ten years.

September 2011 to June 2012 would be the worst ten months of my life. I had recently lost an older brother due to a heart attack and my elderly mother had been diagnosed with an aggressive cancer.

The severance package given to me would last a year, but it came with a non-competition clause stating that I would not be allowed to work for a lengthy period of time.

I spent the next eight months visiting my dying mother in the Barrie hospital. I made the drive there and back home to Ottawa in both clear conditions and through snowstorms. I wouldn't even recall the long drive sometimes. I was on autopilot, thinking of my saintly mother, recalling childhood memories and listening to a lot of music. I knew she was proud of me. She watched me become independent at an early age. Barb taught me very well. I put myself through college. I eventually assisted her financially many times as I was a successful broadcaster in her eyes. It was painful to tell my dying mother I was laid off. I told her to not worry about me. I was so angry and bitter at my former employer, knowing that my mother's last memory of me might have been that I was no longer employed. Not needed. Not successful.

I also spent my time at home updating my resume. I hadn't sent out a resume in twenty-four years. My time was also spent hosting a steady succession of friends checking up on me.

I read a lot of online messages. I felt the love of thousands of viewers telling me I was missed. I read countless messages from people who expressed that they didn't watch the previous channel anymore, especially because I wasn't there. I answered countless private messages asking, "What happened?" and, "Where are you?"

As in many industries, no position is secure. I suppose I was one of the lucky ones, staying employed while seeing valued people all around me get severance packages. That was the new normal. Hundreds underwent career shifts. I watched layoffs all around me, almost on a weekly basis.

Things happen for a reason, although it is never clear to us during the process what the reason is. It's not until time passes that we see with some clarity how an unforeseen change could be beneficial.

Getting a phone call in June 2012 from news director Jay Westman (CKWS-TV/Corus Entertainment in Kingston) happened at the perfect time. After the ensuing job interview and being offered a position, my life changed for the better—more than most will ever realize. Please consider this chapter as a sort of love letter to my new adopted home of Kingston, Ontario.

All I have ever done is work hard and contribute. I have always considered my role a big responsibility, and I cherished the chance to once again have the opportunity to educate, inform, entertain and engage with a new audience. I learned in Ottawa that the size of the audience doesn't matter. Yes, Kingston is a smaller city, but I have realized that for me, being happy is about connecting with the audience that is available, whether it be hundreds, thousands or hundreds of thousands. I am fortunate to have forged a strong bond with the community I am now a part of.

Kingston became my home in July 2012, and it took about eleven seconds to fall in love with the "Limestone City." I wasn't a stranger to this city, as I had visited Kingston many times for various assignments when I was with MuchMusic and MuchMoreMusic. But as of now, being here, I am the happiest I have been in a very long time, personally and professionally. Kingstonians are one of the big reasons why. It is a very welcoming city that embraces its past while it looks to its future. It is a very caring city that focuses on community, diversity, sustainability and creativity.

I was filled with pride knowing that I was going to be working at CKWS-TV, one of Canada's heritage TV stations. The station first signed on December 18, 1954. Presently, 170 Queen Street here in Kingston is home to CKWS-TV (Global Kingston) and two successful radio stations, 96.3 Big FM and 104.3 Fresh Radio.

I was first hired to host and produce a 5 p.m. lifestyle show, *Live at 5*. The thirty-minute live show featured community guests, charity endeavours and fun general interest segments. I grew the show to add more musical acts and bigger name guests. That time slot grew larger in ratings, and it eventually evolved into *The WS Daily*. The longer show also featured interviews with music artists, and I was given even more freedom to bring whatever I wanted to the show. We featured a lot of fun eastern Ontario-based stories and we established crucial viewer interactions.

Even before physically moving here, I was making friends. I met news anchor Julie Brown in the lobby at the station on 170 Queen Street while waiting on Jay for the initial job interview. She was very friendly and hospitable, and we would eventually work closely together. Jules remains one of my best friends in Kingston.

I am thankful for one of our technical directors, Rachel Hele. Rachel helped me bring to reality some ideas I had that needed technical help. Her love of television and passion for creativity rivaled mine. I cherish her leadership abilities and knowledge of everything technical. She quickly became one of my closest friends here in Kingston when I first started. She taught me non-linear digital editing and became a close friend that I have relied on many times. She has been an awesome travel companion and a great partner for seeing concerts. Rachey remains very close to me.

In an age of falling ratings across the board, CKWS-TV ratings grew even more. It wasn't long before I realized that my life had achieved a sense of purpose again. My contributions to this talented team that was open to new and exciting ideas proved to be successful. A year after being at CKWS-TV, I was awarded a Corus Entertainment National Samurai Award for best exemplifying Corus values. What? A major media company that instills values in their employees? It's true! Interestingly enough, about a year later, the *Ottawa Citizen* newspaper published a scathing article on the toxic work environment, low morale and continued layoffs at my former employer's newsroom. Yes, the same newsroom where just a few years prior, I had tried to bring numerous concerns to the VP/GM in order to elevate things to a happier place. My concerns had been kicked aside, as I was. While reading the article online, I had feelings of vindication. But, I felt bad for the remaining friends I still knew working there.

I have now been in Kingston for over ten years. I have found the experience joyful, therapeutic, rejuvenating and most importantly, lifesaving. I currently co-host and co-produce *Global News Morning* with the fantastic Maegen Kulchar. She makes me laugh every single day. She is the epitome of awesome. It is an amazing group of people in our newsroom, led by wonderful manager Jay Westman. I brag to friends and family about Kingston's geographic beauty and colourful history. It is where Lake Ontario meets the St. Lawrence Seaway and the Cataraqui River (part of the Rideau Canal waterway). Kingston is Canada's original capital city. I consider myself extremely lucky and grateful to call this gem my home. I feel the support from a community I love with my entire being.

Before moving here, a dear friend I knew in Toronto let me know that he was originally from Kingston, and he told me that I would love it here. That friend was Mauro Sepe, and he had moved back to Kingston a few years prior. I had met Mauro through a mutual friend in Toronto, John Temou. We hung out at my place in Toronto many nights, drinking, talking about music and listening to music until sunrise. It wasn't until I moved to Kingston that I learned from Mauro that he had many connections to one of my favourite bands, The Tragically Hip. Mauro went to high school with all the guys, and he was embedded in many early '80s Kingston bands, including being the drummer in a short-lived band called The Filters. The Filters remain part of Kingston music lore. The band featured young members Gord Downie and Rob Baker, who went on to establish The Tragically Hip. The Filters were formed by a young Finny McConnell, who went on to create Irish punk band The Mahones. Mauro remains a cherished friend, and it never ceases to amaze me how he didn't tell me about his connections to The Hip while I was playing their music constantly during our late-night drinking sessions.

There was a long period in my career where I tried to deny my music background and previously entertainment-focused existence. I wanted to shake that weight off and transition into something else. My time here in Kingston has allowed me to be open to all kinds of community endeavours *and* once again be very involved with music, and importantly, *local* musical acts. I am blessed to pick and choose what artists to feature, whether local or national or international.

Many musical acts I have featured on CKWS-TV have told me that *localized* TV supports music interviews more than a lot of traditional outlets. These music artists say that no national TV music channels exist anymore, so smaller market TV press is more important than ever. I have been told numerous times that shows like ours on CKWS-TV are desperately needed by the music community.

I thank Kingston for many things. I thank this city for allowing me to do what I do and for the acceptance. I am Kingston's biggest fan of its history, its geography, its attractions, its lively arts scene and its beautiful people working together for many charitable endeavours. We possess a true sense of community with many charity efforts that are taken care of by generous citizens. We can boast that our city truly cares for all who live here. I eagerly accept most appearance requests to emcee dozens of charity events each year.

I could easily fill a book writing about the many individuals and groups that devote their time and attention to help shine a spotlight on many charities. The Kinsmen Group are tireless supporters of donating to charity, and so are the Rotarians. The Easter Seals folks do awesome work. I love Lionhearts Inc. for their endeavours too. Bhavana Varma was the president and CEO of United Way Kingston, Frontenac, Lennox and Addington for many years. Her and the United Way team's love of community and assisting many organizations was infectious.

I became friends with Gord Hunter and his beautiful wife Ginette Blais early when I moved to Kingston. I would take a bullet for this couple. Not only do they have exceptional taste in music, but they are devout *givers*. Their time is devoted to animal welfare and ending Parkinson's disease.

Another person I met here was Amanda Alves. This woman changed my life in a huge way. How huge? I asked her to marry me in late 2022! I had resolved to be single forever, but that ended quickly when I met Amanda on Brock Street, around the corner from the TV station, in late 2016. We ran into one another for months during our lunch breaks. We'd see one another and smile and walk and talk, as she worked around the corner from me. The timing felt like fate, and I would get to see her randomly once or twice a week. Then my work schedule changed, and she sadly disappeared from my life. Months went by before Amanda reached out to me in a private Facebook message. I told her that I had been thinking of her. She later admitted that her sister, Christina, convinced her to message me after a few glasses of wine. We exchanged numbers and talked frequently. Amanda was a very talented hair stylist, esthetician and makeup artist. I always found it odd that this in-demand makeup artist made others look beautiful and feel confident, yet she was all that herself even without any makeup on. Our first date was in early 2017. It was a remarkable and phenomenal night that I will never forget.

We bonded over food and similar tastes in music (including The Tragically Hip), and I fell in love. We became inseparable. She was soon spending a lot of time at my place. She added her spare toothbrush to my toothbrush holder. Eventually, she needed a drawer for some clothes. Then two drawers. Within a year, she had moved in.

In short time, I met Amanda's parents. I immediately fell in love with Judy and Armindo. Soon, I was invited to all the Alves's family functions. At the time of me typing these words, Amanda and I live in a beautiful house I bought in the spring of 2022 in Kingston's east end. She has decorated it and designed the rooms with impeccable taste. Amanda has been a huge figure of strength for me and continues to be a positive guiding light for me.

I distinctly remember looking at her left hand when we first met. I was searching for a wedding ring. Luckily, I didn't see one. I could never predict that six years later, she would be wearing an engagement ring from me. Thank you, Amanda, for bringing value and class and most importantly, unwavering love to my life!

· · · · ·

Kingston's community works hard to take care of their young, old, sick and poor. It is a tireless battle to end poverty and to fight for many issues. But our community always steps up and always shows love.

There are so many reasons why I love Kingston. We can lay claim to having the most restaurants and pubs (per capita) in Canada. If visiting, I recommend Tango Nuevo, Wooden Heads, Pan Chancho, Harper's Burger Bar, Chez Piggy, The Grizzly Grill, Olivea, Atomica, Tir Nan Og pub, Chien Noir Bistro, Heist, The Iron Duke pub, The Duchess Pub, The Toucan pub and so many other fabulous, fun, indie and delicious destinations.

I have never seen a city that shows such huge support for its arts and music scene. The arts community and its energy are incredible. There are many painters and visual artists, photographers, authors and poets here. Film and TV productions are abundant and we now posses a burgeoning film industry. There are many art galleries and live music venues. Besides The Tragically Hip, there is a huge music legacy in Kingston that includes Sarah Harmer, The Glorious Sons, the Headstones and The Mahones. Bryan Adams was born here. Musician Chris Koster and his brother Dave are from here. Dave Koster, a.k.a. "Billy Ray," is The Hip's long-time guitar tech and the unofficial sixth member of the band. Some of the guys from Moist are from Kingston. Also from Kingston are Dan Ackroyd and hockey legends Doug Gilmour and Kirk Muller. Controversial figures Sir John A. Macdonald and Don Cherry are from Kingston too.

There is a healthy and vibrant live music scene here, with a myriad of venues of all sizes. I want to draw attention and shine some flashing lights onto many great musical acts from Kingston, including Kasador, Miss Emily, Greg Ball, Michelle Kasaboski, Jack Mead, Bon Evans, Luscious (featuring Brielle LeBlanc), Abby Stewart, Logan Brown, Lotus Shaker, Mauricio Montecinos, Ryan Gollogly (Goldwing, Reckless & Banded), Erika Lamon, Jay "Smitty Kingston" Smith, Celtic Kitchen Party, The Wilderness, Doug van der Horden, Oakridge Ave, Chris Morris, Spencer Evans, Tony Silvestri, Tom Savage, Christopher Jackson, Alexa Goldie, Jordy Jackson, Luther Wright, Tim Aylsworth, Dave Bull (The Tone Kats), Kris + Dee (Kris Abbott and Dee McNeil), Rob Watkins, The Codas, The Gertrudes, Lowery Mills, Trevor Walsh, Michael George and so many others.

Michael George became an executive producer, teaming up alongside music impresario Dave Wreggit, to establish the QR The Band project in Kingston in early 2022. The two spearheaded the unique program to give a leg up to Kingston area musicians. Artists were given an afternoon to record an original song at The Bathouse Recording Studio while cameras recorded a music video. The bands were showcased live on stage at The Grand Theatre in Kingston in December 2022. An album called *Give Me a Break* is slated for release in 2023, featuring the studio recordings and live tracks captured from the concert. The concert also served as an awards show. I was honoured to receive a trophy that recognized my contributions to showcasing Kingston-area music artists. I must credit CKWS-TV for providing me a platform to do what I love!

Speaking of music, there are more than a few music recording studios based around Kingston, aside from the most famous being The Tragically Hip's Bathouse studio, located just west of Kingston in Bath, Ontario. The nineteenth century Victorian home was purchased by the band in the early '90s and converted into a full-on recording facility. It is one of the last and best residential recording facilities in Canada.

A month or so after moving to Kingston, I ran into Rob Baker and Paul Langlois from The Tragically Hip. I wrote earlier that I have been an enormous fan of the band for many years, even before I first started interviewing the boys in the mid '90s. It has become a big privilege for me to now call The Hip guys and many of their families my *friends*. It is a wonderful perfect circle scenario for me.

August 20, 2016 proved to be a very emotional day for The Tragically Hip and for Kingston. The city asked me to emcee and host those gathered in Springer Market Square to watch The Hip's final show of their

Man Machine Poem tour, broadcast on a huge stage and screen just four blocks away from where they played at the Rogers K-Rock Centre (now, Leon's Centre). There are some estimates that put the numbers in Springer Market Square that day at around thirty thousand. People still talk about the beautiful light that shone on our guys and our city on that day. Fans gathered from all over Canada and the US to come to Kingston to show support for the band and to rally behind singer Gord Downie, who had been diagnosed with an invasive brain tumor called glioblastoma. The average period of survival following diagnosis of glioblastoma is less than two years. Although it was never said publicly, most felt that this day would be the final time all five members would play together. The day was beautiful, emotional and filled with love. It was impossible not to feel the great community spirit. People still talk about how unforgettable and inspirational that day was.

When news broke about how the City of Kingston had asked me to emcee the public screening of The Hip's concert, I was blessed to read hundreds of messages expressing positivity and encouragement. Hosting the stage festivities for thirty thousand at Springer Market Square was a huge honour and very humbling. The true blessing came from The Hip's Paul Langlois's wife Joanne. It was as if I was anointed by the Queen! She expressed how the city "couldn't have picked a better guy." Wow. That's all I needed to represent our great community with much pride and love. It was a giant privilege to be an ambassador for our city and to remind visitors why Kingston is so awesome and about what The Hip represents to us and Canada. I love that music and five guys can inspire so many amazing feelings of positivity.

The widespread heartfelt feelings of all those that descended on our city will never be replicated ever again with a size that large in Kingston. That day needed to be commemorated somehow, in some way. That day arrived on February 2, 2017.

I would do anything the city asked, especially if it had to do with elevating our Hip guys and their legacy. It was a ginormous honour to emcee the festivities for the revealing of the commemorative Hip brick.

At the public ceremony, Mayor Bryan Paterson exclaimed, "From this point on, countless numbers of visitors to Kingston and its residents will stop here, reflect and remember what was a very magical and special evening. This stone is really about saying, 'Thank you.' Thank you for all you have done for your hometown." Rob Baker and Paul Langlois were in attendance to unveil the brick with Mayor Paterson.

Langlois had taken a break from working at The Bathouse studio, producing Greg Ball's album. Following the unveiling and posing for pictures, he headed back to Bath to resume work on the forthcoming album from his friend. Langlois said, "It's an honour! It's a bit surreal, but only in a good way."

The brick is embedded in Springer Market Square on the northwest corner. I joked at the unveiling, "Take pictures, but don't actually step on The Tragically Hip." The large stone features The Hip's lyric, "Everybody was in it from miles around," from their song "Blow at High Dough." The lyric was chosen by the public in an online survey that drew more than eleven thousand votes from across Canada. The marker also contains the date of the band's final show.

The brick will be there long after we are all gone, inspiring many and remaining a reminder for all of us who feel blessed to have witnessed the magic of The Tragically Hip's music, their legacy and their final show. The brick also became the focal point for hundreds of fans to gather around following the very sad news that Gord Downie had passed away on October 17, 2017. A makeshift memorial began in the morning and lasted well into the late evening. I stopped by early in the day. I recall kneeling, saying some prayers for Gord and lighting some candles I had brought with me. Fans came in from all over the region, Toronto, Montreal and upper New York state to place candles, flowers, pictures and even hockey sticks around the brick.

Gord Downie's passing had a huge impact on me, and of course, on thousands of others around the world.

CHAPTER EIGHTEEN
DEATH AND GORD DOWNIE

As I get older and reach what people call "middle-age," I think about death a lot more. I suppose many at my age begin to consider it a simple fact of life that we must eventually die. I am not afraid of death, but again, like most people, I feel there is not enough time to accomplish everything I need to do or want to do. I know I am very lucky. I have experienced much of the world and accomplished more at thirty years of age than most people have at ninety. But that fact doesn't negate the notion that I still have much to do.

I have considered the concept of death a lot more lately, but not in a sad, suicidal way. I am just reminded of it more and more. I hear on a semi-regular basis about the passing of classmates. Or older relatives. Death becomes more prominent the older we get.

The older I get, the more I realize the importance of expressing to people how much they are appreciated. We seem to only praise people and express our love for them when it's too late. It's the same with music artists. Why do we usually only talk about artists' contributions and their greatness when they pass away?

I only cite music artists here, but obviously I refer to *anyone*. But with me, music artists have had the biggest influence on and have brought the most joy to my life. We don't know them personally, but we feel a tangible bond to them. Their music has been comforting to us. Their music has been a friend to us when we needed it most. Even if we have never met an artist, their passing still hurts.

I love celebrating people while they are alive. And it's always been bittersweet to see an older interview clip of mine that airs when someone passes away. It is a pleasure to be reminded of the moments where we met and conversed, but it always comes with sadness. I recall that the first time this happened was when country legend Conway Twitty passed away on June 5, 1993. I had interviewed him for MuchMusic in July 1992, just thirteen months prior to his passing. I was (and still am) a huge fan of Conway, his voice and his contributions to both rock 'n' roll and country. Rightfully so, he went by the moniker "The High Priest of Country Music." MuchMusic ran some of my interview the day following his death. I was working that day and stood in the middle of the studio watching the interview clips being run live. I wept and after going home from my shift, I played a lot of Conway's music.

The same has happened too many times with awesome and influential artists I have interviewed who are no longer with us. Some of these people include Johnny Cash, Waylon Jennings, George Jones, John Prine, Lisa Marie Presley, Gordon Lightfoot, Scott Weiland (Stone Temple Pilots, Velvet Revolver), Taylor Hawkins (Alanis Morrisette, Foo Fighters), Stompin' Tom Connors, Meat Loaf, Jerry Lee Lewis, Adam "MCA" Yauch (The Beastie Boys), Prince, Malcolm Young (AC/DC), Tina Turner, country singer Hal Ketchum, The Doors' Ray Manzarek, pro-wrestling WWE Hall of Famer The Iron Sheik (although not a musician, he *was* in a Cyndi Lauper video!), Lemmy Kilmister (Motörhead), David Bowie, Billy Joe Shaver, John Entwhistle (The Who), Robin and Maurice Gibb (Bee Gees), Paul Humphrey (Blue Peter), Eddie Money, John Morris Rankin (The Rankin Family), Eddie Van Halen, Jeff Healey, Les McKeown and Ian Mitchell (Bay City Rollers), James Gray (Blue Rodeo), pop singer Aaron Carter, Peter Tork and Davy Jones (The Monkees), Juno-winning Haydain Neale (jacksoul), Dan McCafferty (Nazareth), Kenny McLean (Platinum Blonde), Andy "Fletch" Fletcher (Depeche Mode), Canadian country music legend Ian Tyson, Doug Fieger (The Knack), David Cassidy, Charlie Daniels and sadly, many others. These were artists I had spent a lot of time with and forged bonds with. Some of these artists' music had a great deal of impact on me and thousands of others around the world too.

The Cranberries' Delores O'Riordan was someone I was a big fan of who I had also spent much time with, conducting several interviews. She was only forty-six when she passed away on January 15, 2018. Her death came as a shock globally to many of the people who had purchased some of the Irish band's forty million albums.

The Cranberries had come out of nowhere in 1993 with their debut, *Everybody Else Is Doing It, So Why Can't We?* They had a cool and edgy sound with sometimes politically inspired lyrics and were led by a female in the sometimes male-dominated music industry of the early to mid-'90s. The band had an interesting dynamic: a hard-crunching, three-piece gang of blokes backing a somewhat diminutive female. But Dolores's voice was a true gift. It was her unique instrument. Loud and powerful and yet, when she wanted it to be, soft and tender.

The Cranberries' success wasn't a fluke in the 1990s, with four top-twenty albums on the Billboard 200 Chart. They were awarded with many accolades, even a Canadian Juno Award. That's not luck. That's talent and hard work.

My first interview with Delores and the band was in 1996 in New York City for the release of their album, *To the Faithful Departed*. I remember thinking that this unit was definitely led by their strong front person, and Delores was the ultimate spokesperson for the band. I also recalled the band being omnipresent, and they ultimately knew she was to be protected. I sensed a huge love and trust amongst them. I was struck by her lyrics on that particular disc. It was very anti-drug.

My last time seeing them was in Montreal in 2001 for the album *Wake Up and Smell the Coffee*. I had been sent on assignment to interview The Cranberries for an hour special I hosted and produced to air nationally for MuchMoreMusic. I have a wonderful memory of Delores rushing up to me with a big hug, saying, "How are ya, mate!? I miss ya!" She was so warm and welcoming and beautiful.

She not only brought up our first interview five years previous but had also watched a lot of my work while she was in Canada. She had married a Canadian and spent much time in Ontario in the late '90s and into the early 2000s. She even joked that she was half Canuck. A toast to one of my favourite Irish people of all time.

In my life, single-handedly, Gord Downie's death had the biggest impact on me. His death was like a punch to the gut, and I am sure it felt like that for every fan of The Tragically Hip, globally. One of many amazing things about moving to The Hip's hometown of Kingston in 2012 was renewing my friendship with the guys. I had been interviewing them since the mid-'90s with MuchMusic. I had interviewed them countless times in Toronto and on the road. I had interviewed them in LA, New York State, Cleveland, Chicago and some other places over many years. Even though I had cultivated a connection and friendship with the guys, I was always a fan first and foremost.

In many ways, I find it anathematic to put anyone on a pedestal. Inevitably at some point, one will become disillusioned or feel let down by unrealistic expectations. Bruce Springsteen would even lose some fans in July 2022 after they found out they would have to hand over $5000 for a concert ticket due to Ticketmaster's controversial "dynamic pricing" policy, which automatically increased ticket prices when demand was high. Where was the empathetic everyman figure pandering to a working class fan base? Many fans took to social media voicing their displeasure with their hero.

I have made it a point to publicly declare my dislike for most entertainment news shows. Interviewers are constantly elevating celebs to a god-like status, forever gushing about how fabulous they look and how wonderful their work is. These celebs are simply human beings who will fail sometimes, garnering headlines about spousal abuse or drug addictions or (oh, my gosh!) weight gain. The public then reacts with shock and horror that they are *not* infallible. I have been very fortunate to not have been let down by any artist I have looked up to, and it's a long list that encompasses The Cure, Waylon Jennings, Blue Rodeo, Garth Brooks and many others. Topping this list is The Tragically Hip.

The Hip hold a place in my heart where only a few music artists reside. All the boys possess grace, humility and carry a penchant for contributing to many worthwhile charities. I always found it easy to be a fan. Is it difficult to cherish a band or artist and their music, but also have to interview them? For me, it's not difficult. I learned quickly to separate *that* side of myself from being a professional that had to conduct interviews.

A HAPPY HAS-BEEN

Sometimes in the process of interviewing somebody repeatedly—and I did so many times over thirty-plus years—there is a sense of becoming acquaintances or even friends.

I place The Hip on the same level as Canadian icons who are known globally, like Rush, Neil Young, Gordon Lightfoot, Joni Mitchell, The Guess Who, Bryan Adams, k.d. lang, Celine Dion, Drake, Justin Bieber and a few others.

I have said publicly numerous times that I love The Hip, and I have since their first EP. That self-titled debut in 1987 was my first exposure to The Hip. I was studying radio and TV broadcasting at Seneca College in Toronto. I had a radio show on campus with CRSC. I played that first EP a lot. To this day, I still play the songs "Last American Exit," "Highway Girl" and "Small Town Bringdown" at home and on my MP3 player.

Years later, I have come to appreciate the story of five school friends getting together to play music by their rules and standards and on their terms, and who kept on doing it right up until the very end.

I have seen The Hip live at least a dozen times. A Hip concert wasn't just a night out. It was an experience one would never forget. No two shows were the same. The band reinvented the show every night. It's this quality that fans appreciated and went ballistic for. The Hip had a reputation as a band to be reckoned with when playing live. Gord Downie's imagination was played out spontaneously in front of thousands. No other front man was as enigmatic or captivating as Downie. He drew the audience in with his dreamscapes. His actions, mid-song rants and movements invited us into a strange yet fun world. The audience was attending an amusement park watching Gord Downie live. I caught myself many times at Hip concerts singing along to the songs with eyes closed and happily, joyously lost in a world created by Kingston's own, The Tragically Hip.

They have won sixteen Juno Awards and, in 2005, they were inducted into the Canadian Music Hall of Fame. The year 2022 saw them receive a second star on Canada's Walk of Fame. The Hip have also received the Order of Canada, as well as honourary degrees from the Royal Conservatory of Music.

In 2021, The Hip was bestowed with a Juno Humanitarian Award. Very few outside of Kingston can appreciate how much the guys do for charity. The band has given back to Kingston millions of dollars over the last twenty years. The Hip collectively, and the individual members, have always shown support for their community and countless numbers of charities. Organizations that have benefited from The Hip's endeavours include ALS research, Parkinson's research, AIDS awareness and fundraising, the White Ribbon Campaign, food banks, the University Hospitals Kingston Foundation, many environmental issues including Waterkeeper Alliance, the Special Olympics, the Limestone Learning Foundation, War Child Canada, B'nai Brith Canada, Camp Trillium and many other endeavours. Their commitment to charity is just one of many reasons why I love the band.

It is an easy argument to cite The Hip's proclivity to proudly sing about Canada as a reason to love the band. But aside from Stompin' Tom Connors and Gordon Lightfoot, no other act surpasses The Hip's penchant for lyrics and imagery of Canadiana. Napanee and Pierre Trudeau are referenced in "An Inch an Hour." Terry Fox is given respect in "Inevitability of Death." Other songs referencing Canadian geography or subject matter include "Goodnight Attawapiskat," "Train Overnight," "The Bear," "Thompson Girl," "Summer's Killing Us," "Silver Jet," "The Dire Wolf," "Courage (for Hugh MacLennan)," "Bobcaygeon" and "Wheat Kings." These songs and many others inspire, elevate and provide the audience with a love and pride of Canada.

"At the Hundredth Meridian," released in 1992, is about the hundredth meridian west, specific to Canada and how it is considered "where the great plains begin." Even the video features a nod to another Canadian geographic landmark: although shot in Australia, Gord Downie is wearing a Gros Morne National Park baseball cap. Newfoundlanders are proud of this historic site. I am proud to say I have visited there, and all Canadians should be proud of this site.

The first and what could be the only song *ever* to mention a Canadian "toonie" belongs to The Hip's "Heaven Is a Better Place Today." The song was dedicated to the NHL's Dan Snyder, who died in a car accident in 2003.

Downie introduced many hockey references into his lyrics. How Canadian is that? "It's a Good Life If You Don't Weaken," "Fireworks," "Fifty-Mission Cap" and "Lonely End of The Rink" remind us that hockey is in our blood. Gord Downie even wears a retro Boston Bruins jersey in the video for "Courage (for Hugh MacLennan)" and also references Bruins great Bobby Orr in "Fireworks." Hip fans know that the Downie brothers grew up being big Boston Bruins fans. By the way, my namesake grandfather William Peachy is in the Bobby Orr Hall of Fame. I never did get a chance to share that with Gord Downie, but I did tell Gord's brother, Mike.

Fans south of the forty-ninth parallel should note that The Hip also utilized many American pop culture and geography references too. The band toured all around the globe and Downie was a sponge, soaking up all he learned and turning those experiences into cryptic but heartfelt lyrics.

The Hip's individual members were also very prolific with side/solo projects. I even consider Paul Langlois's first two solo discs amongst my absolute favourites in a collection of CDs numbering in the thousands. The Hip guys simply love creating, writing, playing, producing and even fostering others' talents.

The most important reason I can offer on why I love The Hip? There are so many moments of brilliance on every album they put forth. Just when you think you have your favorite Hip songs figured out, you continue to find new favourites within their huge catalogue. Yet another song from their past will move to the top of my playlist.

All of my interviews with the guys over the decades were amazing. Only one negative experience stands out. It was an ordeal that gave me nightmares for years. It was an interview I did in 1998 with The Hip's Gord Downie and Gord Sinclair. We did the interview at the battleship that was docked in Toronto for many years at Harbourfront, the HMCS Haida. We did the interview in the engine room. The cramped quarters contained many dials and gauges that resembled the album cover for the forthcoming *Phantom Power*. It was the perfect location.

MCA Records gave me an advance cassette of *Phantom Power* to get acquainted with the release. This was standard practice for interviewing an artist before an album's official release. The record company rep gave me explicit instructions to not lose the tape. They reminded me that Jake Gold (part of The Hip's management) would get very angry if I lost the tape and, worst case scenario, it got leaked. I had met Jake a few times and although I always got along fine with him, he had a bit of a reputation in the industry as being "intense."

After the interview, I accidently left the cassette in the engine room. I didn't notice until I got back to the station. I raced back to Harbourfront. Some school tours had followed our interview and to my dismay, I could not find the cassette.

I spent the next two weeks worrying and sweating until the day the album was finally released. I prayed each day that whoever found the cassette, didn't know about its importance. The great news is that the music was never leaked.

・・・・・

Gord's passing in 2017 brought a lot of attention to not just his art, but to Canada's search for truth and reconciliation with our Indigenous citizens. Gord Downie's legacy also included creating a focal point for the fight against the rare cancer, glioblastoma. If there was one single positive outcome from Mr. Downie's struggle, it was the huge awareness that developed around this type of cancer and the fundraising effort that has happened since the announcement of his cancer was made on May 24, 2016. The funds raised due to his affliction were astounding. Lives will be prolonged. Brain cancer research conducted here in Kingston fifteen years ago at Queen's University extended Gord Downie's life. Research continues and breakthroughs are consistently happening.

Dr. James Perry, Gord's neuro-oncologist at Toronto's Sunnybrook Hospital recently stated, "Sadly, in the next year, nearly four hundred [Canadians] will develop a glioblastoma. And four hundred more the year after that. And the year after that too. But there is hope. We are making progress in treatment advancements and support like yours helps us continue our work."

Everyone who watched the final Kingston concert has their favourite moments. For me, seeing Gord kissing and embracing each bandmate prior to even taking the stage was powerful. I lost it and started sobbing. We were all witness to a gang of brothers off to battle the odds. The global audience was blessed to see for themselves the courage and bravery Gord Downie and our boys possessed.

Watching Gord battle his cancer was a reminder to us all of why cancer is such a horrific disease. It brought back memories of when my own mother, Barb, was dying of cancer eleven years ago. I witnessed a lengthy, painful and brutal battle. Everyone around her knew *how* she would die, but none of us knew exactly when. Watching someone die from cancer feels as if we are mourning the loss of our loved one while they are still with us. The pain of losing someone we love is always difficult, whether it's a sudden heart attack or a tragic car crash. The pain is sudden and real. When a loved one is losing a battle to cancer, the pain lasts a lot longer.

It is an awful wait. We feel their pain and would do anything to take it away. All we can do is let that person know they are cherished, loved and very much appreciated. We can remind them how their positive influence affected us and how their influence on us elevated us to be a better person and how their time on Earth made the world a better place.

One of Gord Downie's biggest legacies is teaching many Canadians a part of our history we really didn't learn in schools. He taught us hope for reconciliation with our Indigenous brothers and sisters. Mike and Gord Downie established The Gord Downie & Chanie Wenjack Fund in 2016. According to the group's website, The Gord Downie & Chanie Wenjack Fund is part of Gord Downie's legacy and embodies his commitment, and that of his family, to improving the lives of First Peoples in Canada. In collaboration with the Wenjack family, the goal of the fund is to continue the conversation that began with Chanie Wenjack's residential school story, and to aid our collective reconciliation journey through a combination of awareness, education and action. In The Hip, Downie was always an advocate for social justice, with particular sensitivity to the plight of First Nations communities and families. He used his final years to shine a light on the social ills that inundate many Indigenous families.

In 2022, I had many conversations with Gord's brother Mike, who is helming what he calls the "definitive documentary" on the band. Mike Downie is slowly uncovering pictures and videos the band hasn't even seen, to be shown in a four-part series set to be released in 2024 on the streaming service Amazon Prime. The documentary series will serve to mark the fortieth anniversary of the band's formation in Kingston, Ontario. I have been helping Mike source some of my previous interviews with The

Hip. I have also helped locate and pull some archived moments from the CKWS-TV video library.

I just can't imagine a world without The Tragically Hip and their music. Gord Downie with his Hip bandmates and friends Paul Langlois, Gord Sinclair, Johnny Fay and Rob Baker (and the sixth unofficial member, Dave "Billy Ray" Koster) have indeed made the world a better place. Thank you so much, guys. Your music means more to me than you'll ever realize, which is a thought I know I share with millions around the world.

CHAPTER NINETEEN
A SINGLET AND BLACK WRESTLING BOOTS

When I look at my career, I recall many occasions in which I have indulged in assignments that were totally outside of my comfort zone. But I have always maintained that anything deemed "scary" is worth doing once. And it usually makes pretty good television.

I have always trusted the true professionals who were by my side while I was training to conduct certain acts. I have bungee jumped for TV assignments in Daytona Beach, at the West Edmonton Mall, at the Calgary Stampede and over the Ottawa River. The secret to a successful bungee jump? Just close your eyes and jump. It works!

I have gone skydiving in Gananoque. I have flown with the Snowbirds, the Royal Canadian Air Force's military aerobatics flight demonstration team, and I didn't vomit! I write that because another journalist did. It's a fun game the pilots have while taking newbies up in their jets—especially journalists.

I was stoked to partake in a demolition derby in Ottawa. I suffered whiplash. I participated in a couple of polar dips for charity. Jumping into a frozen body of water through a small hole in the ice while wearing only swim shorts will take your breath away. The air rapidly leaves your lungs. Even after a hot shower, your body doesn't really warm up until the next day. And it's awkward having one's private parts retreat inside. Yes, there is extreme shrinkage.

I have been parasailing in Jasper, Alberta and I've learned to rappel many times. And I hate heights.

I have been white water rafting on the Ottawa River and dealt with the experience of falling overboard, going *into* the river. Our raft hit a big rush of water and several of us were thrown overboard. My friend John Temou flew over with his side of people on the raft, taking out our side, and we all ended up in the water. I tried not to panic, as I was underwater for only a few seconds, not knowing which way was up. Those few seconds seemed like a few hours. All of us climbed back into the raft. I regrouped with Johnny and exclaimed "My knee is bleeding. I think I scraped a rock!"

Johnny replied, "No, I think it was my teeth that hit your knee!"

There were experiences that I couldn't say no to. I knew the TV audience would be entertained by hanging out with the Ottawa Roller Derby girls for a practice. Sure! Why not? Except for the fact that I was knocked on my butt five times. On the same side. I had a bruise the size of a dinner plate on my left butt cheek for a month.

I thought it would be good television to be tasered *and* pepper sprayed on the same day by the kind folks at Ottawa Police Services. It was great television! All went well except that our cameraperson double-triggered, pressing "record" on the camera too fast and inadvertently stopping the recording. He then began recording two seconds later. The recording didn't capture the taser darts going into my back. The resulting TV footage was the Ottawa Police Services instructor aiming a taser gun at my back and asking, "Are you ready?" before cutting to the last two seconds of me yelling "AAAAGHHHHHH!!!!!!" We had missed the actual taser shot and the first three seconds of my body reacting in a way I had never felt before. After being helped up from the ground by two kind officers, my cameraperson asked, "Can you do it again?" I thought, *REALLY? NO WAY!*

I broke a rib in a charity hockey game, courtesy of Ottawa Police Chief (now Parliament Hill Senator) Vern White. I might have deserved it though. The game was in Ottawa for a fundraiser for the Make-A-Wish Foundation. Breaking a bone was the worst part. The best part was playing with four-time Stanley Cup winner Denis Potvin.

Earlier in the game, I went low trying to get the puck and inadvertently took out Vern. After he flew over top of me, he got up from the ice and I distinctly heard, "You're done, Welychka!" A few plays later, I was checked into the net. Instant pain. I was helped off the ice with what felt like a hairline fracture in a left rib.

I made it home and later that evening I sneezed and heard a cracking sound. I screamed in agony! After a trip to the hospital, it was diagnosed as a broken rib. I was off work for two days. When I went back to work, Chief Vern showed up at the TV station offering BBQ ribs, explaining, "I give you what I broke." He also presented me with an Ottawa Police Service water bottle, saying, "I couldn't find a baby bottle for all your whimpering and whining. Have this." I love Vern White!

I maintain that a life lived in fear is a life half-lived. But I have gone through a "dust settling" phase where I now realize that I am older, and I don't want to partake in dangerous activities anymore. I find myself becoming less brave and adventurous. Only cats have nine lives and even if I did too, I might have used up eight of them already. I will carry on being amused and/or disturbed by clips online of other idiots being daring and adventurous. At least I can say I got paid for it.

I am a big fan of pro wrestling, so I am enormously proud of my wrestling adventures. I loved and yet dreaded showcasing my experiences in a wrestling ring. Being body-slammed by Greg "The Hammer" Valentine? It really hurt. It was a painful honour. I have received a leg drop across my chest courtesy of Ottawa giant wrestler The Hickster. I was body-splashed by TNA/Impact wrestler, the 270-pound Awesome Kong. Before the match, I was warned to keep my face forward. She told me in the dressing room to not look at the fist coming and that she would merely nick my chin. But she connected with the entire side of my head with her closed backhand. I fell to the mat and then she did her full-on body-splash. I was truly dazed and sore. As I was leaving the ring, the referee was holding me and helping me walk. He was telling me, "Keep on selling it!"

I whispered to him, "No! I'm really hurt!" I did manage to high-five a few wrestling fans along the barricades while exiting the ringside area. This ordeal in the ring wasn't even me wrestling! I was only acting as a manager for Awesome Kong's opponent, Gail Kim.

In fact, during many pro wrestling assignments, somehow, I was drop-kicked, body-slammed, body-splashed, leg-dropped on my neck, chest-chopped, slammed through a table, kicked in the gut, punched in the face, Vader Bomb-ed, thrown out of the ring, and even DDT-ed multiple times. All of the above pain and punishment came without even being in a match!

When I was a kid, I loved Saturdays. Every kid does, but for me, Saturdays were spent staying inside watching pro wrestling on TV. All of my friends were watching cartoons or riding their bikes, but I tuned into a steady succession of broadcasts by Maple Leaf Wrestling, Stampede Wrestling, the AWA and the NWA.

I was drawn to the larger-than-life characters, the classic good versus bad guy scenarios and the colourful names. Ray "The Crippler" Stevens, Angelo "King Kong" Mosca, "Blackjack" Mulligan, Sweet Ebony Diamond (The Rock's father), Jimmy "Superfly" Snuka, George "The Animal" Steele, "Jumping" Jim Brunzell! OK, maybe Jim Brunzell didn't have a cool name. And he didn't even really jump!

Pro wrestling comes with storylines. It is like a soap opera. One follows along and there are twists and turns to each plot and loyalty sometimes shifts. It is very athletic and hugely entertaining.

Years later as an adult, I found myself interviewing many of the legends I watched as a kid. I am proud of my long history of getting up close and conversing with some of pro wrestling's biggest stars while being a MuchMusic VJ. My favourite interview was Dwayne "The Rock" Johnson. Other MuchMusic interviews included Brett "The Hitman" Hart, Shawn Michaels and Hulk Hogan.

Here at CKWS-TV in Kingston, I have conducted interviews with pro wrestlers Cody Rhodes, Sheamus, Jake "The Snake" Roberts, "Hacksaw" Jim Duggan, The Iron Sheik, Mick Foley, Ken Shamrock and my favourite pro wrestler of all time, The Honky Tonk Man.

One of my proudest wrestling-related moments came when I was covering the 2005 multi-network tsunami relief telethon, *Canada For Asia*. Musical acts Rush, Barenaked Ladies, Bryan Adams and Tom Cochrane were mixed in with athletes, actors and other pop culture celebs as presenters for the weekend at the downtown Toronto CBC headquarters. I filed hourly stories to MuchMusic and MuchMoreMusic with interviews and coverage of numerous press conferences. WWE superstar Christian was a presenter on the broadcast and during his press conference he was asked, "With all the big stars here this weekend, who are you looking forward to meeting?" His response knocked me off my chair. "I grew up watching MuchMusic. I just met Bill Welychka. That was cool." OK, *that* was weird. Awesome, but a little surreal and weird.

The connection between rock music and pro wrestling has a long lineage. I believe the first major cross-promotion between rock music and pro wrestling was the boringly titled *The Wrestling Album* released by the WWF in 1985. The cooler one in my opinion was 1987's *Piledriver: The Wrestling Album 2*. It featured the entrance theme for the awesome Honky Tonk Man.

The pro wrestling and rock connection extended to Triple H (real name Paul Michael Levesque, a.k.a. Hunter Hearst Helmsley). His entrance theme was always Motörhead. Way cool! The Rock and I have talked about the comparisons between pro wrestlers and major touring rock acts. There are many similarities: packed arenas and stadiums with screaming fans, limo rides, merchandise being sold, sometimes pyrotechnics and magical light shows and the entertainment of thousands each night.

I have huge respect for the men and women who train for many years to get into the ring and abuse their bodies for our entertainment. With only limited training, I have entered the ring and experienced pain, welts and soreness all over. My time in the wrestling ring was for many TV assignments. They included refereeing, being a manager and ring announcing. Despite the "safe zone" of not being a wrestler but still being in the ring, I have received punishment. In addition to being body-slammed by Greg "The Hammer" Valentine and punched in the face by female wrestler Awesome Kong, I was once also on the receiving end of a sleeper-hold given by Brutus "Beefcake" Barber. Luckily, my hair was not sheared off.

My actual ring matches were always part of a tag-team. It's relatively easy getting into the ring when you know that your tag partner can come rescue you. If hurt, you can hopefully crawl or dive to your corner to tag your partner in to take over while you quickly recuperate.

When I first donned the tights, it was for a tag-team match in Ottawa, and although I did have *some* skills and training, my partner did most of the work. Poor Caster McFear! Whenever he went to our corner to tag me in, I was always distracted, either bending down to lace up my boots or off chatting up a pretty girl at her ring-side seat. I felt awful when he would get dragged back to the middle of the ring to take more abuse by our opponents. At one point, he managed to get one of our opponents down, and I tagged myself in to get him out of the way and pinned our opponent. I won, er, *we* won! My arm was raised in victory, but my poor beat-up partner was left dealing with most of the pain.

Upon moving to Kingston, I was lucky enough to meet Jan Murphy. He was another pro wrestling aficionado. He was a writer and editor for *The Kingston Whig-Standard* (Canada's oldest published newspaper) and he also co-managed the local independent Chinlock Wrestling organization. I respected his and co-manager Justin Cousineau's approach to local indie wrestling: provide a platform for eastern Ontario wrestlers and make everything about charity! It was easy to say yes every time he asked me to step inside the ring. At first, I told him that I only wanted to be part of tag-team matches. I considered it an honour to promote the Kingston wrestling events on CKWS-TV because I knew the money being made would stay in Kingston and be directed to charity, namely to Youth Diversion.

My first time in Kingston wearing my singlet tights and wrestling boots was in 2016. I was once again part of a tag-team match. That night featured Myzery The Barbarian paired with me against Freak Nation and CJ Felony. Again, my tag partner did most of the work and somehow, I was last in the ring pinning CJ Felony for the win! WWE referee Jimmy Korderas raised my arm in victory, and so did special guest WWE Hall of Famer Ted DiBiase "The Million Dollar Man."

I was thrilled to be feted in December 2018 when at a Chinlock Wrestling event that featured WWE Hall of Famer Tito Santana and former WWE general manager Vickie Guerrero, I was honoured to learn it was Bill Welychka Appreciation Night. A video was played showing clips of all my interviews with wrestlers over the many years. Again, my nemesis CJ Felony made an appearance and attacked me with two DDTs. A DDT in pro wrestling is a highly dangerous move where the opponent's head is driven into the mat. It can result in a broken neck or spine. Its least severe outcome is temporary confusion. Out of nowhere, and as a total surprise to me, The Honky Tonk Man ran towards the ring to chase CJ Felony out. His surprise appearance saved my head from being busted wide open with a garbage can CJ had brought with him. After I gained my bearings, I actually began to cry. My pro wrestling hero, The Honky Tonk Man, was present for Bill Welychka Appreciation Night. I had interviewed The Honky Tonk Man (real name Roy Farris) many times, but seeing him in the ring with me? It was very emotional for me. I've looked at some of the pictures that were sent to me from that evening and yes, I was actually in tears.

I had to take two days off to recover, but regardless of the pain, I smiled for many days following that night, thinking of the gathered wrestling fans that had had a great time. I smiled knowing that our community had come together for charity. I was very proud of my Bubbas Jan Murphy and Justin Cousineau for a beautiful night. I met many people that had shared their love of pro wrestling with me and I was grateful for the high school friends that had visited from Toronto to lend their support: Vania Gallant, Beverley Michelle, Gordon Macleod (RIP) and Ranjan Das.

There were some other charity nights that followed, but the biggest match of my career came on June 15, 2019. Chinlock Wrestling 5 was billed as Kingston's biggest day ever for pro wrestling. Wrestling fans descended on Kingston and to the Leon's Centre to take in the legends convention during the day and match mayhem in the evening. Chinlock 5 drew bigger numbers than any WWE event that had previously come to Kingston's biggest venue.

For me, the night was about proving something to myself. I was going to wrestle in my debut singles match. I would have no partner to tag me in. I was on my own. It was the culmination of a lifetime of following pro wrestling and occasionally dabbling in the world of pro wrestling. But I wasn't just dabbling this time. I was fully in.

Of course, the entire day's net proceeds went to Chinlock Wrestling's primary charity, Youth Diversion. But there were other notable worthy recipients. A huge thanks went out to the Kingston Kinsmen charity service club for being a huge sponsor and supporter.

Admittedly, it was a true honour to be a tiny part of such a historic day. In addition to seeing fans get up close to their favourite wrestling legends and heroes for pictures and autographs, the evening showcased live matches in conjunction with wrestling superstar Tommy Dreamer's House of Hardcore wrestling company.

It's important to note that *no one* will ever condone attempting any moves or actions witnessed by the pros on TV or even live yourself. Many years of training and learning come with entering the ring. All my experiences came with training and coaching and learning from the best. But even with many years of training, accidents still happen.

In a live Global TV interview here in Kingston, WWE Hall of Famer Mick Foley (a.k.a. Mankind and Cactus Jack) expressed to me, "People ask if wrestling is fake. Look at this!" He proceeded to remove his dentures. He has lost many teeth being a pro wrestler. Mick Foley is considered one of the most professional, experienced and exciting pro wrestlers in history. Real hits. Real pain. Real injuries. I consider it more than sports entertainment. It is a real art form, albeit a dangerous and highly physical one.

I cherish all of my interviews with pro wrestling's best. I love these guys and girls, but I am saddened to see them, years on, most walking slowly, hunched over and dealing with major issues in their knees, backs and necks. Many have had multiple surgeries. Some are even in wheelchairs. It shows dedication and love for the sport, but eventually the multitude of injuries can catch up.

It was easy for me to occasionally stick a foot into the ring and then pull it back. But the true pros do it for a living on a frequent basis. Sometimes three hundred days a year. Ten days prior to Chinlock 5, I hyperextended my left knee while training. During my intensive lessons I took a suplex, but my knee was not bent enough and I landed on my back with my left heel hitting the mat first and my knee absorbing the momentum the wrong way. I finished the training session, but the pain really kicked in the next day. For the following week, I iced and heated my knee constantly. I wore a knee brace to help it straighten. No amount of discomfort would keep me away from my match at the Leon's Centre against CJ Felony.

The night meant that I would finally deal with the unfinished business and differences I had with CJ Felony. He is no doubt Canada's indie-circuit's best heel (in pro wrestling terms, a heel is "the bad guy"). He has cheap-shot attacked me and others. He has even bullied kids and women. To me, our match was not about who would win. It was about realizing a dream and also proving that bullies could and would be dealt with by someone smaller standing up to them.

Prior to the evening's matches, the big screen played greetings from Kingston Mayor Bryan Paterson and The Tragically Hip's Paul Langlois. Both sent messages welcoming fans to the Leon's Centre and to Kingston. Their words were met with huge cheers from the nearly sold-out arena of fans in attendance.

I have dealt with goosebumps a lot in my career, but what an amazing thrill it was walking out to an arena full of screams and cheers and applause. After I was introduced and entered from behind the giant curtains, I ceased to exist as Bill Welychka. I was now a pro wrestler on my own. As I circled the ring and shook hands with the ring-side fans, about seventeen things were running through my head . . . *Walk and strut with confidence, engage the crowd, give hi-fives to the kids . . . What's my first move? Where are the ring steps? Is my singlet too tight?*

The match lasted around twenty minutes. I was proud of the back-and-forth physical action. I don't remember much of the match and it's only after watching the video highlights that I can say, I did pretty fuckin' good. I lost, due to a metal garbage can being brought down hard on the top of my head. I went down and I was out.

In the locker room, after my shower, I was told that a young boy was crying hysterically following my loss. He was pretty shaken up. After I got dressed, I had someone take me to him. I recognized him as being the kid I gave my bCLUTCH headband to when I had circled the ring. I calmly explained to him that I was fine and that it was OK to lose, as long as you tried your best. I gave him a hug and told him that we were now great friends. He stopped crying and smiled. That kid made my night.

I have wrestled since that evening and torn both of my pectoral chest muscles. They will never be the same. I do still have my wrestling singlet and leather wrestling boots. I don't think I'll enter the ring again. I fulfilled a dream a few times over and I think I will stop there.

One of the most interesting things about the pro wrestling world is getting used to an entirely new language. Pro wrestlers speak in codes and use words that require a specialized dictionary. For the uninitiated, what follows is a very short glossary of pro wrestling terminology that can be heard backstage:

- *Bump*: Taking a bump is the first move any new wrestler must learn and master. It involves hitting the mat hard on one's back while keeping the arms out level with the shoulders and keeping the chin tucked in. A perfect bump happens quickly, with a loud thud, and the back of the head doesn't touch the mat.
- *Heel* and *Babyface/Face:* A heel is the bad guy/villain, and the face is the good guy/hero.
- *Turn*: When a wrestler switches their persona. The wrestler goes from being a face to a heel.
- *Put over*: When a wrestler will lose to allow another wrestler to win and advance their stature.
- *Card*: The night's scheduled matches. Mid-card wrestlers are considered somewhat respected. Low-card wrestlers are there to learn and expect to be jobbers.
- *Jobber*: A hard-working wrestler who gets a lot of matches but usually loses. Their role is to make their opponent look good.
- *Mark*: A wrestling fan, a paying attendee at a wrestling event.
- *Kayfabe*: Used as a secret word to warn other wrestlers around that a mark is present. It also generally implies that pro wrestling is very legit and unscripted.
- *Pop*: The positive reaction from fans. When all things go right and the audience yells with appreciation.
- *Gimmick*: What a wrestler needs to establish to make a name for themselves. A trait that sets them apart. It's their persona and attitude.
- *Heat/Bringing the heat*: Creating drama or a strong rivalry between two wrestlers.
- *Lucha Libre*: The Mexican style of pro wrestling. It usually involves colourful masks and a high-flying, very fast style of wrestling with many holds and maneuvers.

It is integral that I acknowledge and thank all of the indie wrestlers that I have worked with, shared a dressing room with, learned from and whom I respect so very much: Myzery The Barbarian, Deeno Benjamin and

Cheeky, Tommy Dreamer, Danny Franchise, Fear The Beard, Charming Chaz Lovely, Freak Nation, The Immaculate Ray St-Jean, Nova, Showtime Shaun MacMillan, KL Shock, Hotstepper Macrae Martin, The Hickster, Caster McFear and the most important figure in my indie-wrestling "career," CJ Felony.

This chapter is dedicated to the greatest WWE Intercontinental Champion of all time and WWE Hall of Famer, The Honky Tonk Man. Thanks Wayne for all of our cherished times together. You continue to inspire, entertain and bring joy.

CHAPTER TWENTY
EGOS AND EMPATHY

I have always considered myself very fortunate and lucky to have maintained one single career. As I wrote earlier, I love the entire process of creating television, whether it's on air or behind the scenes. I am fully aware many people go through lives having to enter multiple careers. We are in an age where many people must shift careers. It isn't like a generation or two ago when people had the security of holding onto a single tenure. My field of employment has been very good to me. I've had the pleasure of working in some excellent environments in some wonderful cities under some caring and nurturing bosses and managers. I'd like to take what I have learned about life and work and relay it to you.

We all know that shit happens. To every single one of us. It's a terrible cliché to offer the trite sentiment that things happen for a reason. But I have seen it come true many times. We may not know it at the time, but weeks or sometimes years later we realize why something had to happen to get to where we wanted or needed to be.

I once interviewed author Eric Mosley, CEO of Globoforce. Mosley has written numerous books pertaining to workplace positivity. One of his books is entitled *The Power of Thanks*, and it is all about increasing performance and success in any work environment. The book examines the most powerful word in our vocabulary. The title gives it away. It is "thanks." He maintains that gratitude is one of the keys to a successful business. The practice of mutual appreciation, and even trust, rewards higher performance and loyalty. It can lead to stronger, more unified teams and departments, which can lead to a fun but hardworking work culture. After the interview, I was reminded of my own previous workplace experiences and what I have learned about my industry.

Communications (print, TV and radio) is a shrinking industry. Everyone knows about the thousands of layoffs that have taken place in the past fifteen or so years. I have been very blessed to have worked in many positive, hardworking and creative newsrooms and TV environments.

Yes, there are occasional run-ins with egos in the television business, but I take a pretty simple approach to such things. To me, television personalities are not heroes. We certainly are not special. True heroes are those involved with charity and the advancement of humanity. They are not rock stars or media personalities, but teachers, members of the military, doctors, nurses, spiritual leaders, police, firefighters and first responders.

Here in Kingston, at my current job, we have Corus Values. They are as follows:

- Win Together. Be approachable and actively help others succeed.
- Think Beyond. Challenge assumptions, imagine what's possible.
- Make it Happen. Focus on priorities, take ownership to deliver.
- Learn Every Day. Be curious and look broadly for answers.
- Show We Care. Support each other's personal well-being.

Our company name, Corus, is derivative of the word "chorus." A chorus describes a group of people working together successfully in harmony.

I must add the word "elevation" as a value I have carried for a long time. I try daily to elevate those around me. I try to inspire. I also say "thanks" as often as I can. Simply put, elevate everyone around you, in *any* work environment.

The treat for me in doing what I do is the audience. They are the most important factor in the communications business. I really enjoy when a stranger on the street or on the bus tells me that they watch faithfully, they enjoy the work and they see the fun and respect my co-workers and I have for each other.

I want nothing more than hardworking people to be happy and to love their craft. I thank *you* for following me. And I thank all my co-workers for creating an awesome workplace.

Try it. Say "thanks" to people around you. Tell them they are appreciated. It will feel awesome to you and them.

I have had the honour to work with some amazing bosses and supervisors. I have learned that there are many types of management styles, just as there are many personalities. It has been said that the best bosses possess vision, are democratic and aspire to be great coaches. The best bosses I have had have shown patience. They believed in teamwork and accountability. They executed their directives with passion and knowledge. They secured safe work environments by highlighting respect, gender equality and diversity.

But there are also bosses that are described as *autocratic*. Autocratic management is the most top-down approach to management, where employees at the top of the hierarchy hold all the power. They make decisions without collaboration or without informing their subordinates. The decisions might be the wrong ones, but there is no wrong in their minds. After the leader delegates duties, they expect immediate acceptance and execution from their subordinates with no questions asked. Basically, they demand underlings to jump, and the employee must respond with "How high?"

In an autocratically managed workplace, there is no room for creative thinking or discussion. Often, autocratic management stems from people being put into manager roles without proper management training. Their style of wielding power is usually an indication of insecurity within themselves. If one of their employees doesn't follow orders or disagrees with them, they punish the employee by chewing them out or threatening their job. They may even publicly humiliate them in front of their peers if they really want to make a statement to their team. Fear, guilt, intimidation and shame are an autocratic manager's main weapons of motivation.

Autocratic managers are also the ultimate micromanagers. They police their employees' every move to make sure they're obedient, allowing little to no flexibility. Employees do what they're told and managers don't want to hear any feedback. They believe that *their* way is the only way to achieve greater financial success and to appease *their* bosses.

Teams and companies led by autocratic managers don't usually reach great financial success because they can't innovate. Often, they won't let their employees, who have differing perspectives from them, share their new and possibly *great* ideas. Autocratic managers don't try to convince their employees to buy into their vision, they force them to. Even though coercion might work in the short-term, it won't last in the long-term. No one likes to be controlled. And if people don't know why they're supporting the company's vision, morale will plummet, leading to low-quality work and a high turnover rate.

Managers that lead with an iron fist often surround themselves with proverbial *yes-people*. These employees are usually insecure themselves and bend over backwards to please their bosses. This scenario often leads to much dissension and division amongst the ranks.

The autocratic management style is one of the most ineffective management styles. It is regarded as old-school and thankfully, is the last of a dying breed.

I wholeheartedly admit that management is one of the hardest jobs in the working world. But in my opinion, and from what I have witnessed and heard from others, ego can be to blame for most ineffective management types. Ego is the reason for not admitting one's mistakes. Ego is the idea that the world revolves around us. Ego can lead to workplace politics. Yes, absolutely, everyone has an ego, but in this case, size does matter! By definition, an ego is a person's sense of self-esteem or self-importance. Having an ego is not a bad thing. Everyone should feel important and possess self-esteem, but when you feel you are better, more important, more intelligent or more valuable than others and you don't have to try to improve yourself, then to me, you're an egomaniacal asshole.

I recognize that people like this have a sad and desperate need (and expectation) to be worshipped and catered to. I think a large ego was to blame for the sexual harassment charges against Jian Ghomeshi, Harvey Weinstein, Kevin Spacey and so many others. These guys, I believe, had super-inflated egos that dictated a sense of being untouchable and having superiority over others. In their narcissistic minds, they believed that they were immune to standards and proper behaviour in their allegedly imposed actions on others.

A good example of egos that are out of control are some celebrities' expectations. Many touring musicians and celebs working on projects are offered extra items for their work areas and dressing rooms. In the industry, it is quite normal. These stipulations are called backstage "riders." A rider is a set of requests that a performer has for their performance. Often, it is a list of demands the artist has for their dressing room.

It sometimes seems that the marquee value of an artist directly reflects the size of their ego and their list of demands. TheSmokingGun.com website provides many leaked revelations of artists' contracts and requests. Mostly they are normal expectations: bottled water, food requirements, brands of alcohol, etc. But sometimes extreme egos are at play and an artist can appear as though their self-worth is miles beyond us mere mortals. Leaked clauses in a Mariah Carey contract stipulate "Cristal champagne with bendy straws" and that her dressing room be outfitted with two dozen white roses and vanilla aromatherapy candles. Also, only sixteen-ounce plastic bottles of Evian water are allowed.

I have interviewed Mariah previously, and although the request wasn't made of me, I have heard that other journalists were told to tell her she looked beautiful and thin. How much adulation does a person need? Don't get me wrong, I like compliments, but I don't believe they should be solicited. I would never instruct my handlers to ask others to tell me flowery things, even if I had handlers!

Another leaked backstage rider shows that on one Britney Spears tour, she specifically requested Pop Tarts, Froot Loops and Cap'n Crunch cereal. (Hey, if I were a pop star, I'd probably request those too!) On another tour, she requested a phone backstage equipped with outgoing calls only. If the phone rang, the promotor would be fined $5,000.

Lady Gaga has had a cool and unique request: notifying security to look out for fans bringing political banners into her shows. That's kind of cool.

TheSmokingGun.com offers that Canadian mega-seller Drake expects E-Z Wider brand rolling papers and one pack of Dutch Masters President cigars. On the beer/booze front, the rapper needs a bottle of Pinot Grigio, a case of Heineken, and bottles of Jack Daniel's, Patrón Silver, Hennessy or Courvoisier and Grey Goose. Geez, I guess I'd be thirsty after a lengthy concert too.

A search for Justin Bieber's backstage requirements unearthed some egocentric demands. According toBusinessInsider.com, the megastar expects a convoy of ten luxury sedans and two buses, rooms at two different five-star hotels and twelve white handkerchiefs. Also, "an entourage of 120 people will be joining him, along with ten shipping containers with items he desperately needs on the road: sofas, a ping pong table, a massage table to be used backstage, to name a few. He'll also dine in style with a personal chef who will name dishes after some of the singer's hit songs." It is also stipulated that Justin's thousand-square-foot suite should be decorated with carnations in his favourite colour, purple, with nothing smaller than king size beds. There should be a private jet for him on standby, and he reportedly flies into stadiums on a chopper.

At MuchMusic, a VJ I once worked with threatened to stop playing a certain record label's artists' videos until they were given all of the week's new releases (free CDs). That is an example of an out-of-control ego. That particular VJ was eventually let go.

A co-worker I once knew, when on assignment, used to want to see the hotel rooms of the cameraperson and their producer after being checked in. This person wanted to see who had the biggest room, and if they thought their room wasn't the biggest, they would ask to be moved to a bigger room. Sheesh. Whenever I travelled, simply having a bed and a working shower sufficed.

Another co-worker would hate when the live audience applauded for me when I entered the studio. This person would belittle the crowd and insult me in front of the guests. Their precious ego was upset that the positive audience reaction wasn't for them. If the roles were reversed, I would be proud of my co-worker for getting a big, happy reaction from the audience.

I have said many times before that the viewer is the most important part of the equation. Without an audience, people on TV wouldn't have a job. I have worked with shameful on-air people who have believed that they were doing a favour to the viewer simply by being on their TV screen. No, the viewer is doing *us* an immense favour by watching and hopefully enjoying and appreciating what they see.

I have learned and offer this: anyone with a public personality has a responsibility to show humility and grace. I am referring to local or even national on-air news people, reporters and politicians. I am referring to athletes, music stars, TV and film celebrities and even social media influencers. Be kind to others and use your stature to improve others and the world around us. As someone who has been fortunate enough to have had a tiny impact on those around me, my advice is this: understand that being recognized by the public is simply a platform to inspire others in a positive way. It is a God-given opportunity that allows you the privilege to inspire change. Once you are recognized for the work you've done, it's time to give back to those in need. We should all strive to be humble and to possess empathy and gratitude.

According to Arshi Gupta, a blogger who writes for yourdost.com, research has shown that the ego can be held responsible for many negative human traits, including (but not limited to) criticizing and judging others. It can lead to acting in a manipulative fashion. It is responsible for being inflexible and rigid, and for possessing a constant need for praise and approval. It can bring on a need to feel superior to everyone around you and can make one feel resentful towards others. It can create the need for power and control over others.

A bad or big ego is a poison. It can be more lethal to our well-being than anything else. If we allow our ego to take over, we can destroy personal relationships, work relationships and friendships. An inflated ego has the power to make us see things differently than they truly are. Ego is the idea that the world revolves around us.

It has been said that the opposite of ego is humility. Humility is not necessarily about thinking less of yourself but thinking of yourself less. To me, the night cleaner is just as important as the company's CEO.

Money doesn't buy happiness. Yes, you can buy things that will make you feel less miserable, but the Internet is full of wonderful life truths pertaining to why money alone shouldn't be one's sole focus…

> Whether we drive a $150,000 car or a $30,000 car, the road and the distance are the same, and we reach the same destination.
>
> Whether we drink a $300 or $10 bottle of wine, the hangover is the same.

> Whether the house in which we live is 300 or 3000 square feet, loneliness is the same.

> True inner happiness does not come from material things of this world.

> Whether you travel first class or economy class, if the plane goes down, you go down with it.

These insights into life are an extension of the motto shared by the global charity, Rotary International. They preach Service Above Self.

I believe my lack of ego is what made me realize a very long time ago that I am much happier in a smaller television market, even though I make a lot less money. I applaud many I know for having the drive and desire to achieve a bigger existence and profile by chasing their dream of fame and money to the USA. Personally, I never thought it was worth it to double or quadruple my salary to pursue a position that wouldn't necessarily make me less miserable. I am perfectly happy doing what I am doing and very happy doing it where I am.

I credit my mother Barb for instilling in me a strong work ethic. There is a feeling I get from doing a job the best I can, always. I take pride in the fact that I never procrastinate. Co-workers always find it amusing that I clear out my email inbox daily.

If I am asked to perform a specific task, I never say, "That's not my job." I will gladly get it done, or if I can't, I will offer, "I will look into that. Let me get back to you."

I have learned that it is never too late to learn. We all must embrace new technologies and there is always someone eager to share their knowledge. I have not been afraid to ask for help. I also love being that person that can share knowledge. I have also learned that it is never too late to change. I have been stubborn in the past about certain beliefs, and I now embrace the chance to hear other sides and others' opinions. Listening to others is how we can all expand our belief systems and take in more empathy and awareness.

It has become imperative for me to learn from mistakes and to embrace the past. Those experiences paved the way for where I am now. I have learned to welcome change and to be aware that no matter how old I get, I can still change for the better.

We must love and accept everyone, despite differences. People thrive on love and acceptance and belonging. If we want that for ourselves, let's encourage it and show it to others.

CHAPTER TWENTY-ONE
ADVICE AND TIPS

It is very odd to think about or even relate to, but I may have been a resource for many media students. I remember after my first year on air at MuchMusic, I got a letter from a student asking to interview me for their class project. I was very flattered and proceeded to divulge as much information as I could about the industry, my best tips on acquiring a job, on-air interviewing advice, the best part of my job, the worst part, etc.

I have said yes to many interviews with grade school, high school and university students who have been curious about or had chosen media as a career endeavour. Despite an industry that has massively changed in terms of ownership of media companies, technology and downsizing, many of the same answers I've given still apply.

What follows are the most often asked questions I have answered over the decades.

- How do you prepare for an interview?

If I book an interview, it is usually from an email offering a pitch. Often, there is a news release associated with it. I will read thoroughly. From there, I will research extensively. An interviewer must know their subject matter. If it is an author, familiarize yourself with their book. If it is a music artist or band, listen to their music and read their bio.

The interviewer is the conduit between the subject and the audience. The worst interviewers say with laziness, "Tell us about yourself." They don't make it a conversation. A great interview is not an interrogation.

It is a relaxing conversation that lets the subject speak freely. Prior to the actual live interview, there is time to go over the subject matter with your guest. The pre-interview chat is very important.

- How do you choose a topic to focus on during an interview?

The interview subject has a message to deliver. Concentrate on *their* message. What do they have to say? Why is the message important to them? Often, an interview subject might have to do three or ten interviews that day. Make your interview somehow special by asking a question that you think won't be asked by anyone else that day. Make it a great experience for them.

- What is the process of creating an interview?

Every interview subject is different, but the end goal is always the same: to provide a platform to get their message across. Your interview subject will range from a local city councillor to a local hockey player to a major music artist or a "man on the street." Treat everyone the same. The task of any interviewer is to obtain a great and memorable sound bite from your subject, a succinctly expressed offering that the audience will take with them. And again, know the topic as best you can.

- What is the most difficult part of preparing for an interview?

Occasionally, there isn't a news release. Google can be your best friend. Sometimes, you may have to elevate your interview subject. Sometimes, the subject is nervous or too prepared (they are relying on notes to provide answers) or they have never been interviewed before. It is the interviewer's job to relax them, make them feel comfortable and make them realize that this is their opportunity to get their message out. There is always a story behind the story. Get those fascinating details from the interview subject.

- What is the easiest part of preparing for an interview?

The news release should highlight all the imperative details. Do not be afraid to ask for talking points. Also, if you have interviewed the subject before and are highly familiar with their work or message, it will make the interview much better.

- How does timing affect the way an interview is produced?

This is a great question, especially if one is working in the realm of live television. For example, a live morning show segment will need five minutes and forty-five seconds to take you to the next commercial break. Everything must be delivered in that allotted time.

The host/interviewer must fill exactly five minutes and forty-five seconds, knowing that there are a few seconds with pad going into a commercial break with prepared stingers/bumpers (industry talk for the bit of music and visuals used as a buffer going into the commercial break). You are relying on the technical director in your earpiece, or the floor director, to give you hand gestures and cues letting you know how much time is left.

A host/interviewer in this position must know when to ask the final question and steer the conversation to a recap, then a goodbye and then a throw to the commercial break, all while making it feel seamless and natural. This can only come with time and much practice, experience and confidence.

- Are there any specific rules or qualifications that need to be followed when doing an interview, and what are they?

It depends on the interview subject. If the interview is conducted off-site and in the field, media passes may be required. Often, the station's assignment editor or news producer will secure those.

There have been times when I have been asked to stay away from certain subject matter when interviewing a person who might have dealt with a controversial past or an uneasy topic. In this situation, it is always a delicate balancing act to appease the interview subject and show respect, but also allow the audience to hear what needs to be addressed. There is usually a way to make it work.

As I have offered, do research and then do more research. Make your interview the best your subject had that day.

- You can't control what the guest will say, so how do you make sure the interview is what listeners or viewers want to hear?

The interviewer will know beforehand who their subject is and what their messaging is. Are you interviewing a crude stand-up comic on your morning show to promote their appearance later that night in your city? Politely remind them prior to the interview that they can't swear and have them be respectful towards the audience.

A TV host will never make the entire viewing audience happy. Interviewing a controversial or opinionated guest will sometimes lead to comments like, "Why didn't you go after them?" or "Why were you so harsh?" You can't make everyone happy. But were *you* satisfied with the end result?

- What is the most rewarding part of an interview?

After the segment when the subject says, "Wow. That was great! Thanks!" Or a few weeks later, talking to the subject and being told their event sold out because of the interview being watched on TV or shared online.

Sometimes, an interview subject has a reputation for being "difficult." I dreaded interviewing Mick Jagger in late 2001 in LA knowing that he wasn't the easiest subject to interview. He hates interviews. But within forty-five minutes, he was laughing and having a great time. It made for excellent television and resulted in an awesome Rolling Stones national TV special I hosted and produced. The same happened with Oasis's lead singer, Liam Gallagher. He sometimes made interviewers cry, but I had nothing but amazing experiences with Liam, and even a hug during our last interview in 2005.

- What is the difference between preparing for a musical guest interview as opposed to an event-based interview?

There really is no difference. Treat every subject the same. Again, it's all about research.

- Is there a difference in preparation for an interview on the radio versus TV?

I believe TV interviews are not exactly interviews but rather conversations. They should be friendly chats. The camera is on you. Do not read notes or look down when engaging the guest. The audience is watching.

With radio, hosts can get away with a lot more. And, they don't have to dress as well as TV people do. Hahahaha!

CHAPTER TWENTY-TWO
BIRTHDAYS AND GOODBYE

I realized in my early twenties that my birthday was not worthy of being recognized and that I shouldn't be on the receiving end of heaps of praise. Why? Because I had nothing to do with it. My mother did all the work giving birth.

My mother often reminded me as I got older that my birth was difficult for her. I was the last of six children and there were complications. The doctors gave her options, and she carried through with the pregnancy and birth. I am sorry, Mom, that I was such a painful birth, but thank you for having faith!

Around the age of twenty-one I started to refer to my mom by her first name, Barb. It was endearing to me. I would also call her on my birthday to say, "Thank you for giving birth to me." Again, I had nothing to do with being born. I just popped out. Barb did all the hard work. I was simply along for the ride.

Sadly, I lost my saintly mother in the spring of 2012. I am sad that I can't call her on my birthday anymore to say thank you.

I am also uncomfortable with the attention birthdays bring, though I am entirely grateful for the positive and loving messages. We all feel the love from friends and family on the day we were born, and, due to social media, we are also wished well by total strangers. But I cower a little at being the focus of attention. I would much prefer to let people know they are loved and appreciated every day. One shouldn't rely on a day in their calendar year to tell others how important they are.

People say, "Age is just a number," or, "You're only as old as you feel." Those adages are somewhat true. I sometimes still feel as if I am twenty-nine, but my body has lately reminded me that I can't stay up as late as I used to. I am not as athletic as I once was. I dread the loss of wonderment in things I was fascinated by in my teens or twenties.

For many years, when someone found out it was my birthday, that feared question was asked: "How old are you?" My answer was always the same: "I loved turning twenty-nine so much, I am doing it again this year!" Turning thirty was weird. It felt too "adult." I had purchased my first condo by then. Luckily, my job and lifestyle kept me feeling young. By thirty, I would periodically run into friends I knew in grade school or high school and think, "Where did that belly come from?" "You have three kids?" "Wow, you're bald!" Of course, all those things are normal and natural. But they were foreign to me.

I had heard before that turning thirty was tough but that forty would be much easier. Really? Not for me. I found turning forty very difficult. I had a hard time coping with it. I think it was because when I was twenty years old, forty seemed so far away! It was "old" to me. I couldn't accept it. My sadness continued and I wondered why getting older and aging was becoming an issue with me.

I recall an interview with The Cure's Robert Smith. Robert cited that turning thirty was difficult for him too. Hence, The Cure's landmark album *Disintegration*. It was about how he felt as if he was falling apart, and it explored the negative aspects of getting older. He too felt like turning thirty was the beginning of the end. But when he turned forty, he admitted that he had become fine with aging and even embraced the idea of getting older. Even now, in his sixties, Robert Smith is still touring with The Cure. He still has his exploding-mushroom-cloud black hair and trademark eye makeup. I admire that. Even at eighty, he will still pull it off! The Cure's fans will still love him.

I fully admit that my life has been blessed with seeing and doing much and travelling the world well into my twenties, but I sometimes look back and realize the biggest laughs and the most fun times I had were when I was in my twenties and early thirties. Whenever I get back to Toronto,

I am constantly reminded that those fun, crazy, reckless days are well behind me.

I do admit that having a birthday means that one is another year older, living life on this (mostly) beautiful planet. I have learned that it sure beats the alternative . . . death.

The week I turned forty, I noticed that I was holding a newspaper further away from my face in order to have the words come into focus. I now need reading glasses. My hair has slowly started to turn grey. A small balding area has developed on the top of my head. I suffer from sleep apnea and so I go to bed with a nozzle attached to my nose to provide clean air to my nasal passages so that my heart doesn't work too hard and I'm able to sleep. I know I can't fight aging. For many, and me, getting older might mean losing passion and that sense of wonderment and interest in the things we used to get excited about.

About fifteen years ago, I became active in again building up some collections I'd had when I was a lot younger but had since lost or thrown away. I used to collect hockey cards when I was about nine years old. Sadly, I had stored them in a giant garbage bag. The cards had become bent as I hadn't had the foresight to collect them proudly with care. That garbage bag was eventually thrown out. I am sure I had multiples of Wayne Gretzky's rookie cards in there somewhere. A mint Gretzky rookie card is now worth hundreds of thousands of dollars. I have now rebuilt a giant collection of Chicago Blackhawks hockey cards. I have been a fan of The Blackhawks since before I was born, I think. My collection of Blackhawks cards now spans about seventy years' worth of cards. This enormous collection is well taken care of, painstakingly organized into many binders and proudly displayed on custom shelves in my home office. My collection consists of old cards, rookie cards, autographed cards and many memorabilia cards. Memorabilia cards were introduced in the mid-'90s, and they contain bits of a game-worn hockey jersey, hockey stick or even hockey gloves embedded into the card. They are numbered and certified with an authenticity guarantee on the back of the card. All these cards bring a huge amount of joy to me.

I have spent the past five years purchasing and collecting old *MAD* magazines. I was an avid reader of *MAD* from about grades two to seven.

Acquiring many of these old issues brings back similar feelings as my hockey cards do. They inspire cherished memories of a much younger age. With my hockey cards and MAD magazines, I am easily transported to simpler and carefree times. They represent a time of family and youth and not having to deal with death and depression and pain. These artifacts tap into my inner-child and bring me comfort.

Officially, I am fifty-five years old as my fingers are pecking at this keyboard. But in many ways, I still feel twenty-nine. I continue to maintain a sense of wonderment and curiosity about things and people. I am grateful I still live a life where my job's focus is interviewing fascinating individuals and sharing their stories and messages.

Getting older also means dealing with a glaring reality and awareness that there is less life ahead. There is a tangible sense now that the grains of sand are slipping slowly through the tiny hole in the hourglass. There is more sand at the bottom than there is on top. And those grains of sand continually fall. But I have recently sensed around me that others are in large need of being reminded of their pasts and are trying to latch onto a time that they too have cherished.

Nostalgia and retro became big again in the 2010s and early 2020s. It is a shared theory I subscribe to, that the decade prior is not cool. One needs to be twenty years or so away to look back at a decade and see it as being cool again and for that decade to become appreciated. Apparently, the '90s are now considered retro-cool, and its musical offerings are being welcomed as big again!

There has been a big rise in podcasters in the past several years. Podcasts on every topic one can imagine are available to be downloaded for the user's listening pleasure. I found it interesting that for much of late 2021 and well into 2022, I was asked to be a guest on many podcasts that featured retro music or were focused on looking back at '90s broadcast trends. I learned that there was a building reverence for my career and what I did and who I interviewed. I usually thought these podcasters were getting in touch with me by mistake, but no. There was a big audience actually wanting to hear from me and to listen to some of my experiences.

It occurred to me that perhaps I have sort of become a source of nostalgia for many! It is odd for me to realize and understand that I have become a perfect circle for some. I have cherished all of the perfect circle moments in my life, so there was no way I could say no to becoming someone else's perfect circle.

All of the podcasts I was invited to be on were fun and engaging. The public's interest in the '90s became a growing trend, and I was on the receiving end of many emails and private messages inviting me to numerous events and broadcasts. One of MuchMusic's original and most famous VJs, Erica Ehm, invited me onto one of her podcasts in 2021. It was a great experience catching up with her. She really did create the Canadian template for what a VJ was and could aspire to be.

In late 2021, CBC Music published an online article about the MuchMusic compilation CD series, *Big Shiny Tunes*. The successful CD releases were amongst the biggest-selling Canadian music compilations of all time. I believe there were seventeen collections in all. Many artists and MuchMusic insiders were interviewed about the CD compilations. One of my favourite singer/songwriters of the 1990s was New York City's Poe, known for her alt-rock hits "Trigger Happy Jack" and "Angry Johnny." She was featured on the very first *BST* in 1996. She was quoted as saying, "Bill Welychka was really soulful. He cared a lot about artists and the first question he asked was always, 'How are you feeling?' People would just spill their guts to him." Thanks Poe! As I expressed to you many years ago, dynamic and talented people that have something worth saying will always have an audience.

I was interviewed in 2021 for a documentary that will be released in 2023. I agreed to be part of the doc after hearing the project's directive to showcase MuchMusic's contributions to Canadian pop culture and to the Canadian music industry. I was excited to be asked to be a part of it. My experiences were only a tiny fraction of what MuchMusic was all about and what it meant to so many people. The two-hour doc, *299 Queen Street West*, is directed by Sean Menard.

I was asked to be part of an outdoor live music event in July 2022 in Brantford, Ontario. The sold-out WTFest gathering featured '90s hip hop legends Maestro Fresh Wes, Rob Base and The Beastie Boys' DJ Mix Master Mike. Also on the bill were MuchMusic VJs Steve Anthony, Master T, Rick Campanelli and me. We had a beautiful time catching up, reminiscing and laughing. The coolest part of the night was meeting viewers who simply wanted to say hello and grab a picture. I met so many people that expressed the same things: "I grew up watching you!" or, "You were part of my life!" or, "I love and miss those days!" Guess what? I miss those days too and I am thankful and blessed I could share them with you.

In the fall of 2022, I was asked to emcee the Toronto screening of the documentary *Doug and the Slugs and Me* by director Teresa Alfeld. It was her very emotional project that brought the Vancouver '80s band Doug and the Slugs back to Canadian consciousness. At the premiere, I saw another MuchMusic original, Michael Williams. Also present was my favourite woolen curmudgeon, Ed the Sock (Steve Kerzner). We all had dinner together and shared many fun stories. It was very cool to also see cameraperson Tim Crough at the event. Tim was the cameraperson that shot my last Robert Smith (The Cure) interview in 2004.

Also in 2022, as yet still another throwback and sign of nostalgia, I was asked to curate and host many music video playlists for a new digital platform called Viewistic. It was a thrill to choose themes and host and produce about ten, hour-long playlists of videos of my choosing. It really did bring back memories of introducing music videos. I did it with great pride and excitement, selecting themes and videos that anyone would enjoy.

It is sometimes difficult to reconcile one's past with one's present. Everyone walks this path. Many people look at old family photo albums or open long forgotten high school yearbooks to revisit their pasts. My past is something that I have been reminded of on a weekly basis for a few decades. But really, isn't that the goal in any life? The longer we live, the more stories and experiences we all have. Those stories and experiences keep getting lengthier for all of us who are still living. We should be grateful to all be continuing to add to our lives' experiences.

To me, the popular notion of a "has-been" implies someone who did something admirable earlier in life but who hasn't amounted to much lately. But, it's all about perspective. From my point of view, I'd say the past ten to twenty years have been amazing and enlightening. I have achieved things, learned many lessons worthy of sharing and have grown to be the kind of person my mother Barb and my father Alex would have been proud of. Hell, I am proud of me! I have nothing to prove anymore and nothing to chase to bring me to a higher level. But to someone who only knew me twenty or thirty years ago, the perspective certainly looks a lot different. Professionally, I am not on a national radar anymore. But I am perfectly fine with that.

A happy life to me means being proud of the job I currently do. To be living in a city I love and to feel the warmth from that city. I love feeling that I contribute in some sort of minor way to making this world a better place. I need to go to bed feeling exhausted from giving my all and I need to wake up refreshed and ready to do it all over again. I now know a happy life means being loved and giving love. (Thank you, Amanda!)

I am probably the world's first has-been who is loving life and is grateful for everything they have.

But before I could even wind down this book, 2023 would bring me yet another bizarre and surreal experience. Days before this book was sent to my publisher, I was asked to attend a meeting by Kingston filmmaker Jay Middaugh of Happy Kid Productions. He explained to me that he was writing a script for a film loosely inspired by my story. And he asked me to play the lead role. WHAT!? My life is worthy of a film? Sometimes, I suppose the truth *is* stranger and more interesting than fiction.

I will play a fictionalized version of myself in a story about a middle-aged, former high-profile entertainment journalist who moves to a smaller city. The lead character gets offered a chance to be national again and tries to recapture the glory of his youthful fame as he interviews local musicians. Can he turn back the clock and relive his glory days, or is it too late? Or is there maybe more to his new community than he expected? What I love about Jay's pitch and his story is that music and local musicians (playing themselves) will drive the narrative. Jay loves Kingston too and is also a big supporter of local musicians.

At the point of typing these words, initial filming is set to begin in early summer 2023 here in Kingston.

I wrote earlier that I believe everyone has a story worthy of a book. We all possess experiences that we can learn from and share with others. We all have moments in our lives that are funny, sad, heartbreaking, fantastic, wondrous, glorious, momentous, shocking, enlightening, surprising, educational and unbelievable. My life has been filled with such experiences and I am grateful for the chance I've had to share them with you. I thank you so much for reading my words. I hope you've felt the time doing so was worth it. I cherish you.

God bless ya and cheers!

ACKNOWLEDGEMENTS

This is another part included in most books and again, a crucial part for the author to share with others. But like the Preface, many people also skip past the Acknowledgements. So, thanks for still being here, reading! My theory about this part of any book is that some readers will look for their name to see if they were mentioned. I have done it when reading bios by people I know or consider acquaintances.

But I totally understand why it is important for any author to print the names of people they deem necessary to mention. This is the chance for the author to say out loud, with pride and joy, THANK YOU!

If your name is not mentioned here, it doesn't imply that you were not important to me. There is a good chance that somehow, no matter how long we've known each other, I took something away from our experiences with one another. I have been blessed with many friends, acquaintances and strong influences.

I have always been a big believer in elevating everyone around me. A part of that desire is to see and share in others' successes. One is only as happy as those around them. Do whatever you can to make others around you feel happy and appreciated. You will then feel better about your life and surroundings as a result.

I would love to take this opportunity to simply recognize people who believed in me, inspired me and loved me. These are people that were close to me, patient in teaching me lessons and have made a positive impact on me. Some were also lifesaving friends and people that made me smile, laugh and appreciate life.

My parents, Barb and Alex. Both are no longer with us, and they are missed every day. My immediate family of siblings, Ed, Gerard, David, Len and Maria and their families. Sadly, three siblings have passed on. I think of them daily too.

Thank you to my former co-workers, Sherry Greengrass, Rob Brown, Denise Donlon, Chris Ward, Craig Halket, Steve Anthony, Erica Ehm, Cara Daley Nye, Sandra Pappas, Michelle Newby, Michael Haydon, Dave Azoulay, Janice Groom, Mike Rudolph, Simon Evans, Dave Russell, Joni Daniels, Paul Templeman, Moses Znaimer, Matt Phillips, Steve Gelder, Jay Mirus, Tony Wannamaker, Dave Hurlbut, Aly Thompson, George Lagogianes, Monika Deol, Isabelle Pelletier, Jordan Kawchuk, Corinne McDermott, Morgen Flury, RT Thorne, Bruce Turner, Kerry Hittinger, Jamie Corbett, Tim Crough, Tracy Hugo, Steven Fine, Jodi Stansfield, KCC, Mike Campbell, TD Mulligan, Sheila Sullivan, Neil Staite, John Martin, Dave Kines, Deno Saunders, Chris Duncan, Melissa RC, Mike Haslett, Richard Gray and Peter Angione. Many have become very close to me to this very day.

Thank you to record company and music industry friends for the many years of concert tickets (not for personal pleasure but, ummm, for research purposes?), backstage passes (again, for research purposes?) and CDs: Ken Bain, Andrea Orlick, Kevin Shea, Attila Somogyi, Dave Watt, Brian Hetherman, Rob Chubey, Tony Szambor, Ivar Hamilton, Karen Pace, Kim Cooke, Steve Waxman, Ron Harwood, Eric Alper, Shawn Marino, Liz Doyle, Anastasia Saradoc, Richard Flohil, Karen Bliss, Bernie Breen, Patrick Sambrook, Jake Gold and Dale Peters. These people's passion for music and specific artists was contagious.

Some portions of this book's contents are based on my previous columns originally published by *The Kingston Whig-Standard*, a division of Postmedia Network Inc. The idea for a monthly column came from them, so thanks to *The Whig* for being interested in my life.

I want to recognize cherished supporters and friends. Some of these people I haven't spoken to in a while, but their presence in my life remains integral. Thank you to Jeff Parissi, Ranjan Das, Ed MacLaren, Sue Parkinson, Vania Gallant, Vicki Ludwik, Beverley Michelle, Mark Turner, Eddie Burkholder, Fred Dunn, Jason Taylor, Sue Loveless, Allyson Tonelli,

A HAPPY HAS-BEEN

Fay Chapple, Brent Nurse, Doug Jeffries, Mark Potter, Sgt. Steve Koopman (Kingston Police Service), Jimmy Hassan, Christina Alves, Pat Johnston, John Temou, Tina Cerilli, Katie Matchett, Julie Hill, Dahla MacKenna, Kirsti Stephenson, Anna Macina, Lori Anne Stoute, Jill Forristal, Tea Cheney, Kim Van Nieuvanhusse, Shelby Lewis, Sandra Blaikie and Dr. Tim Bell, Dan MacNeil, Frank Boldt, Angela McFarlane, Steve Winfrow, Julie Brown, Vern White, Anne Mathieu, Bon Bon, Carole Rhude, Karen Campbell, Faye and Ray Goudreau, Michelle "Bopers" Beaupre, Jan Murphy, Justin Cousineau, Gary Cork, Ryan Dennee, Pat Murphy (80s Enuff), Graham Forsythe, the LeBlancs, James McColl, Jason Rees, the Paquettes, the Hurtuboises, the Greengrasses, Mauro Sepe, Kris + Dee, Greg Ball, Gord Hunter and Ginette Blais, Miss Emily Fennell, Dave Pinkerton, Jeff Reitzel (SkEye Stream Inc.), Dave Bastedo, Joseph Casnaw, MP Mark Gerretsen, Kingston Mayor Bryan Paterson, Kingston Town Crier Chris Whyman, Jacquie Collier, Matt Lee, Dave Bull and JP Rayne, Queen's Gaels football coaches Pat Sheahan and Steve Snyder, Lynda Colgan, Maddie and Kiki Longo, the Harts, the Wards, Dwayne Henne, Janette Ewen and my Tragically Hip friends and their families.

At the point of writing these words, I want to acknowledge current co-workers Rachel Hele, Maegen Kulchar, Paul Black, Nick Lansdown, Mike Postovit, Darryn Davis, Derek Bolduc, Ryan Peddigrew, John Lawless, Paul Soucy, Mike Wheeler, Jay Westman, Bill Hutchins, Aryn Strickland, Fawwaz Muhammad-Yusuf, Sideshow, Monica Lapajne, Jesse Reynolds, Amanda Knott-Smith, Mackay Taggart, Ward Smith and many others who allow me to continue to feel part of a talented team and who assist me in living my dream of making television in a community that feels absolutely perfect. Corus Entertainment's Global Kingston (CKWS-TV) provides me with all that I need to be *actually happy!*

Thank you to Bridget Stuart and Jason Rees for the book cover ideas. Many thanks to Dee Dee, Scott Donovan, Lee-Ann Jaworski, James Stewart and FriesenPress for having the faith in me to bring my story to anyone interested.

But most importantly, this is for Amanda Alves and her family. Thank you, Judy and Armindo, for giving birth to Amanda and raising a beautiful daughter. Thank you, Amanda, for being patient, for having my back, for guiding me to a healthier lifestyle, for teaching me how to love again and for making me laugh. And for laughing with me. I cherish the day we met on Brock Street. It sent into motion the events that would allow me to become happy again.

Printed in the USA
CPSIA information can be obtained
at www.ICGtesting.com
JSHW072317080823
46146JS00018B/558